Fans

Fans

A Collector's Guide

Nancy Armstrong

SOUVENIR PRESS

First published 1984 by Souvenir Press Ltd,
43 Great Russell Street, London WC1B 3PA
and simultaneously in Canada

Reprinted 1990

ISBN 0 285 62987 5

Filmset and printed in Great Britain by
BAS Printers Limited,
Over Wallop, Hampshire

Contents

For Peter, my dearly loved and eldest son.

List of Illustrations

COLOUR PLATES

BLACK AND WHITE PHOTOGRAPHS

Acknowledgements

Many people in the 'fan world' are generous to a fault with their help and encouragement. I could not have written this book (or my previous one) without the aid of the following:

Hélène Alexander, Felicity Barnett, Sam Farr, Madeleine Ginsburg, Grace Grayson, the late Bertha de Vere Green, Peter Greenhalgh, Avril Hart, Milne Henderson, Betty Hodgkinson, Pamela Hudson, Dr. Richard Illing, Neville Iröns, Prue Lachelin, John Lawson, Margaret Little, Santina Levey, Miss Lintott, Michel Maignan, Susan Mayor, Jane Mitchell, Esther Oldham, the Rt Hon Lord Oranmore and Browne, Geraldine Pember, the late Eleanor Robinson, Anne, Countess of Rosse, Larry Salmon, Miss Smedley, Sheila Smith, the staff of the Spanish Institute, Katy Talati, Edward Thornton-Vincent, Georgette Tilley, Gillian Troche, Anthony Vaughan, Ian Venture and Martin Willcocks.

1 Collecting Fans

We feel attracted to fans not simply because they are old—not even because they are necessarily beautiful. Their most magnetic appeal comes from the glimpses they give us into the lives people lived long before we were born. For an antique fan should not be an object simply to possess and invest in, but a chink in the door of the past, a whisper through a bygone age that thrills the collector like a signal from a distant planet. Historians may unfold for us the panorama of great events without wringing out a single tear; a lonely Victorian child's fan can fill us with tender amazement. It is just because this small fan appears to be so trivial, and so everyday, that the insight we can gain from it gives it such poignancy. Fans seem to have a life of their own: they are intensely personal because the majority have been owned and used. Writers about fans today are constantly driven by the questions, 'When was it made? Why? Who used it? Which was its country of origin? How was it made?' Following up the answers to these questions provides the collector with a whole new world of sheer delight.

There has been a sudden and dramatic re-awakening of interest in the subject of fans during the past twenty years. Firstly, Nancy Armstrong wrote *A Collector's History of Fans*, which was rapidly followed by seven other books in English, and the establishment of collectors' societies. As a result, prices of fans began to rise very quickly and most collectors, eventually, chose to specialise in types.

The overall interest seemed to trigger off a spate of exhibitions, generally in top museums, first in the United Kingdom, then Europe, followed by the USA and the Orient: the accompanying catalogues were, and are, extremely costly, each liberally illustrated in colour and black and white. They are, however, essential works of reference for the collector, and are bought—regardless of cost.

These books and catalogues, in various languages, have contributed a great deal towards a deeper knowledge about fans: if mistakes have been made they were not deliberate or dishonest, for in this new field we have all progressed and matured by error. No one has exclusive knowledge, more research is being done all the time on different aspects of fans, and it becomes more and more evident that they are inescapably tied in with social history.

Until 1974 many people felt that fans meant 'frivolous ladies in fashionable dress semaphoring prospective suitors'. To a certain extent this might have been so—but only for a very short period of time. On the whole the fan, the fly-whisk and the umbrella were symbols of social position which, in the majority of cases, meant that they were used by men.

The word 'fan', therefore, is a very loose term overall, encompassing many different things, and more and more books are necessary to explore the wide variety of specialist categories which have emerged. Serious collectors, academics and historians now seem to be concentrating on the following main themes:

1 Oriental fans for the home market
2 Export fans from the Orient
3 Ethnographical fans
4 Ceremonial and religious fans
5 Historical fans
6 European fans *c* 1650–*c* 1930
7 Modern fans

In the past collectors were free to make their choice between these categories; today the value of a fan has sharpened so much that it would be senseless and untrue to suggest that a new collector has all that much choice, especially with a limited pocket.

Obviously historical fans in museums will stay there, and so will most religious fans in temples (although, naturally, the social historian can write them up very fully). If the new collector has the nerve to back his or her own judgement, the area least explored today is that of ethnography; otherwise I would suggest buying some unmounted Oriental fan-leaf that caught the eye. It is always wisest to buy the best you can afford; quality is a sound investment, and much Oriental art is still undervalued in Europe. However, it must be remembered that ethnographical fans are not sold as such in auction sales, but under the section 'African works of Art', etc., and Oriental fan-leaves are sold within 'Oriental Painting' sales.

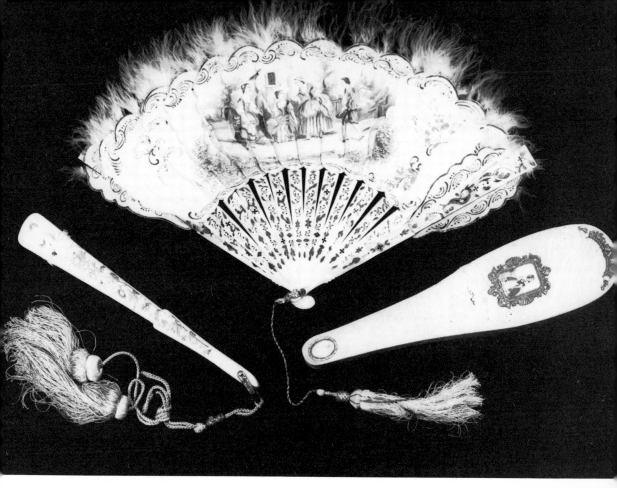

1. Left: a closed fan, showing the guard with shibayama inlay. Possibly mid-19th century. Japanese. 11″ : 28cms. Centre and right : the leaf painted with a scene from 18th century life but in the 19th century manner, each leaf edged with maribou feathers, mounted on pierced and gilded mother-of-pearl sticks. Possibly French, made for the Spanish market. c 1860. 11″ : 29 cms, shown with its original case. By courtesy of Bonhams, Knightsbridge.

In Category 1 (above) only artistic content and merit should be considered. In Category 3 it is extremely important to have a full provenance. In Category 6 craft comes before art in the main and, at best, is an amalgam of the two. This is the area from which most new collectors enthusiastically gather their fans and where one can begin extremely modestly. Then, in time, a personal statement can be made which reflects either the state of one's purse or one's taste.

The most important aspect of collecting is that each major purchase (it cannot happen every time) should have an impeccable provenance: it is pointless to boast that your fan was once owned by Marie Antoinette or was painted by Michelangelo unless there is positive written proof—word of mouth does *not* count.

A fan known to have been in any Royal hands (almost any country, almost any period) is generally much more valuable than it actually warrants; the same applies, to a lesser degree, to fans once owned by people in the theatre, or by artists or authors. Fans bought from the sale of a well-known collection should always keep their sale tags on them, together with the sale catalogue for proof.

The best advice that one can give to prospective collectors is to buy what they really like and to pay as much as they can afford at the time for one fan, rather than buying a selection for the same price—for quality costs money and you have to live with your enthusiasm every day. Nothing is more soul-destroying than to hear of people buying what they do not really care for, purely as an investment, and then

2. Italian fan, the black kid leaf painted with Adonis surprising the sleeping Venus with an audience of putti; mounted on ivory sticks painted in the chinoiserie manner. c 1700. 10½″ : 26.5 cms. By courtesy of Bonhams, Knightsbridge.

putting the purchase away until it can be sold at a profit—why not just buy stocks and shares?

Some people feel that brand new collectors should buy some exceptionally cheap fans (say about five) merely as a starting point: to get the feel of them, learn about them, handle them and compare them with illustrations in the standard books. Then, when they feel confident enough, they should branch out into a chosen field and throw the original five away . . . or sell them.

Most new collectors set out with little or no idea of where their preferences lie and think of fans as being merely charming and colourful adjuncts to dress. Some are brought into the collecting field because they discovered a cache of fans in the dressing-up box, or because their grandmother left them a treasured marriage fan which she, in turn, inherited from Victorian times. Gradually, as the collection grows, so does one's knowledge, until suddenly a shape appears to the collection. That is the time to sell or exchange the unworthy and start to specialise. A guide to both expensive and cheap fans is tabled below:

Expensive fans of top quality
> Seventeenth century varnished fans
> Eighteenth century cabriolet fans
> Eighteenth century lace fans
> Oriental fans for the home market
> Oriental fans leaves
> Mask or Domino fans
> Mica fans
> Fans with real gemstones
> Eighteenth century commemorative fans
> Some ethnographical fans
> Gut fans

Cheaper fans are found amongst the following
> Advertising fans
> Small wooden brisé fans
> Plastic fans
> Gauze mounted fans
> Fans with machine-made lace
> Fans with plain satin mounts
> Any fan which is badly damaged

Other fans come in the price range between these two categories and you pay what you can afford.

There are three ways in which to buy fans: privately, through a dealer and at auction sales. The first is done mainly by the very experienced collector, often at the end of an auction sale and especially if the fans have been sold as a lot. Beginners who buy privately are really asking for trouble, partly because they have no idea of prices and partly because they foolishly trust the owner for genuine details.

Buying through a dealer is a very good idea. Most dealers are well-known in the collecting world and they have a reputation to maintain. They allow you to handle a fan for some time and, should you buy, you know you have bought the fan which you handled and not another: i.e., you can handle during the preview of an auction, but so can others, and you may emerge with a fan that has been damaged after you saw it. Also the dealer gets to know your tastes, looks out on your behalf, or even buys in for you at auction so that others do not know the fan is really for you. Dealers are patient people who enjoy what they sell; I have heard several say, after attending an auction sale, 'Two for me and one for stock.' They know a very great deal on their subject but, at the same time, they do not expect the customer to 'pick their brains'. Their stock may be a trifle more expensive than fans at a sale, but they show a choice and it is *they* who have had to fight to get to a big sale, *they* who have had to take the risks and *they* who have had to spend their time and money in acquiring stock. Many dealers keep a small selection of 'cheapies' for beginners to buy to practise upon, and, naturally, they always have their customers in mind. It is sensible for beginners to work up a good relationship with some dealer for they will rarely be let down and, when the time comes (as it will) that the owner needs to sell an unwanted fan, then the dealer might take it in part-exchange or even arrange a sale.

The other side of the coin is the fun of a gamble in the auction sale. Beginners should go to the preview before the sale and immediately buy a catalogue. They should study this first, marking any lots which seem to appeal, and then go and look at their choice. Equally important is to study the 'estimated prices', a present-day advantage to all buyers which lends a good deal of spice to the proceedings.

In the past few years, in London, fans have emerged into a category of their own: no longer do they lurk among toys and costume, and

3. An eminently collectable painted decoupé fan depicting figures in a landscape, on pierced, carved and painted ivory sticks. c. 1770. 11½" : 29.25 cms. By courtesy of Bonhams, Knightsbridge.

no longer are they sold in miserable lots, bundled up together, but as single items.

Catalogues are the fan buyers' bible. Most enthusiasts have the catalogue for each fan sale sent to them whether they intend to buy or not, and use it as reference material. Some people buy two catalogues, one to mark with comments—the price fetched and who bought it— and one to keep as an investment with any acquired fan. In this way the movement of prices can be seen, the new categories noted (i.e. advertising fans are now sold singly on occasion) and, occasionally, an 'old friend' may come up for sale a second time and the collector might pick up something that was missed before.

An 'estimated price' is just that. No auction house can guarantee what the day will bring: how tastes might suddenly change or if all the 'big' collectors have gone away on holiday at the same time. You can pick up a bargain if you are quick; you can lose something that you dearly want because you are intimidated, for the moment, by glares from the opposition; or you can find something that attracts you enormously that you missed at the preview.

To buy without having seen and examined a prospective purchase is sheer folly; but, once seen, to leave a bid with the sale room staff is an extremely good idea—they will not go mad on your behalf and you can rely on them.

Many 'big' collectors are tough, single-minded and ruthless. Once the catalogue of any sale has been studied you can learn to guess who will be present to buy the best. Watch who is at the viewing, or at the sale, and watch when the important people swiftly and silently leave the room. Many collectors are secretive for two main reasons: firstly for security and secondly because it is the very nature of the species. It is always wise not to enquire too closely what a collector has bought or has in his collection; it seems as impertinent as asking to look at his bank balance. Wait for an invitation!

Buying (or selling) through auction houses can be great fun and there is always the chance of a bargain. However, it is wise to examine with great care all the fine print, discover any hidden charges or premiums, and to remember that the auctioneers never take any risks themselves.

2 Historical Background

The use of the fan dates from the dawn of time as it accompanied the sun around the world, cooling people down. Today, in spite of the availability of air-conditioning units, fans are still being made, and used, in hot countries.

The earliest fan may have been a large leaf, or plaited straw in the same basic shape, with an added handle. At the same time fans were made from bunches of birds' feathers.

All over the world pretty feathers from rare birds have always been used for decorative purposes. One of man's earliest diversions was to tame or cage birds, to listen to their song and to admire their plumage. He would take a feather which attracted him and place it in his hair (some tribes still do, especially in Borneo) as a sign of comparative wealth, privilege or social standing. This use of a feather 'on high' is still retained today although few people really know the reason why. Feather shapes in diamonds (*aigrettes*) are worn by ladies in society, feathers curled around hats are worn by ambassadors, feathers in ceremonial head-dresses are worn all around the world, from crack Italian regiments to doormen outside first-class hotels—and feathers are even featured upon the heads of the magnificent Lipizzaner horses in Vienna.

The bird in the cage would beat his wings and provide a cool breeze, so what more natural than for the owner to pluck out a few brilliant feathers and make his very own 'bird's wing', the first real fan? In the sub-continent of India the Hindi generic term for a fan is *pankha*, from *pankh* meaning a feather or bird's wing. In China the archaic symbol for a fan looks like, and means, 'a bird's wing', and the newer word *shan* means 'feathers under a roof'. The same basically applies to Japan. Surely all of this is no mere coincidence?

There are three main shapes for fans: the fixed fan, the brisé fan and the folding fan.

THE FIXED FAN

This is rigid in shape and generally has a handle to hold. It can measure between six inches (15 cms) and two feet (60 cms) across, but is rarely larger. It can be shaped like a leaf, circular, like a spade or a flag, or sometimes indeterminate. I came across a beautiful one recently, painted upon a terracotta jar, *c* 380 BC, at the Museum in Benevento, near Naples (No. 372). The leaf was spade-shaped and dropped into a long wooden handle. The fixed fan has both advantages and disadvantages in its rigidity: the advantage being that it can be decorated on both sides in the most elaborate way; the disadvantage that if it is so decorated it cannot be put down on any surface but needs to be placed in a fan-holder. These holders seem common enough in the East but are never seen in the West.

An example is one of those delightful Chinese *pien-mien* which are

4. Pair of Handscreens, made of cream silk, double, stretched over strong wire frames and bound in blue silk, oversewn with twisted threads, formerly silver. Shaped handles. The central embroidery is in narrow ribbons, chenille, silk braids, silk threads, aerophane. Refs: Needlework Through the Ages by Symonds and Preece and Domestic Needlework by Seligman and Hughes. Third quarter of the 18th century. Total length $16\frac{1}{2}''$: 42 cms. Total width $5\frac{1}{2}''$: 14 cms. Owned by Mrs Pamela Hudson.

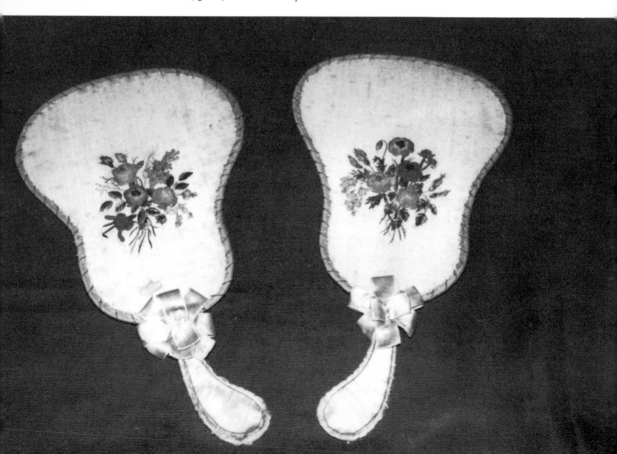

5. Ivory brisé fan, very rare, in the form of a double barrelled flintlock sporting gun, the sticks pierced, and the guardsticks silvered with the lock-plate, and carved to form the barrels, trigger and lock-plate. $11\frac{1}{2}''$: 29 cms. c 1780. (Fetched £1100 in August 1981.) By courtesy of Christies, South Kensington.

basically made from paper stretched over a wire frame, liberally coated and strengthened with glue, covered by pure gold-leaf and then elaborately decorated with a scene of birds and flowers made from tiny, iridescent kingfisher feathers held in gold wire. These flowers and birds can stand proud of their background by up to two inches (5 cms)— nothing will crush as the fan does not fold; it is carefully held in the hand by an applied handle, often of carved ivory.

THE BRISÉ FAN
Whether the brisé fan originated from China or from Japan is a matter of dispute. Its shape probably came from the use of writing tablets held in the hands of court officials. These were made from various materials, mainly wood or ivory, which were thin and light and easy to write the characters upon, from top to bottom. In order to keep them tidy and in order, a hole was made at the bottom of each and a cord used to tie them together. There appears to be certain evidence from paintings and carvings, and an example was found inside an image

6. *Chinese ivory brisé fan of a very high quality.* $7\frac{1}{2}''$: 19 cms. *Made in Canton, c 1780.* From Fans of Imperial China, *by Neville Iröns, by courtesy of The House of Fans Limited.*

of Kannon (at the Toji temple at Kyoto), which shows that the slips or tablets might *just* have been the origin of the brisé fan, but there is no definite proof to be found anywhere.

Whatever its origin, the brisé fan as we know it takes the form of thin, light slips of ivory, wood, etc., which are held firmly together by a rivet or cord at the base and, along the top, initially by connecting threads, and later, by fine, thin connecting silk ribbons. This thread or ribbon is passed through or round the slips (or sticks) so cunningly that the brisé fan can fold up when not in use. On the whole this type of fan relies for its appeal upon the crafting of the material (carving, piercing, lacquering, etc.) or upon a painted scene. Any extraneous decoration (shibayama inlay, etc.) would only be placed upon the outside of the guards.

Oriental brisé fans place far less emphasis upon the guardsticks than do European brisé fans; indeed, the earliest Japanese brisé fans made no attempt to distinguish the guards at all: the fans were made of many sticks, identical in length, breadth and thickness, and held together with either a metal rivet or a cord, with a decoration which spread right across all the sticks. Later, the end sticks were made thicker for protection, and often decorated in a different manner from the sticks, and we now call these 'guards' because that was their function.

It appears that the earliest wooden sticks were wide (about one inch

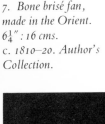

7. Bone brisé fan, made in the Orient. 6¼″ : 16 cms. c. 1810–20. Author's Collection.

8. *English fan, the leaf with a central masked mezzotint printed in bistre probably by Bernard Lens, the reserves painted with two fishermen, and a farmer and his wife, within garlands of exotic flowers; the ivory sticks inlaid with tinted mother-of-pearl flowers. $10\frac{1}{2}$" : 26.5 cms. c 1720. (Fetched £520 in July 1982.) By courtesy of Christies, South Kensington.*

or 2.5 cms) and the earliest pleats for folded fans took on the same width. In either case the need for a careful balance was paramount and explains why earlier, pre-seventeenth century brisé fans lacked heavy guards.

THE FOLDING FAN

The folding fan may have originated in either China or Japan: in view of the fact that so much Japanese art and culture stemmed from China, it seems probable that folding fans were a Chinese invention. No one knows for certain, and very few people care (except for a little pedantic in-fighting which goes on from time to time), but it seems generally agreed that the folding fan is Oriental in origin and that it emulates a bird's wing—many are referred to as 'bat fans'. In the past, relying heavily on the painstaking research of MacIver Percival and Wooliscroft Rhead, authors stated that the Japanese invented the folding fan and that the Chinese first had the idea of decorating it with a painted scene; recent equally painstaking research contradicts these statements, and only the dedicated scholar of the future will be able to provide proof one way or another. (For a description please see Chapter 3, 'Parts of a Fan'.)

Pleated or folded fans have been known in Europe from earliest times as well, originating more from the folding or pleating of fabric—some religious and some ceremonial. The earliest (on public display) is that presented by the sixth-century Queen Theodolinda of the Lombards to the Basilica of St John the Baptist at Monza, near Milan.

There is no real start to the history of the fan; in each warm country in turn people have used them, and their decoration has altered in tune with all other decorative arts. In a way, the use of a fan to cool oneself has been as natural as the use of a drinking vessel to hold liquids—and no one has thought very much about either until their manufacture and decoration became refined.

We rely very much on early bas-reliefs, sculpture and painting in order to learn about contemporary fashions and customs. In this way we know of Egyptian fan-bearers, and proof has been provided in the handsome example discovered in the tomb of King Tutankhamun (c 1350 BC): a gold pole for a standard fan with a chased design upon it of the young god/king hunting ostriches—presumably for their fine white feathers.

Another historic example is the fan owned by Montezuma which can be seen today in the Museum für Völkerkunde in the Hofburg, Vienna. It was one of six pieces of the Montezuma Treasure sent over by Cortez to the Hapsburg King Charles V of Spain in 1524, then transferred to the Hapsburg Castle Ambras, and finally taken to the Hapsburg Palace in Vienna. It was more valuable than gold, for it was his symbol of authority. This example is a circular fixed fan, a mosaic of bright feathers applied to a wood and leather base and surrounded by an iridescent ruff of quetzal feathers; it was held on high on a bamboo pole.

Through writings, poems and excavations from tombs we also know of many ancient fans from the East. For example, in a burial mound of the sixth century AD in Fukuoka prefecture, on the island of Kyushu, are what are probably the earliest representations of fans in Japanese art; or again, in the Ma-wang-tui tomb site near Changsha in Hunan province were found two woven bamboo side-mounted fans of the second century BC, the earliest extant Chinese examples.

I am inclined to believe that fans were so universally used in warm areas that they were not dramatically introduced into Europe in the sixteenth century at all (as some previously believed) but, through the newly developing trade routes, new types of fans came through from the Orient to add to those already here. These new styles excited the interest of the ladies of the courts of Europe and they were pounced upon, used, and proudly displayed. Their display coincided with the new fashion of having portraits painted of people other than royalty, so the wealthy merchants and their wives were portrayed sporting the latest fashions in dress, and ladies' fans were seen at last, together with the newest accessories, such as gloves and handkerchiefs.

The history of the fan in both China and Japan is voluminous, and one can only suggest that the new collector slowly and steadily devours all the books listed in the Bibliography. In Chapter 3 some of their many types are explained, but it is only fair to stipulate that writers of the Orient always consider fans as a vehicle for various stages of

9. Rare Oriental fan, possibly made for export. The leaf is of paper, symmetrically cut out for mica panels to be inserted (now missing) and, in between, there are painted panels with mother-of-pearl chips. There are painted ivory sticks and pierced and painted guards, terminating in a reversed tulip-shaped finial and having a domed metal pivot. Late 17th century. Private Collection.

painting, etc., in their very long art history—that is, when they are discussing fans which were painted for their home market. 'Export' fans are a different matter. The artists and craftsmen of both China and Japan are extremely well documented; happily for us, many artists signed their names on any fan they considered worthy, often applying a date mark as well. If a collector has access to Chinese or Japanese libraries, and to scholars, then the task of identification and dating is much easier than with European fans.

In Europe the matter is considerably more difficult. As with all art history, the trained eye will be able to date a fan and even, on occasion, accurately suggest its country of origin. However there remains the question of whether a fan was made throughout by one person, or is a composite of styles and craftsmen. Mrs Pamela Hudson of Cirencester, England, once showed me a fan with French, Flemish, Persian and Chinese influences 'all thrown together with abandon' most successfully. Many people associate fans only with the French, or only with the Spanish, yet a hurried glance through any recent sales catalogue will show that they were made in Russia, Germany, Austria, the Netherlands, Italy and England, too. Some countries had Guilds (see Chapter 6), which helps identification; other areas, such as Germany or Italy, were not as we know them today but still divided into States, so that one should rather consider the arts of a city, such as Venice or Berlin.

Fans are not evaluated merely as an accessory to dress, although the less worthy ones can be directly tied to fashion, but in many cases they form part of European art history. They also reflect the best of the miniature crafts, especially those in which weight is no consideration. One must also bear in mind that the fans of the sixteenth, seventeenth and eighteenth centuries were generally extremely expensive and that the prices they fetch today may still be relatively cheap. European and American fans of the nineteenth century eventually became astonishingly cheap (some were sold for one farthing) when they were machine-made or imported by the thousand from the East. The prices fetched for a fan twenty years ago were, clearly, a great deal cheaper than today, but I believe that a clever collector can still build up a splendid collection and, in a few years' time, find that all the hard-won expertise has been more than worthwhile; aesthetically, a whole new world will have opened up, and dozens of new friends will have been acquired along the way.

3 Catalogue: Fan Types, Styles, Materials

The Bibliography at the end of this book gives a comprehensive list of books about fans. In addition, more and more exhibitions are currently being mounted, with catalogues; and endless articles about fans find their way into antiques magazines—too numerous to mention here. The older books are mostly out of print, but can sometimes be bought in specialist shops (such as K. E. Skafter, DK-4800 Nykobing 3/Falster, Denmark) or at auction sales.

Information can also be gleaned at museums, especially where they hold a collection of fans which has recently been updated. In the United Kingdom most of the modern English books mentioned should be obtainable through reference libraries—certainly the British Museum has copies.

The Fan Museum, 10/12 Croom's Hill, Greenwich, London, is, naturally, the normal place to make enquiries about fans and fan books and, if it is possible to get there, in which to study them—but ALWAYS write to the Curator in advance.

The following catalogue is an attempt to standardise terms used in the fan world and especially to help those who wish to buy at auction.

ADHESIVES
In the past most forms of adhesive were secret formulae which were jealously guarded by different manufacturers. They have already been adequately covered in previous books on fans (see Bibliography).

ADVERTISING FANS
On the whole these were made, not for sale to the public, but to be given away as advertising gimmicks for various hotels, drinks, soap, etc., in the way that plastic or paper carrier bags are today.

They were pretty, cheap gifts with a good deal of public relations impact, rather in advance of contemporary advertising in newspapers

10. Advertising fan, made in Japan and printed in India. The paper leaf is printed in colours; the sticks are of wood. Early 20th century. 8½″ : 21.75 cms. Owned by Mrs Margaret Little.

or journals. They may have been 'give-aways' but they were not 'throw-aways', for those were the days when people were loyal to a shop or hotel, and if they had been given a fan freely they felt that they then had a moral obligation to look after it and continue to patronise that establishment.

They come in every size and shape, smaller fans being more usual. Few were made before 1850 and the majority come from the first quarter of the twentieth century. So far, it is known that one group of collectors has unearthed over 1,500 different types, picking them up casually on bric-a-brac stalls. I know of three similar fans advertising an hotel: in 1970 one was bought for five pence, in 1975 another changed hands for £5 and in 1981 a third was for sale for £85—an indication of the general rise in the value of a fan.

Over 50% of advertising fans started life in Japan with cheap, unadorned wooden or bamboo sticks and a plain or floral leaf made of paper, fabric, chicken skin or even cardboard. Imported by the thousand into Europe or the United States, they were then overprinted by the advertising company with its slogan or decoration; others were merely stamped along the guardstick. It is very easy to find identical advertising fans with merely the names of different firms printed or stamped on them. Most other advertising fans are of a better quality and much more personal.

Collectors are now beginning to specialise: some buy only silk fans, other buy those which have a sample of the goods they advertise (such as Piver scent, etc.), others concentrate on French advertising fans, and so on. Up until now all advertising fans have been lumped into one category, but I believe that shortly they will be categorised in sales; they are a fascinating category for new collectors, with all the separate branches, and a great many can still be had for very small sums. See also COMMEMORATIVE FANS.
Illustration Nos. X, 10.

AIDE MEMOIRE FANS
Towards the end of the eighteenth century there appeared many fans which were designed to jog the memory: printed with dance steps, words and music of a contemporary song, historical data, rules for card-games and a variety of other information. For some there were plans of theatres and their numbered boxes, for others there were details of botanical specimens and flowers newly popularised by the travels of Captain Cook and Sir Joseph Banks. The majority were made during the latter half of the eighteenth century and into the first quarter of the nineteenth. Although they were generally printed, some were then hand-coloured, and often they were mounted on to cheap wooden sticks. The materials used for the leaf were as varied as those for advertising fans. Today they are quite rare.

ALMANAC FANS
During the eighteenth century there were some printed fans, often made of paper, which displayed an annual calender, several incorporating varous events as well; they were meant to be thrown away at the end of the year. In the nineteenth century the makers became far more inventive in their designs and other materials were used, from cardboard to silk and satin. See illustration in *The Book of Fans,* page 26.

APPLIED FACES FANS

These fans were made in China, strictly for the export trade, being highly coloured and having an enormous popularity in Europe, during the nineteenth century. They are normal folding fans with a paper leaf painted with a scene showing Chinese men and women. The figures sometimes have silken robes applied to them and (and this is the main novelty) the faces of the people are of painted, shaped pieces of ivory. They cannot, by the greatest stretch of the imagination, be called 'art'; they are pure exercises in craft, which is both why the Victorians enjoyed them so much and why they were not used by the Chinese themselves. It is also the reason for calling them not 'mandarin fans' (which would be a sarcastic insult), but 'applied faces' fans.

The practice of painting scenes thronged with people, often to commemorate some occasion, is well-known in China; moreover, during the Ch'ien Lung period (1736–1795) there was a vogue for bone and feather pictures which led to fans also being made with applications of mica, straw, feathers and silk. During the same period, similar fans were being made in Europe, but in a different style, with slightly larger applications of ivory for the painted faces, and including a neck as well as a face (several c 1760 are extant). European fans of this period and type are also known, with painted faces made from a soft chamois leather; by their style they seem to be made in France. The European

11. Applied Faces fan, the leaf mounted on ornately enamelled, pierced and carved gilt metal sticks. Probably Canton. c 1850. 11" : 28 cms. By courtesy of Bonhams, Knightsbridge.

I. Telescopic, Applied Faces fan opened to its fullest extent. The leaf is covered with ivory applied faces, and applied silk robes; the sticks are of black and gold lacquer on wood; the double silk tassel hangs from a loop. Made in Macao. 9″ : 23 cms. Mid-19th century. Private Collection.

II. The same fan displayed when 'shut down'.

III. Detail of the reverse showing a central scene, in a cartouche (one of three) of the Port at Macao. This fan could also loosely come under the category of a 'Topographical' fan.

IV. Lace fan. The leaf is of very fine Brussels mixed lace, brilliantly embroidered overall with diamanté which flashes fire as it is fluttered. The sticks are of mother-of-pearl. 14″ : 35.5 cms. c 1880. Private Collection.

V. Detail of the lace fan, showing the superb crafting of the mother-of-pearl sticks and guards, with a 'goldfish' backing and tonal gilding.

versions then had ivory or bone sticks and guards crafted in the chinoiserie style, whereas those made in China were made from a multitude of materials: carved, pierced or lacquered woods, ivory, bone, mother-of-pearl and metal filigree.

The Applied Faces fans of China can be vaguely dated by the number of figures they include—the earliest having the fewest, the latest having a great many—which led to some being named 'fans of one thousand faces', although it is rare to see more than 50 on each side. These fans came from two distinct places, Canton and Macao. Neville Iröns has done some important work on identifying both makers and artists (especially in Macao) and it is worth reading his book *Fans of Imperial China*. One type, from Canton, generally had the figures on both sides and was relatively quieter in colouring, being made 'for the rest of Europe': the other type came from Macao and was much brighter, often with a silvered or gilded paper on the reverse painted with long-tailed birds and large flowers, or sometimes with views of harbours in vignettes; these were destined for Spain or Portugal. In every case these fans give an appearance of being rich, innovative and individual, and they repay hours of study under a magnifying glass to delight the owner; they were made for about 100 years. See also MANDARIN FANS. Illustration Nos. I, 11, 34.

ARTICULATED FANS

These were made in Europe between 1760 and 1830 and were a speciality of the Germans. In appearance perfectly normal folding fans for their country or period, they also have well-carved and crafted sticks and guards. On the upper section of the guardstick there is featured some small scene, often under a protective material such as glass or an Essex crystal, in the shape of an elongated oval: many of these tiny scenes have no decorative connection with that of the leaf. Alongside this scene on the guard, hidden among the general crafting, is a tiny metal rod, and when the rod is either pushed up or pulled down, something in that scene alters; for example, one known scene shows a 'lady of quality' with a tiny mask in her hand: when the rod is moved a hinge at her elbow permits her to raise the mask to cover her eyes. Another shows a gentleman out shooting and when he raises his gun a gamebird drops to his feet; another shows a woman chopping vegetables in a kitchen.

It seems possible that these articulated scenes were made by toy-makers or jewellers, but because of their delicacy they obviously had a short life. There are, however, two types of articulated fan: firstly the earlier ones which are complicated and mechanical with hidden hinged rods activating the movement, and secondly those which tailed off into a more simplified manual movement with no hidden rods, as seen in children's books.

Illustration No. XXXIX.

ASSIGNAT FANS

A British £1 note has the words, 'I promise to pay the Bearer the sum of . . .' and an Assignat fan is a skit on these words (literally: to assign to) dating from the time of the French Revolution, when the French monetary system was in chaos. Many people paid their accounts with IOUs (assignats) and some contemporary fans were made with a scattering of these useless promissory notes on the leaf. Sometimes the design incorporated a playing card showing the seven of diamonds. These printed (occasionally hand-coloured) paper Assignat fans were made between 1789 and 1797; when the monetary system stabilised the fans were no longer made and were either thrown away or stored. They are rather rare, but there is a good collection of them in the Museum in Geneva—understandable with the Swiss interest in Banking.

See illustration in *The Fan*, page 82.

ASYMMETRICAL FANS

The Oriental world was very aware of the fact that the Japanese relished a joke, enjoyed a novelty and were not averse to an object being made with an asymmetrical design. The Chinese, on the other hand, preferred symmetry but, towards the middle of the nineteenth century, they seem to have made some fine fans in an asymmetrical shape for export to Japan, together with asymmetrically shaped porcelain objects. In turn, when released to trade worldwide, the Japanese copied these fans and exported them to France. They are large, generally with either a black or a red background, made of fine linen applied to thick or thin paper, silk or satin, and then decorated with bold designs of flowers, birds, or figures, many in black and white and a good deal of gold. The sticks too are large and made of gold and black lacquer

34

on fine wood. When folded, the fans' sticks give a 'stepped' appearance.

According to *The Lady's World* of 1887, a taste for asymmetry emerged and 'skirts now never have two sides alike'; the Japanese export in folding fans with an asymmetrical shape dates to this period.

AUTOGRAPH FANS

These are almost always of the nineteenth or the early twentieth century. They are either wooden brisé fans of some considerable size, or folding, made of stout paper, because in each case they were designed to be autographed by people unused to 'decorating' a fan. Some merely have signatures upon them, others have sketches or paintings. One of the most famous is the Messel Autograph Fan, one of a collection in private hands, a large wooden brisé fan, now displayed in a splendid case with glass on both sides in order to show the wealth of autographed sketches and paintings made by friends of Linley Sambourne. He was an artist who contributed to *Punch* in the late nineteenth century; the friends included some of the most distinguished artists of the period and it is possible that the fan was decorated in Linley Sambourne's house in Stafford Terrace in London (now open to the public).

These fans also come under the category 'commemorative fans': nothing is more frustrating, however, than to find an autographed fan with absolutely no reference to the event it commemorates.

BALLOONING FANS

Because of its rarity this type of commemorative fan now has a category of its own. It first appeared as part of the widespread enthusiasm for ballooning in the eighteenth century, although there exist pastiches (copies) made in the nineteenth century. The Montgolfier brothers (Joseph and Etienne) invented the first hot air balloon and got it off the ground in Southern France on 5th June, 1783. As a result, some of the earliest fans are also known as 'Montgolfières'. Other inventors created hot air balloons and hydrogen balloons (Blanchard and Professor Charles) soon afterwards. All the fans are hand-coloured, some displaying a flurry of national flags, and all, naturally, have to show the balloon upon them, too. They had a very short life.

BAMBOO

Most Oriental fans are catalogued thus: 'sticks: bamboo', and the collector passes on, unthinking. Yet the bamboo is an extraordinarily 'elegant grass' which occurs naturally in every continent except Europe and Antarctica, but seems happiest in southern Asia. In the world there are about one thousand species of bamboo, of some 50 genera. In Japan there are 662 species, from 13 genera; in China 300 species, of 26 genera. The most striking characteristic of bamboo is its growth—no other living thing grows so tall so fast. Near Kyoto a Japanese scientist measured the world's record: a culm (woody stalk) of *ma-dake* (*Phyllostrachys bambusoides*), Japan's commonest bamboo, grew almost four feet in 24 hours. The Chinese were the first to appreciate the beauty and usefulness of bamboo; their ancient dictionary, the *Erh Ya*, written 1000 years before Christ, referred to it and it is also known to have been both split and glued at that time.

Long before the invention of paper in the second century BC, China's earliest records were written on slips of green bamboo. It is easy to scratch or incise on bamboo's smooth skin, a quality unique in the plant kingdom. To make a bamboo book, strips were strung together with silk or ox sinew—one such bundle of 312 slips was recently unearthed in a Han Dynasty (second century BC) tomb.

Apart from bamboo's practical uses, in the Orient it is considered very beautiful. In China they call bamboo the chief member of the trio of 'Winter friends'—bamboo, Winter plum and pine—and the three occur throughout Chinese art and literature as symbols of resistance to hardship. The plum flowers while snow is still on the ground, the pine flourishes in poor soil and clings to precipitous cliffs, and the bamboo remains green throughout the year.

Bamboo, for many purposes, is lighter and stronger than steel. One of the engineering marvels of the world is the great bridge over the Min River in Sichuan (still in use after more than 1000 years) hanging from bamboo cables nearly seven inches in diameter, wound round capstans so that they can be tightened like tuning a guitar.

Bamboo is said to have a peculiarity: most species flower only at long intervals—30, 60 or even 120 years apart—and then they die. At about the same time, all plants of the same species—wherever they are in the world—will burst into flower. When this happens the culms die, the fallen seeds take root, but it may be from five to ten years before a bamboo seedling reaches full maturity and growth.

In India, it is said, bamboo is the poor man's multipurpose timber and he literally lives with it from birth to death. One-fifth of India's forest reserves are bamboo, from which the people cut selectively. In Japan most of the bamboo flourishes in the mild climate of Kyushu, the southernmost island, although the bamboo capital is Kyoto. The Japanese use bamboo for decoration and the decorative arts far more than do the Chinese; the variety of objects extends from flutes and furniture, via torture instruments, to the comfort of the 'bamboo wife'—a woven basketwork cylinder about five feet long, which the sleeper embraces (on very hot nights) and throws one leg over, so that cooling breezes can pass through.

Bamboo used for fan sticks is often from the 'tea stick' variety, named for its colour resembling freshly brewed tea. It has to be three to five years old before cutting because new culms are mostly water and if you cut them they will shrink and crack as they dry. Once cut they are cleaned with fine sand, then left in the sun for ten days. Afterwards they are straightened over a fire and then cut to length.

The use of bamboo for sticks is not to be lightly passed over, nor is it easy to pin-point which of the thousand species is being used. 'Green-striped', 'Black' (from China), 'Mottled' (from Sri Lanka), 'Golden', 'Giant' (from Burma), 'Square' and 'Tortoiseshell' are but seven different species.

It is noticeable, too, that the guards are very often of a different variety of bamboo from the sticks, often painted to match their colour, the sticks remaining as Nature made them. This is because of the length between 'nodes' or joints of the bamboo: as the guardstick had to be wider or thicker or longer, it often came from a different plant and was then disguised by paint or lacquer.

Since bamboo has a parallel grain, sticks can be evenly and cleanly cut to size and then polished. Bamboo sticks can also remain attached to the culm, leaving it as a handle, when making 'uchiwa' fans. Charlotte Salwey gave this description in her book *Fans of Japan*, published in 1894:

> About eighteen inches of bamboo is cut and prepared, of which about nine inches is split down to the node or joint which prevents further splitting. As the grain runs perfectly straight, fifty or sixty segments are obtained by careful division of exactly the same thickness. In order to keep these in position, a diminutive bow

of thick bamboo is inserted just below the joint, the segments are deftly arranged crossways, and a string having two strands is interlaced alternately between them and fastened securely: by this tension the whole framework is steadied. Though the handle is generally formed by the few inches of bamboo left below the node, other substitutes are sometimes employed for the handles, which are left either plain or embellished: coloured and naturally curved bamboo, notched and carved in an open manner, is frequently resorted to for a change. When this is the case a circular piece of thick paper or thin wood is doubled so that the lower portion of the fan is dropped into a slot and fixed with a small brass nail or rivet; but the framework of this fan is always constructed on the plan previously entered upon.

The Japanese have a reverence for natural beauty so, on the whole, they did not embellish their bamboo sticks and guards. When they did so the decoration was lightly painted in a contrasting but self-colour and the better examples were different on each side of the sticks. However, they also have a keen competitive spirit and when they made fans for the export market they sometimes inlaid the guards with ivory, wood or metals. This attitude appears similar to the change from making fans with a single leaf (which is normal for Japan) to a double leaf (more normal for China) when considering the export trade. Illustration Nos. VII, XXXII, XXXIII.

BAROQUE

This term, derived from the Portuguese word *barroco* (Spanish *barrueco*) meaning a rough or imperfect pearl, was originally used in a pejorative sense to describe seventeenth century Italian art and that of the other countries, particularly Germany, which were under Italian influence. In the decorative arts, Baroque was distinguished by a return to classical forms, but used in a totally unclassical way. Its vogue lasted from *c* 1600 to *c* 1715, when the Rococo began to take over. The earlier period was dovetailed with the High Renaissance and the latter for many years with the Rococo. It is a style of movement and freedom: in architecture buildings were designed to evoke emotional responses from those who entered them; the use of light and shade was treated in a totally different way, perspectives were adjusted, grandeur and magnificence were seen

12. *Italian baroque fan, the vellum leaf painted with Mary visiting Elizabeth, meeting on the steps before a house, surrounded by other figures and putti in a rural setting; the reverse decorated with painted flowers: mounted on carved ivory sticks inlaid with mother-of-pearl and piqué point. In free-standing glazed case, fan shaped. Early 18th century. 10″: 25.5 cms. By courtesy of Bonhams, Knightsbridge.*

from canvases to ceilings, colours were heavy and often dark in tone; 'all the world was a stage' and there was a great interest in classical mythology.

All of this can be seen interpreted on fans from *c* 1650 to *c* 1730, especially those made in France, England and the Netherlands. Many baroque fans had a spread of 18 inches (45 cms), with sticks of tortoise-shell or ivory which bore absolutely no reference to each other in their design and often appeared as a stark contrast. The leaf was dark in tone, whether of parchment or rag-paper; the painted scene continued right across from one side to the other without any breaks for vignettes, etc., and the subject matter was very grand, sometimes being surrounded by a scattering of flowers and leaves outlined with gold.

These fans usually reach a high price in sales, especially if undamaged in any way; some have been removed from their sticks and mounted as paintings. It should be noted that they really *were* easel paintings, cut to a fan-shape and applied to sticks. There is very rarely any indication that the painter wished to follow the shape of the fan in his composition, unlike the Orientals, who always considered the shape. Illustration No. 12.

BATTOIR FANS

This type applies to normal folding fans which had very few, large and curiously shaped sticks called 'battoirs' because they looked like flat guitars, or bats, or racquets for 'bat and ball'. The leaf was usually highly decorated in order to balance the bold design of the sticks—sometimes as few as six or eight in number—which were pierced, carved and generally highly crafted (sometimes interspersed with very plain, straight sticks for practical purposes); the guard-stick did not necessarily have the same shaping but did have similar crafting. Because there were so few sticks, this led to very wide pleats in the leaf and there were endless attempts to balance sticks and leaf in weight.

Most battoir fans are labelled 'Spanish' although, as a very loose rule, those made in the eighteenth century with ivory or bone sticks and guards were actually made in France for export to Spain; it was those made in the nineteenth century of plain or painted woods that originated in Spain for the home market.

BONBORI FANS

The first Japanese fans had only a single leaf, whereas Chinese fans originally had double leaves (and they still like to work this way although there are obvious exceptions). During the Muromachi period (1392–1568) Chinese double fans were introduced into Japan and, to deal with the increased thickness of the leaf, two new types of fan were developed. One type was the bonbori, with guardsticks which bent inwards at the wider end, holding the thicker leaf together (sometimes in what seemed a vicelike grip); the other type was the suehiro (q.v.).

BONE (See IVORY)

BRAZILIAN FANS

During the nineteenth century, a most prolific firm in Rio de Janeiro (M. Luiza Bittacourt) used to make a frou-frou of a fixed fan. These came in cardboard boxes of circular shape, with a handle, about six inches deep, and a well-fitting lid—exactly like a hatbox. The fan was made up of feathers, layer upon layer, upon a canvas support, often with a tiny hummingbird alight in the centre. The colours were of every shade of the rainbow, starting with white or tinted ducks' feathers, the points of their quills to the centre, frothed over by maribou and finally decorated by an iridescent hummingbird, or tiny iridescent beetles, or both. The other side of the fan was kept flat (so that it could be laid to rest) and it was held by a handle of bone, wood or turned ivory. In some cases the fans are made with feathers on both sides, and in others, instead of the hummingbird, there are small, beautifully made silk and feather flowers which come together with a flower wreath—showing that these were made for either a bride or a debutante. The fact that they were exported so often by this company leads us to call them all 'Brazilian Fans', although other firms made them, too. There is an interesting selection in the Museum in Bournemouth. See illustration in *The Book of Fans*, page 90.

BRIDAL FANS (See MARRIAGE FANS)

BROKEN FANS (See TRICK FANS)

CABRIOLET FANS

I have been guilty in the past of misunderstanding the real reason behind the shape of the cabriolet fan; I am especially grateful to Neville Iröns for propelling me towards Peter Mann at the Science Museum, London, for the latter's patient explanations and for information in two books which have helped me: *Carriage Terminology: an Historical Dictionary* by Don. H. Berkebile, Smithsonian Institution, Washington 1978 (page 64) and *Looking at Carriages* by Sallie Walrond, Pelham, London 1980 (page 96).

The cabriolet was introduced into Paris in 1755 by Josiah Childs (who also designed it). A small, light-weight one-horse chaise which could easily be driven by a daring lady driver, it had wheels of a very large diameter. The cabriolet had a curious motion when travelling because of its pair of long, springing shafts which made it buck and prance like a goat—its name came from the French *cabrioler*, to leap or to caper, because it was so light and frisky. The shape was like an elongated comma, or nautilus shell, which was most uncommon at that time. The third curious characteristic of the cabriolet was its hood: in order to leave room for the Tiger (or groom) to travel standing on a platform at the rear of the carriage, it was generally kept half-open when driving by means of a metal bar which radiated across the central section of the ribs of the hood . . . a new technique adapted later for the hoods of baby carriages.

Childs' cabriolet was the first of its type—in fact it did not become common in England until about 1794. Letters flew back and forth between Paris and the other capitals of fashion (especially London), and descriptions are extant of cabriolets being painted onto the garments of both sexes, just as we might buy a passing vogue today. Fans were immediately made to look something like the cabriolets, with the vehicle painted onto them, too.

The cabriolet fan is therefore distinguished by certain features: long, thin sticks like the shafts, an ordinary fan leaf but with the addition of a secondary one, like the strengthening bar across the ribs of the hood, placed across the centre of the sticks and, with the genuine ones *c* 1755–60, a painting of a lady driver with the hood of her cabriolet 'half-up'.

It now seems fairly safe to assume that all genuine cabriolet fans of the eighteenth century were made in France, that they should all have two leaves, that they should have thin, straight sticks and lastly, but by no means least, that they should have painted on them a scene of the driver and her 'cab'. Nineteenth century cabriolet fans are copies and show a variety of other small scenes. The double leaf has been seen on earlier fans (I know of two *c* 1740) so the painting of the vehicle is essential. There is also a ravishingly pretty treble-leafed fan in the Oldham Collection, Museum of Fine Arts, Boston.

CAMIEU FANS

This fan has a painting on the leaf of different tones and shades of the same basic colour, such as rose or blue or green. Shades of grey are better known as 'grisaille' and used for mourning fans.

CANTON FANS (See APPLIED FACES FANS)

CARTOGRAPHIC FANS

These are rare today although they must have been a popular novelty in their time, and they were made all over the world. Mostly made of paper, although silk examples are known, they are generally printed fans on cheap sticks, designed as a guide for the traveller, showing countries, counties or towns, and having been of help on a journey they were then thrown away. Fans known are enormously varied: a map of Switzerland (giving details of how many miles it was from Berne to London or Rome, etc.), another showing the centre of Pekin, an eighteenth century one showing the City of London, others showing counties in England and a rare one on silk showing a map of Gibraltar. See illustration in *Fans of Imperial China*, page 144.

CARTOUCHE

This is a term used to describe certain decoration upon a fan. A cartouche is ornamentation in a scroll form, applied especially to an elaborate framing around a design; by extension the word is applied to any oval shape, or even to a decorative shield, whether scrolled or not. A cartouche then refers to a decoration on a fan which has a scrolled border or framing, isolating that decoration from the remainder of the fan leaf. It can be a painting upon paper, vellum, etc., or embroidery

13. The leaf of this fan is painted with various scenes in four curiously shaped vignettes: the ivory sticks carved, pierced, painted and gilt with figures and scrolling and with encrustations of carved mother-of-pearl. Probably Flemish. 11″ : 28 cms. c 1750. (Fetched £520 in May 1982.) By courtesy of Christies, South Kensington.

14. *French fan, the leaf painted with five vignettes of different shapes, the reserves painted with fruit, flowers and lace with a peacock blue border; the ivory sticks carved and pierced in gilt with dancing figures and musicians, one guardstick set with a mother-of-pearl plaque inscribed with the initials J.J.P.B., the other guardstick set with a mother-of-pearl skull and carved with an ivory pierrot. 11" : 28 cms. c 1765. (Fetched £300 March 1982.) By courtesy of Christies, South Kensington.*

upon a textile, or carving upon brisé fans made from ivory or woods.

A *medallion* is similar to a cartouche, but the framing is either oval or circular and of a dominant size within the area of the leaf. A *reserve* is the smaller oval or shield-shape around a monogram on ivory or woods or around small scenes upon either leaf or sticks. It is possible for a cartouche, a medallion or a reserve to be centrally placed; it is also possible to have several upon a leaf or sticks.

A *vignette* is an overall term for a cartouche.
Illustration Nos. 13, 14.

CELLULOID FANS (See PLASTIC FANS)

CHAPEL FANS
Fans were made for use in churches years before worshippers in chapels decided to have their own version. The church fans (q.v.) are more

elaborate and overtly concerned for the Royal Family; chapel fans do not mention them. The first printed, stipple-engraved, uncoloured chapel fan was dated 1st May, 1796, and is entitled 'New Church Fan Published with the Approbation of the Lord Bishop of London' by the Rev. W. Peters. Chapel fans are usually of paper, but vellum was also used.

CHICKEN SKIN

This is an extremely fine type of parchment which was used for fan leaves. It 'snaps' like paper, is far more refined than the normal soft vellum used for fans in northern European countries and it has no grain. The finest type came from Persia and was used for tracing documents and miniatures, and was also used in the Mughal Courts. It is the skin taken from an unborn kid (killing the mother before its birth) and then prepared as a surface for painting. The earliest reached Europe via Venice, through trade with the Middle East and Levantine countries, and its use for fan leaves spread up through Europe during the

15. An 18th century painted fan, the chicken-skin leaf decorated with Diana and her attendants, mounted on finely worked silvered, gilded and jewelled mother-of-pearl sticks and guards. Possibly Dutch. 10½″ : 26.5 cms. By courtesy of Bonhams, Knightsbridge.

eighteenth century. Many of the finest fans are made with 'chicken-skin' leaves; the name stems from the similarity to the chicken's egg embryo skin, which is equally fine, light, strong and almost transparent when held up to the light. When used for fans sometimes more than one skin is glued together to make it more opaque. See also PARCHMENT. Illustration Nos. 15, 29, 35.

CHILDREN'S FANS
During the eighteenth century children were often treated merely as small adults in society, and therefore wore much the same fashions as their parents, but in a small size. This also applied to fans. Many tiny fans were as beautifully decorated for children as for their parents; some were educational but most were just smaller adult fans. They are much in demand today.

CHINESE IVORY BRISÉ FANS
These were made in China from the mid-seventeenth century as export fans to the West. The first type were small, wedge-shaped, made with

16. Chinese ivory brisé fan, of the transitional period when they began to be carved (for the first time) on both sides. Made in Canton. 7½″ : 19 cms. c 1800. From Fans of Imperial China, *by Neville Iröns, by courtesy of The House of Fans Limited.*

absolutely plain ivory sticks, and painted. Some of the painted scenes show European traders (Dutch or Portuguese) and occasionally there is a small amount of piercing through the ivory. Most of them came into Europe via Holland and were a great novelty. From these stem the 'Vernis Martin' fans (q.v.).

Between 1700–1720 a slightly different type of ivory brisé fan emerged. Again it was wedge-shaped, the ivory pierced in the upper half with a light, geometrical design (or with circular 'cash' shapes) in which certain sections were left solid. These formed 'canvases' for a painted scene, with gilding. The sticks were held by a fine, strong thread (not a ribbon which was not seen until about 1750), the rivet was metal and the guardsticks remained solid and unpierced until *c* 1740.

One point of recognition between Chinese ivory brisé fans and copies made in Europe is that the Europeans always placed their ribbon along the edge of the sticks and the Chinese invariably placed theirs in proper slots well below the edge of the sticks. Until *c* 1830 they also made a feature of the ribbon area, as if there was an implied border. From *c* 1710 the ivory on these fans was pierced through, but after *c* 1760 it was 'ribbed', showing fine, vertical parallel lines as a background, interspersed with small areas of carved ivory in the shape of flowers, leaves, birds, circles and shield-shapes. Small painted scenes were used as decorative motifs on ivory brisé fans from *c* 1710 until *c* 1750, when they finally disappeared, leaving the ivory creamy white, with a matching silk ribbon.

In size these fans were larger, finer and more supple during the eighteenth century and became shorter, cruder and thicker during the nineteenth. Some fans show a central shield shape, developed from earlier vignettes, in solid ivory: these were first painted and then developed into an area where the shape remained, the background was ribbed and a monogram was placed in the centre—carved to order in Europe. By *c* 1750 each individual stick suddenly acquired a rounded tip, and, in the main, the finest ivory brisé fans continued to have this form until well into the nineteenth century.

During the final quarter of the eighteenth century these fans seemed to divide into three separate parts: the area above the ribbon, the area below the ribbon and the area from the gorge to the rivet. Little decorative borders appeared surrounding each area, very fine and delicate, the main decoration within each border being totally different from the others, i.e.—the section above the ribbon could be circular, the central section could have a scattering of small flowers and leaves with ribbing and finely carved vignettes and the gorge section could be both solid and carved with elliptical shapes. At the turn of the century the section above the ribbon ceased to have identical designs on all sticks (usually flowers and leaves) and began to feature different scenes on each, such as those from Chinese life, Taoist or Buddhist symbols, etc.

To coincide with the new European fashions in dress at this time, fans became far smaller, some regaining their wedge-shape and losing their 'finger-tip' outline. The ribbed background persisted, and while above the ribbon the tiny scenes were all different, below it the overall design became fussier, more formalised, with more solid sections of carving showing scenes now of figures (a few to start with, many later on) and some architectural scenes.

Guardsticks throughout the eighteenth century generally appeared 'by a different hand'. From c 1710–1740 they were solid, with occasional touches of paint or gilding; from c 1740–c 1800 they were very often of exactly the same pattern, not necessarily with any reference to the main design, showing fine carved trailing floral patterns, often in definite sections and with a tiny border surrounding the designs. After c 1800 the guards changed from a floral design to depicting scenes from Chinese life or scenes with animals (often of dragons) in heavy raised carving and with no outlining border . . . however, a few floral designs carried on into the century.

By c 1800 Chinese ivory brisé fans suddenly changed to being carved on both sides of the ivory sticks—which meant that the ivory had to become rather thicker and therefore rather heavier. From c 1800 to c 1835 they became somewhat standardised: many were between 7 to 8 inches in length (16–19 cm); the finials of the sticks remained rounded, but bordering and fine inserts disappeared and the area above the ribbon became a sweeping continuation of the design below the ribbon; the gorge area became smaller and more stylised; the main body continued to be ribbed but had far more solid sections of ivory carved with designs showing scenes from Chinese life on both sides of the fan.

By c 1850 the Chinese ivory brisé fan suddenly declined in quality. The rounded finials flattened out, the carving on the sticks became coarse, crude and indistinguishable because it was so shallow: only the guards were still worthwhile. Naturally these are generalisations on the evolution of the Chinese ivory brisé fan: there are of course exceptions, especially when a fan was made to order and not merely an impersonal export from Canton. For Japanese ivory brisé fans see ZŌGE OGI. Illustration Nos. 6, 16, 17.

CHINESE LACQUER FANS

Lacquer fans were made in the East; fans made in the West which look as though they have been lacquered have actually only been varnished. The term 'lacquer fans' refers strictly to a short series of fine brisé fans from China which date from approximately 1790 to 1850. They are small, light, mainly coloured black and gold. Their decoration is almost always in three distinct sections: that above the ribbon (or, in rare cases, strong thread), that of the main 'leaf' and that of the gorge area. Usually each stick is straight except for a small curvature by the simulated gorge and usually each stick finial is curved like a fingertip. They rarely have loops added and the final throat of the guard near the rivet can be unbelievably slender. They are lacquered on to wood. In the main, in the earlier examples, the gold patterning on the black lacquer is of a delicate vine leaf while, towards the end of their popularity, figure and architectural subjects were introduced, some in lavish vignettes. They were generally both made in and exported from Canton.
Illustration Nos. XIII, 17.

17 a, b Chinese ivory brisé fan, finely pierced, lacquered with a scene of a bowl of flowers and two birds in the reserves (the design is identical on the reverse). It has it's original fine cording to hold it together at the top. Made for the European market. Probably late 17th century. Private Collection.

CHINOISERIE

This is a Western fashion of the seventeenth and eighteenth centuries, seen primarily in interior design, furniture, pottery, textiles and garden design, that represents a fanciful European interpretation of Chinese styles. In the first decades of the seventeenth century, English, Italian and, later, other craftsmen began to draw freely on decorative forms found on cabinets, porcelain vessels and embroideries imported from China. The earliest appearance of a major chinoiserie interior scheme was in Louis Le Vau's *Trianon de porcelaine* of 1670–71 (subsequently destroyed), built for Louis XIV at Versailles. The fad spread rapidly: indeed, no court residence, especially in Germany, was complete without its Chinese room, which was often, as it had been for Louis, the room for the Prince's mistress (e.g. Lackkabinett, Schloss Ludwigsburg, Württemberg, 1714–22). Chinoiserie, used mainly in conjunction with Baroque and Rococo styles, featured extensive gilding and lacquering; much use of blue-and-white (e.g. in Delftware); asymmetrical forms; disruptions of orthodox perspective; and Oriental figures and motifs. An entire chapter is devoted to chinoiserie in *Fans from the East*, detailing sources of design (Bérain, Pillement, etc.), difficulties for the fan makers and so on. Another invaluable source is the book on *Chinoiserie* by Hugh Honour. See also my own article on 'Chinoiserie and Japanning' in the *FCI Bulletin* No. 12 (Summer 1979).

Fans made in the chinoiserie style still continue to tease collectors, and many are incorrectly attributed, for the Chinese fan painters who exported fans to the West were very able indeed in interpreting the prevailing tastes. Some fan leaves were separately painted and sent to be mounted on Western sticks; some sticks were made in China from patterns sent out from the West (as they sent out designs for porcelain) and then mounted with Western leaves at a later date. On the other hand there were many equally clever Western decorators who copied Chinese fans or styles and sold them as Oriental in order to receive a better price.

For those who had never been to China (and very few had) the reports which filtered back described an idyllic civilisation. The 'vision of Cathay' evoked a mysterious, charming country, chronicled only by poets and painters; their subjects, apparently, were beautiful landscapes with craggy, snow-capped mountain ranges; grassy plains with cities of dreaming pagodas, intersected by meandering rivers; with

18. Chinoiserie fan in a glazed fan case. The chicken-skin leaf painted with eight shaped vignettes of Chinese figures, the reserves painted with golden trellis against a brown ground; the ivory sticks carved, pierced, silvered and gilt and backed with mother-of-pearl. French. 10½" :26.5 cms. c 1780. (Fetched £260 in July 1982.) By courtesy of Christies, South Kensington.

whole fleets of delicate junks carrying fluttering pennants and precious cargoes which we can be sure contained jades, porcelain, silks, green ginger and delicately scented tea. The people of this land, according to their artists, seemed to be small and neat and all exactly alike, identifiable only by their rich, brocaded clothes. Work seemed forever at a standstill, apart from a few rustics who drowsed on the backs of water-buffaloes; life seemed eternally a warm afternoon, the employment of leisure apparently regarded as the serious business of life. They appeared to paint or write about a country of perpetual Spring, where the prunus was always in blossom and architects had created brightly painted latticed garden-houses to live in, jade pavilions, pleasure domes open to the sky, tall pagoda towers of porcelain and spindly little bridges over good-mannered streams. On the eaves, which were absurdly wide and turned up at the corners, hung tiny bells, set a-jingling by the reverberations of great gongs booming from nearby temples.

That is what was expected from 'Cathay' in the seventeenth and eighteenth centuries by the people of the West, and that is what the decorators supplied on goods (labelled 'chinoiserie' today—it is a nineteenth century term). So, to a certain extent, those scenes are more than slightly suspect when seen on a fan, especially if painted in tones of blue and white. Equally suspect is a scene where the figures all look one way, for while the Chinese enjoy painting a group of people, for instance, walking from the right to the left, they always have a final person on the left walking to the right in order to 'turn' the scene into a harmonious whole. Another clue to what is genuine Chinese (never Japanese), as against what came from the West, is that the Chinese did not paint upon skins but always upon paper or silk.

The whole subject is most tantalising and, without signatures or seal-marks, the best method of identification is to consult academics in the Chinese field and, even then, leave a small corner of your mind open. Illustration Nos. XVII, 18, 23.

CHOWRIES

The word means a 'whisk or fly-flapper', and can be spelled 'chowry' (this word first came into general usage in 1777) or the Hindi spelling of 'chaunri'—the proper name for the bushy tail of the Tibetan yak. Chowries were used in the Indian sub-continent from the beginning of time. In the Exhibition *Fans from the East* (and illustrated in the book of the same title) there was a very fine chowry made of ivory. As it was to be held in the hand it looked like a thin baton of solid ivory, carved with iris and poppy motifs from traditional Mughal miniatures, with a carved pineapple finial at the base, and at the other end it opened up like a vase. Into this vase were fixed hundreds of long, thin slivers of ivory—just as if a potato peeler had stripped off paper-thin lengths of the ivory straight from the tusk. These lengths were very tough and flexible, acting as small whips to any flies which settled. It was probably made for the Ruler of Patiala State in the eighteenth century, and is now in the Victoria and Albert Museum.

CHUKEI OGI

This fan is one of the commonest seen in the West and the type we most associate with the fan makers of Japan. It has simple bamboo sticks and a paper leaf which has been painted to fit in with one of the *No* dramas, and it is carried by an actor in the play. According to Neville Iröns, this type was first introduced in the seventeenth century. If you are able to read Japanese there is a very interesting section in Mr Nakamura Kiyoe's book on Japanese Fans, *Ogi to Ogie* (*Fans and Fan Painting*) in Chapter II, Part Two, where the author deals with (a) The unifying of the four companies and one style, (b) Fans of the *Shité*, (c) Fans of the *Waki*, (d) Resting of the Fan, and (e) Fans of the *Kyōgen*.
Illustration No. XXXIII.

CHURCH FANS

The first of the church fans appeared in England during the 1720s. They gave prayers, the Ten Commandments, the Creed, and special prayers for the Royal Family (unlike chapel fans). In the United States church fans, made from turkey feathers or palmetto leaves, were made available as you went in through the front door (and, in some places, still are). English church fans, printed mostly on paper, but occasionally on vellum or silk, had to have the sanction of the Bishop of London.

CLOUTÉ

This is a term which some auction houses use and tend to confuse the collectors in so doing. It comes from the French word *clou*, meaning a nail (hardware, not on the fingertip) and should mean, when used as a description, a form of 'nail-head' application, generally of metal.

One famous auction house uses the term 'clouté' as 'the application of a solid onto a solid, or encrustation'; i.e., carved ivory sticks may have a further decoration of carved mother-of-pearl set onto the top of the ivory, or even inlaid into a section of it but so that it is raised above the original background rather than being left flush with it.

Clouté always implies an extra ornamentation on top of something which was precious enough in the beginning. One famous collector considers clouté to mean the setting of a tiny solid silver figure onto the mother-of-pearl of a guard, or carved tortoiseshell motifs set onto ivory and so on. However, the simplest use of the term is the basic 'nail-head'. It is usually referred to as a European technique rather than the easily recognisable Oriental styles.

COCKADE FANS

This category encompasses fans of a particular shape rather than of a period or country. Basically the fan opens out into a complete circle, the end-sticks forming a long double handle. Some are made from textiles, paper or parchment, with a great many fine pleats, and others are brisé. The earliest known extant cockade fan (other than small terracotta models of ladies with cockade fans) is that said to have been owned by Queen Theodolinda (sixth century), now at Monza. Some very fine brisé cockade fans were popular from 1785, made from ivory, tortoiseshell, mother-of-pearl and aromatic woods.
Illustration Nos. 19, 20.

19. *Parasol cockade fan, made in Canton, of pierced ivory and with its original carved ivory hanging box. 15″ : 38 cms. c 1820. (Fetched £1100 in August 1981.) By courtesy of Christies, South Kensington.*

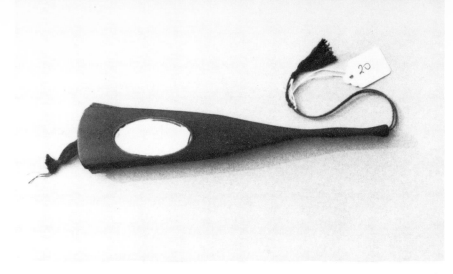

20 Souvenir fan, made of olivewood, the waxed cotton leaf stencilled with vignettes of floral sprays, the leaf is edged with a cotton bobbin-lace border and has a red cotton pull tassel. The guard is incised and decorated with a marquetry inlay of an Italian boy. An oval mirror is set into the reverse. Probably made in Sorrento. 10" : 25.5 cms. c 1870–1900. Owned by Mrs Georgette Tilley.

COMMEMORATIVE FANS

In the past these fans have been lumped into the category Advertising Fans; in some cases they do a double duty but the purest form should be hived off into their own section. They are fans which commemorate some event which is worth recording, from a cricket match between Eton and Harrow (a splendid extant example combines thick and thin paper with silk sections, silk tassels and sequins, and has a pencil attached) to a visit by a royal personage or even, as recently seen, 'General Booth's Welcome Home from Triumphal Campaign in the Far East, December 28th, 1926.' (Miller Collection). They have been known since printed fans began, yet most were made in the nineteenth century; earlier ones were more visual, with paintings of the event, while later ones were heavily over-printed with the facts worth recording. Materials ranged from paper and cardboard to silk and satin. They are not to be confused with advertising fans, although sometimes commercial companies did overprint them, possibly as a form of sponsorship. See AUTOGRAPH FANS, BALLOONING FANS, MARRIAGE FANS. Illustration Nos. 21, 46.

21. The parchment leaf of this fan is printed with portraits of Queen Victoria at various ages and issued to commemorate her Diamond Jubilee; mounted on carved and painted wooden sticks. c 1897. English 10″ : 25.5 cms. By courtesy of Bonhams, Knightsbridge.

CONVERSATION FANS

The 'language of the fan' is discussed elsewhere and, in most cases, could be expressed by means of any fan at all. However, there were some fans made in the eighteenth century with which a complete conversation could be carried on, by holding up the fan and then pulling back a tiny section, revealing a letter of the alphabet behind it. In this way it was possible to spell out each word without difficulty (so long as the viewer had excellent eyesight) rather than having to remember each fan 'signal'. It was a very leisurely way of flirting whilst a duenna was in tow and smacks of a much more pressure-free way of life. There is one in the Messel Collection.

DAGGER FANS

Dagger fans were used in the Orient, in both China and Japan, made by sword-makers as lethal weapons and eventually banned by law. They looked exactly like ordinary closed fans and could be thrust through an 'obi' or tucked into a boot. They were made from wood and came apart into two sections—pull the 'sticks' away and a sharp knife lay inside. Some people in Europe thought that they were made as paper-knives but this is incorrect, they were always made for murder. In Europe, especially in Germany and Austria, small 'daggers' were made of metal, with a velvet-covered sheath, which, when pulled apart, turned into fans acting on a 'half-cockade' principle. Both were novelties and the latter seemed to tie up with the Aesthetic movement. See an illustration of the latter on page 113 of *The Book of Fans*.

DANCE FANS

When, at last, ladies and gentlement danced together rather than as part of a set (contemporary with 'promiscuous seating' where ladies no longer sat at one side of a table facing the men but side by side with them) the gentleman invited the lady for a specific dance within a published programme of dances for the evening. Both sexes wrote down the name or number of the dance, and of the arranged partner— to avoid embarrassing discourtesies. Several types of fan were made to cater for this custom: firstly there were fans with numbered sticks on which the name could be written; then there were small brisé fans, complete with pencil, which would hang from the main fan, on which the names could be recorded; then there were tiny 'aide-memoire' fans

22. Dance fan, the leaf of gauze embroidered with sequins and spangles to look like a butterfly. French or English. Edwardian. With bone sticks set piqué point with cut steels. The loop has an extra attachment from which a tiny dance programme would be hung.
8½″: 21.5 cms. Owned by Mrs Margaret Little.

which were pulled out from the top of the guard; and lastly there were ordinary paper booklets, complete with a tiny pencil, which would be sold with the fan 'of a lady's choice' and which would hang from the loop, nestling in the accompanying ribbons. In the main, collectors like to have fans where the small pencil is still attached to the fan. These were all made in Europe or the United States. Illustration No. 22.

DECOUPÉ FANS
This is virtually the art of decorative paper or skin cutting and the technique originated in China in the fourteenth century. The earliest

known illustrated European examples extant are the sixteenth century Cluny fan (now apparently lost) or the Oldham fan in the Museum of Fine Arts in Boston (others, not previously illustrated, are known to exist). They are made from fine vellum, cut out with tiny sharp scissors or with surgical knives (the latter type has the addition of small mica inserts to add to the effect of texturing). There were later copies of this technique in the seventeenth and eighteenth centuries. Another type of this work is a pricked design executed with pins or fine needles, giving a 'paper doyly' effect—in other words, the design looked like fine lace but the reverse was rough to the finger-tip. In a third type, the fan was mechanically punched out or stamped by paper-makers. I am grateful to Hélène Alexander for this information; Ref: Diderot: *Encyclopédie* section Découpeur et Gauffreur d'Etoffes en Planche 1ère; see Nos. 5 and 6—Fer à piquer autre fer à piquer on emporte, piece. In other words the paper makers had a mechanical punch which worked on alternate leaves and the work is recognisable as a technique.

23. Chinoiserie decoupé fan, the leaf finely painted with a Chinaman and fruit, the background decoupé with punched-work (possibly Chinese): mounted on carved mother-of-pearl sticks (the guards repaired). c 1760. 11″: 28 cms. By courtesy of Bonhams, Knightsbridge.

Another collector of note feels that this type of work was mostly carried out in China, using the 'fish-scale' motif (which is often seen in Chinese carving and piercing of ivory), probably also used with a small punch. In either category the paper decorator takes care not to interfere with any painted designs upon the leaf and works around it.

These fans were made in the various techniques mentioned above from the sixteenth to the nineteenth centuries.
Illustration Nos. XV, 3, 23.

DIRECTOIRE FANS

This type was made c 1789 to c 1805 and was the evolutionary link between the great, grand fans of the eighteenth century and the tiny Empire fans. They remain fairly large, are often made of ivory (brisé) or of embroidered textiles, and carry Neoclassical decorations. None of them have jewels but rely on slenderising lines and often reflect a post-Revolution 'serious' approach to life. See also NEOCLASSICISM, although not all Directoire fans carried Neoclassical motifs.
Illustration No. XXIII.

DOLLS' FANS

Small fans, exact replicas of fans for ladies, were provided for the exquisite dolls sold for children from c 1785 to the end of the Edwardian period. Nothing distinguishes them from adult fans other than their size.

DOMINO FANS

To attend a risqué play during the late seventeenth century and into the eighteenth, ladies were expected 'not to be there', in the same manner as Orientals in some high position who, on meeting a colleague, and with no time to spare for all the normal courtesies, would raise a fan across their face to say 'I am not here' . . . and no one would expect to be offended. Ladies would therefore go to the play with a mask, or domino, across their eyes. Later they carried fans with slits cut across for their eyes to watch the play, or which had small inserts of mica which acted as 'windows' for the lady to look through. During the nineteenth century some fans of this type were made, often of white silk or satin, with a black domino, edged with lace, set on a slant on the fan. See also MASK FANS, MICA FANS, GUT FANS.

EMBROIDERED FANS

The Chinese have always been famed for their superb embroidery techniques, sometimes so fine it was known as 'needle painting'. They made many embroidered fans on silk or satin, some of double but mostly single leaves, with the design so perfect that it is difficult to tell which is the obverse and which the reverse. They used, in the main, satin stitches (and Pekin knot on the many fan bags) and at least one fan is extant where there is fine embroidery on one side and the fan is painted on the other. In the East the embroiderers imitated contemporary paintings; in Europe the whole approach was that of exhibiting a craft, so that they used a great many types of stitches, i.e. gold thread tambour stitch on silk leaves, gold 'bearding' embroidery on Empire fans, etc. European embroidered fans were mainly produced in the nineteenth century; embroidered fans of China have been extant for much longer.
Illustration No. 4.

EMPIRE FANS

This period (c 1804 to c 1814) derives its name from the era during which Napoleon reigned as Emperor, starting in a simple enough manner and enriched as the years went by. Fashions for fans took a lesson from the Revolution and followed dress most carefully—they became, at last, a pure accessory—so where there were dresses of white muslin, batiste or embroidered cotton hugging the figure and slimming the silhouette, the fans followed suit. They were now small, even tiny, and were sometimes named 'imperceptibles' or 'minuets', but not 'Lilliputians' (q.v.). Fine paintings were 'out', sequins, spangles and gold net backing were 'in'—one is even known made from ass's hide. Sticks were made of less costly materials such as wood, horn and bone, some embellished with gold paint or cut steels. The leaves of nets (metallic or otherwise), silks or gauzes were decorated with sequins or spangles. The sequins are always circular (spangles are shaped), of gold, gold-colouring, silver or silver-colouring: they could become foxed in time and the real silver often turned black, leaving the cheapest type to remain bright today. Gold or metallic threads were used to embroider some Empire fans and there was the occasional use of paper-thin mother-of-pearl. The sticks were worked with care and guards occasionally had real gems randomly ornamenting them. Otherwise, in order

to break away and initiate something new (rather than imitating known decorations) marcasite was seen, as was jet, coloured glass, pastes, Wedgwood cameos or medallions and very colourful metallic backing foils. One special feature seen at this time was the 'barrel' rivet, and another was the fact that each fan appeared to have been made throughout by the same hand rather than piecemeal.
Illustration No. XXXV.

EUROPEAN IVORY BRISÉ FANS

Although a very great deal is known about ivory and the fact that it was carved in European countries, there still remains much controversy over whether ivory fans were carved in Dieppe, Paris, Holland or Switzerland. It is probable that they were carved in all these places and it is known that, early on, Chinese craftsmen were brought into Europe to carve ivory. During the nineteenth century some fine fans were made; those of the Empire period were often unbelievably fine (frequently with pastes or diamonds set at the rivet), and later there were many which were quite plain but had extremely heavy guards covered with carved flowers (possibly from Dieppe), or mountain goats in an Alpine scene (possibly from Switzerland), or with painted birds, insects and flowers along the edge, sometimes with straw or feathers applied (possibly from Holland). Spanish, Austrian and German examples are prolific and very accomplished.

ÉVENTAIL

This is the French name for a fan. A fan maker is therefore an *éventailliste*.

FAN OF ONE THOUSAND FACES (See APPLIED FACES FANS)

FEATHER FANS

As explained in Chapter 1, these fans were probably the first type to be used and have continued to be popular ever since. Feathers can be used for brisé fans (especially during Edwardian times) with huge ostrich feathers (dyed or left plain) mounted on tortoiseshell sticks. Or feathers can be used to edge textiles, sandwiched between a double leaf. Or fans can be made from one huge wing of some bird—see page 52 of *The Book of Fans*, for an asymmetrical fan of eagles' feathers.

24. *Commemorative fan, made by the Goldsmith and Jeweller, Tom Dobbie. Three pure white ostrich feathers, from the male bird, are held in a silver handle. This has an applied gold emblem showing the Prince of Wales' feathers set within a gold crown and the motto 'Ich Dien'. On the reverse is the logo of the Fan Circle International and the engraved words THE MARRIAGE OF THE PRINCE OF WALES AND LADY DIANA SPENCER 29 JULY 1981. At the base is the number within this Limited Edition of 25, plus the Hall marks. Overall height about 15″ : 38 cms. Author's Collection.*

There are many varieties, probably the most famous feather fans being those made to signify social position: those carried until recently on either side of the Pope; the sixteenth century fan made for Montezuma;

VI. *Japanese ogi. A delicate painting in watercolours and inks of a landscape and three
small figures. The sticks and guards are of ivory with takamaki-e incorporating shibayama
inlay ; there is an engraved silver loop and twin silk tassels. This fan is very large and was
extremely popular in both Europe and the USA c 1870. 13½" : 34.5 cms. From* Fans of
Imperial Japan *by Neville Irons, by courtesy of The House of Fans Limited.*

VII. *Japanese ogi or folding fan. The leaf is of a silk and paper mixture and shows a scene
of people in traditional costume against a harbour landscape. The sticks are of serrated
bamboo, the ivory guards have a shibayama inlay. 10¾" : 27.5 cms. c 1875. From* Fans of
Imperial Japan *by Neville Irons, by courtesy of The House of Fans Limited.*

VIII and IX. Gold filigree fan (18 carat), each stick having been hallmarked; it is also finely enamelled with white, yellow, blue and green. The mount is of Brussels Rosaline lace, the silk tassel has a gold filigree cap. Possibly Spanish. 8″ : 20.5 cms. Owned by Mrs Georgette Tilley.

X and XI. Advertising fan, the paper leaf being hand-coloured and showing the Ironmongers Hall in Fenchurch Street (on the reverse their Arms). It would be interesting to know more about this fan as it was made by Duvelleroy, 167 Regent Street, W., and the writing is in French: l'Hotel des Ferronniers dans la Rue de Fenchurch á Londres. The sticks are of bone with a gilt decoration. Late 19th century. English. 10″ : 25.5 cms. Owned by Mrs Georgette Tilley.

XII. *Two fans from Java. Each is made from buffalo hide, held by carved buffalo horn. The brisé one on the left shows the normal Wayang shadow puppet designs carried out in gold and red (8″ : 20 cms) : the fixed one on the right shows the Pertala Indera Maha Sakti, or stylised peacock (9¼″ : 23.5 cms). 19th century. Owned by Mrs Margaret Little.*

XIII. *Chinese lacquer brisé fan, made in Canton. 7¾″ : 19.75 cms. c 1840. Private Collection.*

XIV. *Varnished fan, European, possibly Dutch. This is a brisé fan, of ivory sticks, painted with a scene of 'Eliezer bearing gifts to Rebecca at the Well' and then varnished. This could also be called a 'Lilliputian' fan. 8″ 20.5 cms. c 1740. Private Collection.*

XV. *Decoupé or Punched-work fan, the leaf showing a painted scene on paper with an elaborate background of punched-work (either French or Chinese). The ivory sticks are finely crafted and colourfully painted and varnished. 14½″ : 37 cms. c 1760. Private Collection.*

the fans made for Tutankhamun and those made for tribal chiefs in Borneo, parts of Africa and for the Indians in North America. Quite one of the most delightful is the fan made to commemorate the wedding of the Prince of Wales to Lady Diana Spencer in 1981. The celebrated goldsmith and jeweller, Tom Dobbie, made 25 of these, with silver handles, into which dropped three white ostrich feathers, similar to the insignia of the Prince. Permission had to be granted from the Royal couple that such a fan might be made, and it is known that the Princess was presented with one for herself. These fans will one day be great collectable items. They are numbered and dated, engraved with the commemoration details and have the logo of the Fan Circle International upon them, together with the hallmarks of the goldsmith, the London Assay Office and the year mark. It is a splendid link between the original material for fans (feathers) the ancient insignia of the Princes of Wales, the Fan Circle International and our future King and Queen. See COMMEMORATIVE FANS, OSTRICH FEATHER FANS. Illustration Nos. 24, 45.

FILIGREE FANS

There are several types of filigree fan. Basically the filigree is made of a soft (pure) silver or gold; the silver can also be gilt to prevent tarnishing and this metalwork is made by jewellers and sold by weight. They are delicate, valuable, impractical; many must have been melted down at times of financial stress and were probably made for presentation purposes.

The filigree was made in many countries: Norway, Malta, Italy, Spain and Portugal in the West, and China in the East. Some Chinese filigree fans also had enamels incorporated on them and 85% must have been exported from Canton.

Filigree was used in two distinct ways: for brisé fans, and as sticks for folding fans, occasionally interspersed by sticks made from other materials. The first fans of this category were made in China. Illustration Nos. VIII, IX.

FLABELLUM

These fans are religious and can never be collected today. They have been written up at length in all the standard works on fans, but need hardly concern a collector in the 1980s.

FLAG FANS

In the Prado, in Madrid, there is a painting of Venus and Adonis by Paolo Veronese, where Venus is seen to be fanning Adonis as he sleeps, with a flag-shaped fan. (This painting is also to be seen on page 7 of that fine catalogue *Fans in Fashion*, an exhibition at the Fine Arts Museums of San Francisco in 1981.) Fans of this shape, as well as heart, spade and circular shaped, have also been made throughout the centuries in the Indian sub-continent. They are generally about 10 × 8 in (25 × 20 cm), with a stiff handle running down on one side. Some of them are single in construction, some double, with an inner lining. The handles can be simple polished wood or sumptuous solid silver or silver-gilt. The flag area may be made of a multitude of materials, from woven reeds or porcupine quills to peacock feathers or textiles . . . several known examples, made in the Indian sub-continent, are of cloth of gold.

In the main the flag-shaped fan would be hand-held. They have been seen in paintings from the thirteenth century and theories have been put forward that they may have been brought into Europe by returning Crusaders. They were very fashionable in Europe (especially in Venice) during the sixteenth and seventeenth centuries, but they occur far more frequently in Persian and Mughal miniatures and show what was in common use there over the centuries. Several fine examples were on show in the exhibition *Fans from the East*.

FLY-WHISK

Fly-whisks are as old as the fly. They are known worldwide throughout history: in the records of the Chapel of St Faith in the old St Paul's Cathedral in 1298 there is a mention of 'a muscatorium or fly-whip of peacock's feathers' and even in the 1980s various leaders of African countries carry one in the hand both for practical reasons and as a symbol of authority. See also CHOWRIES.
See illustration in *Fans from the East*, Plate 20.

FONTAGE FANS

This type of European folding fan was made *c* 1890 to 1935, the name delineating its shape. When open this fairly small fan appears to come to a point in the centre; when folded the fan leaf appears to zig-zag from the centre to the top of the guardstick. They were decorated

in the prevailing styles from Edwardian Rococo to Art Deco. See PAL-METTO FANS, SHELL–SHAPED FANS.
Illustration No. XXI.

FOUR SCENES FANS

Normally a fan will open from left to right exhibiting a decoration upon the obverse (front) which is finer (and shown outwards when held), and another on the reverse which is seen by the holder. That gives the owner, at most, two decorations (which are most often a painted scene) upon a folding fan.

A 'four scenes fan' is generally a brisé fan, most popular c 1815, made in Europe and the Far East from ivory, bone or horn. This small brisé fan has a central section where there appears to be a crowding of sticks behind the decoration in the centre. You can open it normally from left to right and it shows two scenes. Then you can open it from right to left and a third and even fourth scene appears on both sides. It is done by a most elaborate form of ribboning by the maker.

It is possible to have the fans made in this style with a textile leaf and, occasionally, the 'extra' scene turns out to be vaguely porno-graphic: the Chinese specialised in this. In Europe the decoration was often Neoclassical in style, or with small baskets of flowers or figure paintings, and the technique of 'half-painting' each stick in order to provide four (or three) scenes was most exacting work . . . taking one apart reveals great discipline on the part of the painter.

GLUE (See ADHESIVES)

GUMPAI UCHIWA

According to Joe Earle of the Victoria and Albert Museum, this is a rigid handscreen owing its origins to the late Muromachi period (1392–1568) and still used by the umpires at Sumo wrestling matches. They were generally made of metal and a sharp tap with one would soon part these giants.

GUNSEN

This is a 'war fan' which was first introduced in the Muromachi period (1392–1568), all examples being very tough and durable. (Another author dates this type back to the twelfth century.) The purpose of

25. Gunsen, the gold leaf painted on both sides with the rising sun: mounted on iron sticks with the guard decorated with a dragon. Late 18th century. Japanese. 15″ : 38 cms. On the right a Tanto, dagger, in the shape of a cased fan. c 1800–1820. Japanese. 13″ : 33 cms. By courtesy of Bonhams, Knightsbridge.

the fan was to signal, so it was carried by battle commanders. Normally the fan would have sturdy wooden or bamboo sticks, iron or brass guards and very thick (double) leaves. Neville Iröns tells us that the only decorative devices were the moon on one side (with a black background) and the sun on the other side (with a deep gold background). Illustration No. 25.

GUT FANS
During the first half of the eighteenth century some fans were made which consisted of a leaf created of knotted gut or horsehair. Almost

colourless, the gut is knotted in simple geometric patterns and applied across the sticks. Applied to this curious background (one noted collector has suggested it might have been a poor person's attempt to own a real lace fan) is a pattern of coloured paper or silk making designs of figures or 'lace'. These fans are rare and deserve deeper study. It has often been suggested that the majority were made in Germany.

Gut inserts were used in other fans as well, mainly during the eighteenth century. They were used where it seemed necessary to have an open 'window' for people to look through; one case is known where this 'window' is disguised as a birdcage. These gut inserts were quite small and must have been not only practical but a great novelty.

HANDSCREENS

This is another word for a rigid fan with a handle. It acts as a normal fan, it screens you from other people's sight or from the heat of a fire,

26. A pair of 19th century handscreens, the central vignettes decorated with three-dimensional birds made with beading and ringing; mounted on turned gilt sticks. c 1860. English. By courtesy of Bonhams, Knightsbridge.

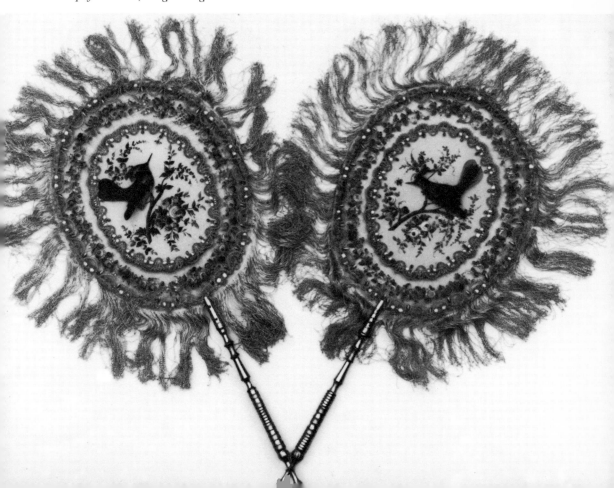

and it can be angled by some artificial means and used as an umbrella or sunshade. Handscreens have been used throughout history all over the world. See *Collecting Fans*, page 61.

European handscreens were heavier, more 'mechanical' than Eastern ones which were used personally as pure fans, whereas ladies in the West and the United States preferred a folding fan and used hand-screens more to shield the face from a warm fire in an enclosed room. Illustration No. 26.

HI OGI

This is a very famous type of Japanese fan and is one of the earliest brisé types. Cypress wood is the normal material used, generally 38 sticks painted all over with gofun (powdered white lead) or gold and silver leaf and then decorated with painted patterns of flowers. The rivet is usually of metal, sometimes shaped like a bird, butterfly or bat, and the fan is held along the upper section by strong threads. On the guards, near the strong top, are suspended multicoloured cords plaited and twisted into various shapes. Mr Nakamura Kiyoe's book (see Bibliography) shows us, by means of a sketch, how this fan, when opened out by the Empress or one of her ladies, is wide enough for the cords hanging from the guards to fall just outside the width of the kimono and cascade to the ground unhampered.

HORN FANS

During the early nineteenth century (Empire period), horn fans became immensely popular. They pandered to the new taste for the simple, they were a spin-off from the prolific horn industry making gun-powder horns, and they were cheap.

During the Revolutionary period it was unfashionable to be seen wearing gold and silver brocades or diamonds, or carrying large painted and be-jewelled fans. Instead you carried a tiny horn fan, known as a 'minuscule', 'imperceptible' or 'pocket' fan, decorated with non-controversial designs of painted flowers or cut-steels piqué—and the social classes could hardly be distinguished.

Horn has been used since the beginning of time. The historian, Theopompus, in the fourth century BC described the Kings of Paeonia (a territory in Northern Greece) drinking out of horns of great size, mounted with gold and silver rims. Since then, horn has been used for up to 180 useful articles such as spoons, beakers, the leaves for lanterns (light horns), shoe-horns, fans and so on. The almost continuous warfare of the Revolutionary period (*c* 1790–1815) encouraged the firearms industry and consequently there was a vast manufacture of containers for both gunpowder and priming instruments. They were made of horn, and the horn industry in Britain flourished.

Every part of a horn has been utilised, from the tips, curled over to make snuff-mulls, to the powder and shavings which are used as nitrogenous fertiliser. Horn is a natural plastic which can be worked in a multitude of ways and its shape altered through heating, carving and pressing. Man-made plastic was invented in 1862, (a form of cellulose nitrate called 'Parkesine' discovered by Alexander Parkes of Birmingham) as an attempt to copy horn more cheaply and using less labour.

There are, of course, many types of horn just as there are many types of synthetic plastic. Ox, buffalo, cow, sheep, goat and antelope horns are hollow and tough and can be split into flexible slices that can then be pressed into flat objects such as fan sticks. Rhinoceros horn is unique in that it is not hollow, has no grain and is very difficult to carve. These different qualities in the horns of various animals have led, to a certain extent, to special uses for each. Ox and goat horn were made into window panes and lantern plates before glass became generally available; deer horn was made into knife-handles, and beautiful ornamental work was usually created in buffalo horn.

Horn is non-absorbent, hygienic and has a wonderful tactile quality; it is unaffected by oils or mild acids and is not easily tarnished. Because of the presence of fibre in its structure, horn is truly a fibre-reinforced plastic. It is also biodegradable—when buried it eventually disintegrates, taking up to fourteen years to do so.

In Britain horn manufacturers was located at the termini of the cattle drives which ran the length and breadth of the country; the cattle were slaughtered and men were employed to de-horn the carcasses and clean the horns for the horn-traders, resulting in hornware craftsmen establishing their workshops conveniently near the slaughterhouses.

In the early 1700s a German named Humpersohn, inspired by the hornware made by the monks of Llanthony Abbey in Monmouthshire, set up the Abbey Horn Works close to a plentiful supply of the source of Herefordshire cattle in Gloucestershire. Humpersohn eventually sold the Abbey Horn Works to James Grove and Sons, horn button makers, and much later, in the 1920s, a new owner, Peter Leresche (of Huguenot descent) moved the business to Kendal, merging it with comb-makers—James Troughton and Sons. In 1955 John Barnes became its proprietor and Abbey Horn of Kendal, Cumbria, is a flourishing business today.

It seems certain that early nineteenth century horn fans were a by-product of the tremendous output of the comb industry. Most ladies then wore a minimum of three combs, one at each side of the head and one at the back; in 1851 the Aberdeen Combworks, to mention one place out of many, were employing more than 600 workers producing nine million combs a year in 1,928 different varieties.

Early in the seventeenth century the art of moulding and pressing horn was devised. One method was to place a piece of horn in a press, submerge it in boiling water (which softened it) and then to screw the press home to give a sharp impression of the dies. Later on horn was worked with gas, heating it in a soft gas flame to render it malleable, and meanwhile bending or twisting it to the required shape. The process is more critical than it appears, for horn has a 'molecular memory': if it is underheated it will slowly revert to its original shape; if it is overheated it will lose its strength and become brittle. Every horn has a different thickness and water content and has to be treated accordingly.

Once correctly shaped under heat the workpiece, such as a fan stick, is placed in a cool press in which it sets permanently into a required shape; on examination it appears that almost all early nineteenth-century horn fans were moulded in presses and not carved by hand; this includes any perforations. These horn fans of British manufacture embody the national preference for peaceful production rather than warlike attributes.

Early nineteenth-century horn fans were generally made from greenhorn, the word 'green' meaning that the horn was heated and plunged into boiling water (where it lost almost all its colour) until it was very soft and malleable, leaving the horn yellow-green in colour and translucent.

Finally there was a painstaking ritual of sanding and polishing to give the end-product the deep and lasting gloss that distinguishes high-quality hornware. One has to be careful not to confuse some forms of 'tortoiseshell' with horn because horn could quite easily be stained to emulate tortoiseshell. Tortoiseshell fans were far more expensive, but fakes can be recognised by the obviously even colouring on the sticks. The method used in the Victorian age was as follows:

Once the hornwork (such as the shaped and perforated fan sticks for a brisé fan) was ready it was softened by leaving it in a solution of one part nitric acid, two parts tannin, three parts wood vinegar and five parts tartar—or two parts wood vinegar, two parts tartar, two and a half parts zinc vitriol, three parts nitric acid and five parts tannin.

Then, to achieve a brown stain, you first painted on an aqueous solution of potassium ferrocyanide, allowing it to dry and then treating it with a hot dilute solution of copper sulphate.

A black stain was achieved by dissolving 50–60 grains of nitrate of silver in one ounce of distilled water—which looked colourless. A small brush was then dipped into the mixture and where a black stain was required (shading the brown into black) the mixture was painted on. When dry the horn was put into the sunshine, upon which the solution turned jet black.

One clue as to whether a fan is genuine tortoiseshell or fake dyed horn is that if the worker went to the expense of buying real tortoise-shell he would almost certainly use either silver or gold piqué on it; on fakes he would use cut steels. This was partly because cut steels were cheaper and partly because piqué work in shell is held by contraction when the shell cools, using no adhesives; horn does not react in the same way as tortoiseshell and therefore an adhesive *is* needed.

Horn fans were made all over the country and sold in local shops; there are records available from various shops (such as Alston and Grey-hurst 'At the Blue Boar within Aldgate 1723'—now called Harvey and Gore in Burlington Gardens, London) where horn fans were sold in the early nineteenth century for a few shillings. The same fans sell today from £10 to £150 all over the land. Illustration No. XX.

IMPERCEPTIBLE FANS (See EMPIRE FANS)

ITA OGI
This is a Japanese type of fan, brisé, made from a great many sticks composed of either a fine wood or a bamboo, and then having a light design painted on them. The fan is generally held by a strong thread near the top of the sticks, sometimes in a decorative pattern, and gener-

ally has a metallic rivet. The sticks (which can be up to 48 in number) occasionally have gentle curves at the edges in the simulated gorge area. These fans can be very large indeed.

IVORY FOR FANS

Most people must be aware that the ivory used for fans is taken from the elephant. Although the teeth of the hippopotamus, walrus, narwhal, sperm whale and some types of wild boar and warthog are recognised as ivory they have little commercial value because of their size and (in some cases) lack of whiteness.

An elephant's tusk is the upper incisor and continues to grow throughout the lifetime of the male and female African elephant and of the male Indian elephant; the female Indian elephant has no tusks or only tiny ones. Elephant tusks from Africa weigh about 100 lb (45 kg) per pair; Asian tusks are somewhat smaller. There are two main types of elephant ivory: hard, usually from the Western part of Africa (and darker in colour), and soft.

All over the world ivory has a tremendous history of being carved and shaped, and fans made from ivory can be extremely fine and delicate. Techniques differ in various countries. Synthetic ivory is generally the use of bone (often the shin bones of horses) or, in the nineteenth and twentieth centuries, of plastics.

JAPANESE IVORY BRISÉ FANS (See ZŌGE OGI)

JENNY LIND FANS (See SHAPED-FABRIC FANS)

KOKOKU

These are Japanese advertising fans of the mid-nineteenth century onwards intended for home consumption. As with all advertising fans, very little attention is paid to the simple bamboo or wooden sticks; their purpose is to get across the advertised message and so the design on the leaf is extremely bold and colourful.

LACE

Lace has been used on fans since the eighteenth century; previous to that, there are sixteenth-century fans extant with decoupé work which imitated 'reticella' lace. Painted laces (on skin or paper) are also known,

27. A fan made in the Fabergé workshops of lace with tortoiseshell sticks and guards decorated with rose diamonds. By courtesy of Bonhams, Knightsbridge.

mainly because real lace was extremely expensive and, for a fan, it must also be shaped rather than made in a strip, cut to shape and turned in. Both needlepoint lace and bobbin lace were used for fans—the former always made by the professional—and finally machine-made lace was used. The year 1800 was quite a turning point because before that time the threads of lace were usually linen; after that time cotton was commoner. Also, laces were now made from silk and metal threads, and occasionally materials such as wool, aloe fibre and hair. Lace was made all over Europe, Russia and South America; it was not introduced into China until the nineteenth century and was not made there.

Only the finest laces are successful on fans, otherwise they appear too thick when folded . . . Chantilly looks delightful. During the eighteenth century lace fans had a leaf entirely made from the lace, often with a coat of arms worked into the design, while in the nineteenth century many fans were made as an amalgam of lace with gauze inserts, painted in pastel shades (or white upon black).

Because of the great expense of lace, the sticks and guards were made to set it off: fine lace is never mounted on cheap sticks. The best lace fans are made as a single mount; during the nineteenth century some lace fans were backed with silk or satin, sometimes as a contrast in colour and sometimes to act as a support. Nothing can look more feminine than a really fine lace fan of the eighteenth century, suitably mounted.

Illustration Nos. IV, VIII, XXX, 27.

LACE-BARK FANS FROM JAVA

The 'lace-bark' tree (*Lagetta lintearia*) originated in the West Indies but was introduced (by the Dutch) to Java during the nineteenth century. It produces a netting-like substance, almost like a net curtain, which has on occasion actually been used for clothing—there are two child's bonnets made from this in the Museum at Kew Botanical Gardens in London. In the *Fans from the East* exhibition, a brisé fan was shown using the 'lace' as long ovals on each ivory stick, strengthened all along the edges by what looked like a border of brown paper. In fact this was flat sections of 'Spatha', the sheath of the fruit of the Mountain Cabbage Palm.

Another strange material formed the tassel, made from the fibre of the pineapple plant, and this was brushed out, as well, to a floss-like texturing, to edge the tips of each brisé section. As an extra decoration delicate dried and pressed ferns were glued across the 'leaf' area.

Two more can be seen on pages 120/121 of *The Book of Fans*: the first in shades of cream, the second in shades of rich brown, with tortoiseshell sticks. Examples are known from both Jamaica and Indonesia, generally made in the nineteenth century.

LACQUER

This is a well-known term for coloured and frequently opaque varnishes applied to metal or wood, forming an important branch of decorative art, especially in Asia. Lac is the sticky resinous secretion of the tiny lac insect, *Laccifer lacca*, a species of scale insect: the word *lac* comes from the Persian word *Lak* and the Hindi word *Lakh*, both of which mean 'hundred thousand', indicating the vast number of the minute insects required to produce lac. In fact about 17,000 to 90,000 insects are needed to produce one pound of shellac. Lac is the basis of some but not all lacquers; in China and Japan it is the sap of the tree *Rhus vernicifera* which, cleaned of impurities, can be used in its natural state. The characteristic constituent of lacquer is called *urushiol*, from the Japanese *urushi*. The names of great lacquer artists are extremely well recorded in both China and Japan.

The base of Chinese and Japanese lacquer is nearly always wood, generally a pine having a soft and even grain; it is extremely thin and in artistic lacquer work is coated with a great many successive layers of lacquer, among which is a layer of hempen cloth or paper. Because each layer takes up to 24 hours to dry, the entire process of producing a surface suitable for an artist to decorate requires at least 18 days. The design may first be made on paper or drawn directly on the object with a thin paste of white lead or colour. Tiny bits of gold and silver may be applied with quill, bamboo tube or pointed tool. Long hardening periods are again necessary during this decorative stage.

In Europe the basic ingredient of varnished surfaces was shellac. Lacquer on fans produces some superb effects (black and gold, silver and gold, red and gold, etc.) and ensures that a fan remains extremely light. It is rarely cheap and often underrated

Many books have been written on both Chinese and Japanese techniques of lacquering and in the world of the fan the biggest accent is placed upon nineteenth-century Japanese fans with gold lacquerwork known as either *takamaki-e* or *hiramaki-e*. The addition of *shibayama* inlay brought Japanese fans to a decorative peak. *Shibayama* work is named after a Japanese family who worked with lacquer (especially on inro) during the eighteenth and early nineteenth centuries, adding tiny sections of carved semi-precious stones into the lacquer. They produced magnificent (thick) ivory guards brilliantly decorated with an elongated scene of a garden, perhaps, with cranes and bamboo leaves in gold lacquer and tiny flowers of carved mother-of-pearl, birds of carved agate and insects of carved jade. Some of these Japanese ivory fans were left quite plain, confining all the rich decoration to the guards: others showed superb gold lacquering (in various subtle colours) right across the brisé sticks. In each case the fan became so heavy it was almost impractical to use but was given as a most acceptable gift.

Illustration Nos. I, VI, 1.

LEATHER (See PARCHMENT)

LILLIPUTIAN FANS

There appears to be absolutely no reason to use the name 'Lilliputian' when describing 'Empire' fans, but to ascribe it to the very small fans of the early eighteenth century instead. It is known that fans were thus named, but the Victorian date is incorrect. *Gulliver's Travels into Several Remote Nations of the World* was written 1721–25 and published in 1726, the author being Jonathan Swift. At that same period there were two distinct forms to fans: that of large vellum or paper fans with an extravagant spread, and that of very small brisé fans; these brisé fans have never been successfully explained before except by being named (incorrectly) 'Vernis Martin' fans. In the past Victorian writers named Empire fans 'Lilliputian', but the title sits far more comfortably in the 1720s when *Gulliver's Travels* was actually written. Therefore, to my mind, early eighteenth-century varnished brisé fans should be named 'Lilliputians'. See also VARNISHED FANS.
Illustration Nos. VIII, XIV.

LOOFAH FANS

I have recently come across the same type of fan made in both Thailand and in remote villages up the Amazon River. They are the conventional brisé type, the upper half being decorated with white ducks' feathers edged with maribou, and with an over-decoration of small, brilliantly coloured parakeet feathers. The curiosity is in the stick area, for the very few, broad, light 'sticks' are made from dried loofahs: they were identified for me as 'Cucurbit', a member of the cucumber family, by the Museum at Kew Gardens in London. It is indeed strange to have sticks made from dried sponges, but they are light and strong and carry out their purpose perfectly adequately.
See an illustration in *Fans from the East*, Plate 24.

LOOPS

The use of a loop attached to the rivet of a fan came in, as a general rule, in the late 1830s. Some have actually been seen from the eighteenth century but are extremely rare and must have been a novelty.

Loops were brought in then because a lady had just too many things to carry and, especially when dancing in the new (modern) style, when both hands were occupied for the first time, she could suspend her fan temporarily over her wrist and immediately have it to hand at the end of each dance.

Loops have been made of many types of metals from gold to a base metal. In the East some magnificent ones are extant and in the West there are some made with real gemstones. They are purely for the ribbon to pass through and are not part of the construction of a fan. See also PARTS OF A FAN and RIVETS.

LORGNETTE FANS
In the past, people who had bad eyesight did not advertise the fact if they could possibly help it; instead they set a magnifying-glass in the most solid part of the guardstick of a fan, or within the rivet area. These fans were seen during the eighteenth century, but as spectacles were used more and more in the nineteenth century there was no more need for them. They are also called 'Quizzing fans'.

MACAO FANS (See APPLIED FACES FANS)

MAI OGI
These are fans used by the Japanese in the dance. When fans have to be in movement with the body (as opposed to being merely waved while the owner is seated) the consideration of balance is of great importance. Fans must be lighter than normal but extremely strong. Most dance fans therefore have only a few supple but strong bamboo sticks which support a single leaf of painted paper or textiles such as silk or satin. Their distinguishing feature is their guards: to keep that balance the guards are either divided into two segments, attached to the end pleat (all the pleats are wide) with matching silk cords, or there are two slender outer 'sticks' attached by cords. These fans appear to have first made themselves a special category from the seventeenth century but those which appear in sales are now almost always nineteenth century . . . an earlier purchase would be a great coup.

MANDARIN FANS
The term 'Mandarin Fan' came to be used, incorrectly, during the nineteenth century, to describe Applied Faces Fans. The Victorians did not realise that the latter were made for export only and assumed that, because a fan showed mandarins in its design (complete with tiny ivory faces), it had been made expressly for the use of a particular mandarin.

True mandarin fans were made to match the clothes of their owners, unless they were a special 'gift' fan, and had designs on them to indicate their status at court. They were specially made to order and were not for sale to the public. See also APPLIED FACES FANS.

MARRIAGE FANS

Another name is a 'Bridal' or 'Wedding' Fan, but 'Marriage' encompasses all the facets of this type. Brides in the past used to have a selection of fans to give out to their attendants or special friends as a commemorative gift. Husbands-to-be used also to commission fine fans for their brides: some were ivory brisé fans with a central cartouche with the bride's monogram carved upon it (or a double one, especially when a coronet of some type was incorporated); others were especially painted with some significant scene.

Another form of marriage fan was some fine fan which was commissioned for the bride and given as a wedding present. In many of these there are portraits of both bride and groom in the design. Various members of Royal families have gone to great expense with these fans and other noble families were never far behind. The decoration generally refers to 'the state of marriage': i.e., some reference to the god Hymen, 'true lover's knots', putti and cupids, hearts and flowers, and so on. None of them set out sternly to instruct, all of them were made to delight and to enhance the happy occasion. They are exclusive, personal and occasionally very rare, but they are only of real importance and interest if the entire provenance is attached and you are furnished with the names of the people and the date.

In the United States today there has again developed a very pretty notion of using marriage fans. Mrs Geraldine Pember in California organises marriages for certain families where the bride carries a white fan with white ribbons and flowers and her attendants all carry matching fans with contrasting ribbons and flowers suitable to their dresses. Illustration No. XXXVI.

MASK FANS

There is a certain very specialist group of fans known as the 'Mask fans' which all appear to have come from the same stable during the first half of the eighteenth century. Basically the fans have a very large mask printed or painted across the leaf with the eyes cut out, and it seems that they were made for ladies going to the theatre. Less than ten are known: four are on display (the Metropolitan Museum, New York; the Museum of Fine Arts, Boston; the Fine Arts Museums in San Francisco; the Kremlin in Moscow), and I know of three others in private collections. Miss Esther Oldham researched her extremely early one over a period of ten years (now in the Museum of Fine Arts in Boston) which has laid very valuable ground for all the others—details are on pages 119–127 in *The Book of Fans*. Some authors refer to this type as 'Peeping fans', especially as John Gay, in his poem 'The Fan', written in 1713, refers to them thus:

> The Peeping Fan in modern times shall rise,
> Through which unseen the female ogle flies.

It is extremely interesting to find that each fan in this specialist category is slightly different in some way: the painted Oldham version appearing to have the fullest collection of illustrations which were inspired by *The Beggar's Opera*, the others (later) in somewhat the same style and taking at least one of the vignettes, while adding other small scenes from contemporary life. It is indeed a teasing type of fan: as much research has been done on this fan as in any other category, yet this very fact has acted as a red rag to a bull and various 'authorities' have attempted to destroy its validity. Why? If any fact is disputed then surely it would be better openly discussed? The type is so very rare it would be a greater service to collectors to illustrate them all and encourage each owner to research his own and publish his findings. This will never happen, of course, but it would be the ideal solution.

MEDALLION (See CARTOUCHE)

MEN'S FANS
In the East various fans were made with a perfectly plain leaf (or brisé sticks) so that the male owner might have something available on which to write notes; fans for ladies always had some form of decoration as it was generally agreed that ladies would not be required to write anything.

In Europe it is known that men, especially in Court circles, carried fans in the eighteenth century. Some people believe that men carried brisé fans, others think they carried large, plain fans; still others assert that they carried fans with small insects painted upon them. All this is pure speculation and there is simply no evidence at present to prove whether there was a special category of fans for men or whether they carried any fashionable fan of the period. Provenance is needed before there is proof. It is, however, generally known that early in the eighteenth century it was said that there were three sexes, men, women and Herveys—referring to Lord Hervey, who appeared to be sexually ambidextrous. He always carried a fan and was laughingly known behind hands as 'Lord Fanny'.

MICA FANS

Mica is the name given to a group of minerals which include muscovite (potash mica) and phlogopite (magnesia mica). It is found in igneous rocks and splits in one direction only. It can therefore be foliated into very thin sheets which are tough and elastic, do not break easily but can be marked with the fingernail. It is mined in large blocks and then split to the desired size with sharp knives.

Mica is an easy material to split into very fine sections and it is also possible to cut it with scissors into patterns. It has often been used as an added material for a fan and it is proof of its strength that some very fine late seventeenth century fans remain intact. It has been used in both the East and the West for four centuries.

There is one extremely interesting group of unique late seventeenth century fans (see page 170 of *A Collector's History of Fans*) of which only four are known, all apparently by the same hand. They are normal folding fans, set on ivory or tortoiseshell sticks with the decoration arranged in three tiers across the sticks to form the leaf. This decoration consists of tiny rectangular sections of paper-thin mica panels set into paper or braid frames and having detailed paintings of busts, flowers, birds or dogs on each. None of these fans is exactly the same (one has to search for the differences) but they are obviously from the same 'stable'. Here, the maker, who may have been Dutch, does not apparently use the mica for its transparent properties but as a smooth and unusual surface on which to paint.

Another very early and interesting fan, made in China for export to South America, c 1700, shows Phillip V of Spain. Then there are others where large masses of mica have been used, lightly painted (in some cases with animals of the Zodiac).

28. Mica fan, made in the Orient. There is a brightly painted paper leaf with mica inserts forming animal creatures from Chinese mythology; pierced ivory sticks, the guards painted in reds and greeny-greys, terminating in a reversed tulip-shaped finial and having a domed metal pivot. Late 17th century or very early 18th century. Private Collection.

During the eighteenth century mica was quite often used as inserts into a scene for a peeping or quizzing fan, or with chinoiserie designs such as the magnificent 'palace' scene in the Messel Collection where mica is set as 'windows' with courtesans looking out (see Plate 15 in *Fans from the East*). The special quality of mica for fans is the fact that the mica does not appear transparent from the front, it just seems a part of the overall design. Once held up to the face, however, the transparent sections all too obviously have their uses.

On the whole mica fans are very much sought after and extremely expensive; they do not often change hands, either.
Illustration Nos. 9, 28.

MINUET FANS (see EMPIRE FANS)

MITA OGI

These Japanese fans are for processions and are huge in size. (Some were also used on the stage.) The general effect is obtained by decorating the leaf with bright colours and leaving the wood or bamboo sticks quite plain. Quite often the leaf is of fine linen rather than paper. They were most used in the nineteenth century.

MONOGRAM FANS

During the nineteenth century it was very appealing to some people to apply monograms, arms, crests, etc., upon a fan in their own homes. The fans were made of sycamore wood, brisé, with wide sticks and, naturally, perfectly plain; some were made in Austria or Bavaria. It was then possible to buy sheets of tiny monograms, etc. from a dealer, e.g. J. H. Kent & Co., Dealers in Crests, Monograms & etc. of 3 Edward Terrace, Cardiff, and cut them out and apply them to your fan. It was more normal to buy especial albums for this purpose; for example, Marcus Ward & Co. Ltd. (Copyright Entered at Stationers Hall) produced small books entitled *Armorie—An Album for Arms, Crests and Monograms*. Upon each facing page would be some form of lightly printed design, such as an outline of a church window which had spaces to infill with the monograms of Bishops. There were pages for the Arms, Crests or Monograms of the Army Regiments, Mercantile Houses, Insurance Companies, Dukes, Towns, the Navy, Earls, Schools, Clubs, Colleges in Universities, Hotels and well-established Overseas Clubs. The entertainment provided was to collect sufficient of each type, cut them out and tastefully arrange them in patterns on the correct illustrated page.

During the nineteenth century people also decorated screens and scrap-books, and it was known that some applied scraps to china, wood or leather objects and to the glass balls which hung on Christmas Trees when they were first in vogue; the art was called 'Decalcomania', from 'decals', meaning 'transfers', and meant the decorating and labelling of any object that cannot be run through a press (see *The New Encyclopaedia Britannica*). One is tempted to call these fans 'Decalcomania Fans' but 'Monogram Fans' would be more readily understood. According to the 1864 *Englishwoman's Domestic Magazine*, another supplier of monograms was Barnard & Sons, 339 Oxford Street, London.

These fans were made from *c* 1850; the basic sycamore fan was also used to paint at home with your own pattern, and others are known from Vienna with white flowers painted upon a red or blue background. The practice of putting monograms, etc., into albums then spread to collecting stamps and putting *them* into albums. As the postal system was rapidly increasing worldwide, and monograms were becoming less interesting because they were already established, monogram fans gradually faded out. See illustration on page 83 of *The Book of Fans*.

MONTGOLFIER FANS (See BALLOONING FANS)

MOTHER-OF-PEARL
Technically this material should come under the heading 'Pearl' or 'Nacre' (from the Arabic *nakar*). It is a material often used in fine fans for sticks and guards and occasionally crushed and used as a mosaic on leaves as well. Early mother-of-pearl came in short pieces which can be seen to be spliced in several sections in order to lengthen them along a stick or guard: because the material is so expensive and difficult to work (it splits very easily), you rarely find an extension of a mother-of-pearl stick made of pearl but from bone or wood instead, secreted between two leaves. The white pearl came from Madagascar, the black pearl from various areas in the East and the 'burgauté' pearl, sometimes also known as 'goldfish', from Japan. This latter has been used in some of the finest fans as a fragile and extremely thin backing for further overlaid designs, sensuous as exotic shot-silk, or winking its rainbow lights from within carved guards. On occasions mother-of-pearl is discovered clouté on wooden or ivory sticks, showing delightful little figures from the Comedia dell'Arte, and attached to the backing material with tiny silver pins.

Mother-of-pearl brisé fans were made in the Orient, notably in China, mainly for export purposes from Canton. In the nineteenth century they came carved on both sides (etched might be a better word) and, according to Neville Iröns in *Fans from Imperial China*, 'from trade labels it appears that a number of specialists existed, foremost Hoaching, followed by others such as Shongshing.'

Mother-of-pearl carved work is never cheap; only when it was machine-made and dyed to pastel shades in the nineteenth and early twentieth centuries did the material become slightly debased and its character altered. A great deal of care must be taken over the material when repairing it.

Illustration Nos. IV, V, XXX, XXXVII, XL, 1, 15, 23, 39.

MOURNING FANS

There are two types of mourning fan: those where an 'ordinary' scene is painted in pale greys, black and white ('en grisaille'), and those where there is a definite 'mourning' scene (classical in essence) with weeping women, weeping willows, funerary urns, etc. The sticks for both are simple, uncoloured, sometimes lightened with silver. During Victorian times many fans were made from plain black satin with black painted sticks; some were for ladies in mourning, others were made because mature ladies never stirred from the use of black in their costume, especially in Spain and Italy.

However, in 1874, Mary Reed Bobbit wrote of the immense painted black satin fans: 'These big fans are all the fashion in London, nobody carries anything else.' So one must not always assume that black satin meant 'mourning', for this was the age of contrasts in dress.

All the same, when in mourning there were very strict rules: a widow wore full mourning for two years (and sometimes for longer); as a parent (or for a parent) for one year; for a brother or sister for six months and for all other relatives for three months.

NEAPOLITAN FANS

In the exhibition 'Fans and the Grand Tour' (Brighton Museum, 1982) a fine collection of Neapolitan fans was displayed with all the 'correct' background material of carved cameos, small bronzes, fine paintings, miniatures, mosaics and copies of books which would have accompanied a wealthy young man as he travelled the Continent.

During this intriguing tour of the Continent a great many souvenirs were bought and shipped back to England, partly as proof that the 'grand tour' had been undertaken at all and partly as presents to give away. Smaller articles such as fans were ideal as gifts, partly because they were 'the latest thing' in use in each country and partly because they were a pictorial commemoration of various places. The most interesting events were the series of eruptions of Vesuvius outside Naples, and many fans were painted to show these and/or the City and Bay.

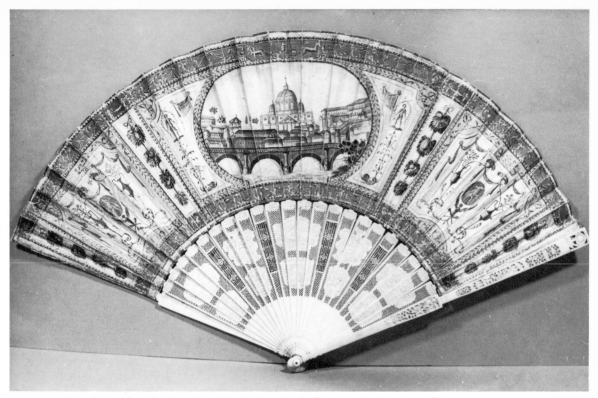

29. Grand Tour fan of high quality. The chicken-skin leaf is painted with a view of Rome and the Tiber, further decorations derived from Herculaneum and Pompeii; ivory sticks pressed and pierced, the guards carved and pierced. The colours of the leaf are of bands of turquoise at top and bottom, all the framing in pink and the ground a primrose yellow. Italian, 11¼″ : 28.5 cms. c 1785. Owned by Mrs Pamela Hudson.

Neapolitan fans were made from *c* 1760 onwards. Some are printed, some painted, many with fine sticks crafted in separate ways and some with an application of coral on them (or simulated coral) to publicise a local craft. Illustration No. 29.

NEOCLASSICISM

This is a taste for classical serenity and archaeologically correct forms that began to be perceptible *c* 1750 and flourished in all branches of the visual arts from *c* 1780 until the mid-nineteenth century. In Europe it represented a reaction against the excesses of the last phase of the Baroque and was symptomatic of a new philosophical outlook. As the Baroque had been the style of Absolutism, so Neoclassicism corresponded loosely to Enlightenment and the Age of Reason, representing an attempt to recreate order and reason through the adoption of classical forms. Coincidental with the rise in Neoclassicism and exerting a formative and profound influence on the movement, was a new and more scientific interest in classical antiquity. The discovery, exploration, and archaeological investigation of classical sites in Italy, Greece and Asia Minor was crucial to the emergence of Neoclassicism.

Neoclassical fans mean those which have some reference in their decoration to the movement from *c* 1780 to *c* 1830. These fans are also often marked by having straight sticks (generally pierced to lighten the weight and design), as the excesses of the Rococo were also frowned upon at that time. Some extremely fine fans were made and enormous trouble seems to have been expended on getting every tiny detail correct. See also DIRECTOIRE FANS
Illustration No. XXXV.

OGI (SENSU)

This type of fan was made by the Japanese for the export market after 1860. It generally has a double leaf of paper, or a mixture of paper and silk, or a very fine linen which has been sized. On this leaf is a well-painted scene from a multitude of different subjects showing life in Japan both in and out of doors. The sticks are generally of wood, bamboo or ivory with absolutely no decoration at all, except for the fact that many have serrations along the edge. The guards can be of a contrasting material and can be lavishly decorated with shibayama or lacquer. It is of interest to discover how many of this type, with ivory guards, have an added ojime (bead) on the tassel. The making of these beads, associated with netsuke and inro, was an art in itself. Their purpose was to keep the cords of the tassel untangled.

OSTRICH FEATHER FANS

The use of ostrich feathers has been known since the beginning of time; many people were intrigued to hear of Tutankhamun's gold and ostrich feather fan found in his tomb, the ostrich feathers being perfect until exposed to the light and air when they disintegrated into dust. When they began to be used in the nineteenth century, female ostrich feathers were seen first as a full spread. There is a publicity photograph in an 1888 issue of *Woman's World*, showing Madame Patti in the newest fashions, using a female ostrich feather fan. Ladies took to wearing two or three ostrich plumes (normally white) in the hair from 1794–1797 and then, slightly modified, carried on as 'Court Dress' into the twentieth century. As a result of this and the use of ostrich feathers in hats and on fans, ostrich farms were established in South Africa, the Southern United States, Australia and elsewhere—but the trade collapsed after 1918. Brown, or brown and white feathers are from the female bird; black or pure white are from the male. The white feathers dyed very well to a multitude of pastel shades. In the twentieth century many fans were carried with either a single feather, or two, placed in a short fan-holder and dyed to match a special dress, often shading in tone.

PALMETTO FANS

This type was made as a European folding fan c 1890–1935. They appear in shape, when open, as a sweeping curve with a slightly flattened central section. When closed they have a zig-zag outline of the leaf to the guard, like the 'Fontage Fans'. See also FONTAGE FANS, SHELL-SHAPED FANS.

PANORAMA FANS

In the past, every attempt was made to amuse ladies of fashion, and this type of fan was the forerunner of the cinema. The idea was to watch changing pictures in the centre of a fan by looking through a central window of a handscreen. Behind this window were two rolls of ivory or wood which were turned round by a handle positioned at the side. Over these rolls was placed a continuous piece of paper on which was painted a variety of scenes which were wound on from one roll to another (like a film spool in a camera). They were made from the mid-eighteenth to the mid-nineteenth centuries. Sheila Smith of Sheila Smith Antiques, Bath, once showed me an extremely rare, matching pair of eighteenth century panoramic fans with turned ivory handles and scenes of Versailles Palace. See also TOPOGRAPHICAL FANS.

PARCHMENT

This material, upon which writing or painting is inscribed, consists of the processed skins of certain animals, chiefly sheep, goats and calves. The name apparently derives from Pergamum (modern Bergama, Turkey) where parchment is said to have been invented in the second

30. English Fan, the vellum leaf decorated with a central stipple engraved vignette, mounted on pierced and carved ivory sticks. c 1800–1810. 10½" : 26.5 cms. By courtesy of Bonhams, Knightsbridge.

century BC. Skins had been used even earlier as a writing material but a new, more thorough method of cleaning, stretching and scraping made possible the use of both sides of a manuscript leaf.

Parchment made from the more delicate skins of calf or kid, or from still-born or newly born calf or lamb, came to be called 'vellum', a term that was broadened in its usage to include any especially fine parchments.

Fan leaves have been made of various forms of parchment, especially vellum in Europe. Asses' hide has been known as a material, as has the leather from the chamois. In the Far East there are many fans made from buffalo hide but, as far as is known, the Chinese did not use any form of skin for their fans. See also SHADOW FANS FROM JAVA.
Ilustration Nos. 2, 12, 21, 30, 34, 40.

PARTS OF A FAN

All the parts of a fan are made to relate to another part and to become a balanced whole. A folding fan is created from two main sections: the leaf and the sticks. This leaf can be made from any material which will fold, and it is set upon the sticks, usually upon the upper half, leaving the lower parts to be decorated in some way; the uncovered part of the sticks is also known as the 'blade'. The uncovered part of the stick is then divided into sections: the shoulder at the leaf end, the gorge or shoulder in the centre and the head at the end. This head area of the fan is of great importance, because in the centre you find a rivet, pierced right through, around which the pivot revolves. This rivet is very often made from metal, sometimes having a form of button to protect each end. The entire fan is then protected by the guards or guardsticks, which are generally much the same as the sticks themselves, only wider.

In France the entire stick area is *la monture*, the sticks are known as *brins*, the leaf or mount is called *le feuille*, the head area is termed *rivure* and the guardsticks are called *panaches*.

In this book I use the simplest terms of 'leaf', 'sticks', 'guards' and 'rivet'. See also LOOPS and RIVETS.

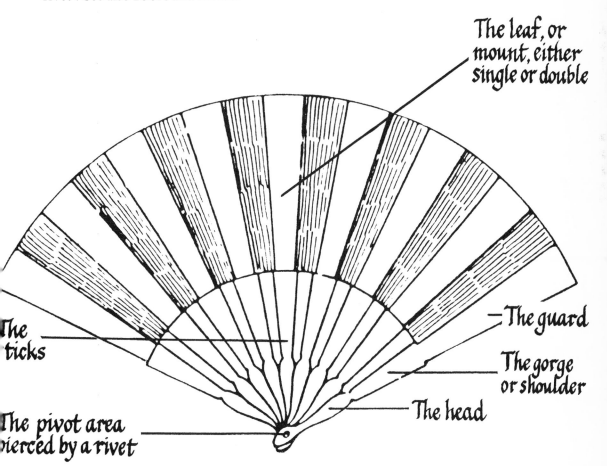

The leaf, or mount, either single or double

The guard

The gorge or shoulder

The head

The sticks

The pivot area pierced by a rivet

31. a&b Victorian fan, the leaf of black satin, painted with a flower design. The sticks and guards are of a black wood, the guards containing two sliding compartments; one having sewing implements and, below, a vinaigrette (inscribed PATENT in gold lettering): the other guard containing a comb and nail-file and, below, a small oval mirror. The tassel opens and probably housed a thimble. See Bertha de Vere Green's book, page 287. English. Private Collection.

PIEN-MIEN

The word *ogi* in Japanese means a 'folding fan'; the word *uchiwa*, a fixed fan. In Chinese the word *pien-mien* means a fixed fan which could be conveniently held in the hand 'to agitate the air'. Therefore

32 Three Chinese pien-mien of the late 18th century. Top: very finely painted with two Chinese ladies in a garden; Chinese calligraphy on the reverse: mounted on a lacquered handle. 15″: 38 cms. Bottom: a matching pair with Chinese figures in a landscape on a gold ground; the reverse (as seen on the left) decorated with birds and flowers made from kingfisher feathers; mounted on carved and pierced ivory handles. 15″: 38 cms. By courtesy of Bonhams, Knightsbridge.

93

it is a very overall term. There are some superb pien-mien to be seen in the Messel Collection, from betel palm stretched over finely split bamboo to K'o-ssu, i.e. shadow embroidery on silk (see an illustration of the former in *Fans from the East*, number 3, page 31; for the latter, see page 125 of *The Collector's Book of Fans*).
Illustration No. 32.

PIQUÉ-WORK

This is a decorative technique, usually employed on tortoiseshell or ivory, in which inlaid designs are created by means of small gold or silver 'pins'. The art reached its highest point in seventeenth and eighteenth century France, particularly for the decoration of small articles such as fans, combs, patchboxes and snuffboxes.

Both tortoiseshell and ivory are animal products of great versatility and both slightly expand when hot and contract when cold. In order to decorate tortoiseshell with piqué-work a fan guard, for instance, is completely finished off and then a pattern is very lightly inscribed on the surface and tiny holes are drilled. The shell is then carefully heated over fine quality smokeless charcoal and either pure gold or pure silver rods are inserted into the tiny holes. When the shell cools down it contracts and holds the gold or silver in place without a trace of adhesive. The metal does not penetrate right through the shell and therefore is not seen on the reverse. As the metal is quite pure it takes a wonderful shine and produces dazzling little pinpricks of light. This technique is known as 'piqué point' or 'piqué d'or' and looks beautiful when in use, but if a fan decorated in this way is put in store, then the piqué-work and tortoiseshell can become dull and lacklustre. To cure that, you must rub in a little gun-oil (or fine machine oil) on the tip of the finger all over the shell and hold it in your hand until the shell is warm and the oil has evaporated, then buff up the piqué work.

During the eighteenth century some piqué decoration became more emphatic, with chased and detailed relief-work, and is named 'posé d'or'; the piqué d'or or piqué point (tiny nailhead work) was then often used as a background to the posé d'or. This is evident during the mid-eighteenth century, especially when you see minute chinoiserie motifs on tortoiseshell. Here the tortoiseshell has some embossing, so the shell was first softened by boiling in salted water so that patterns could be tool-impressed upon it, the motifs appearing in relief. Then the soft metal foil was laid on the embossments and cemented into position. Should a tortoiseshell stick or guard of the eighteenth century have to be cleaned, great care should be taken in case the embossed gold becomes loosened.

In England (as opposed to Germany and France) the gold-encrusted chinoiserie designs were not as popular; instead the English piqué workers developed what is known as the 'hair-line posé d'or', which meant they made their designs (landscapes or pictorial scenes) with lines of pure gold or pure silver, as delicate as pen drawing: the designs became more elaborate in the nineteenth century. Matthew Bolton of Birmingham was a pioneer in working with tortoiseshell in England, gradually incorporating forms of factory production which in no way destroyed the quality of the work. He made and sold lathes for delicate engine-turning as well, and in 1780 he acquired the business of the well-known tortoiseshell craftsman, John Gimblett. One natural result of the Birmingham and Sheffield factory trade in tortoiseshell was that the handcraftsman in piqué turned to ivory, and the loveliest gold stud work of piqué d'or was developed much more extensively than before on this almost equally inviting surface.

The French and the Germans developed the art of piqué work during the seventeenth and eighteenth centuries, especially in tortoiseshell. The Huguenots brought the technique to Britain after the Revocation of the Edict of Nantes, and the styles were treated more 'with the English restraint'. The Italians seemed more accomplished with early silver piqué-work in ivory, but the techniques quickly spread across Europe. During the nineteenth century piqué-work was extensively used on tortoiseshell for jewellery, especially in England after 1872, when a great deal was made by machine in Birmingham.

A third, 'poor man's' technique was that of cut steels piqué. Here the metal is cut steel, rather than a pure metal, the holes are larger, the background material (such as aromatic wood) does not expand, so a strong adhesive is required. It was widely used during the nineteenth century, especially in fans made for Spain.

One method whereby one can determine whether animal products (such as ivory or tortoiseshell) are genuine, without laboratory testing, is that it is almost unknown for fan makers to use pure metals with cheap background materials, nor do they use cut steels with good animal products. Therefore, for instance, cut steels were used on horn but rarely on fine tortoiseshell; on bone instead of good ivory. Also piqué d'or would not have been used on plastics or bone.

Some silver or gold piqué-work can be slightly raised; almost all cut steels work is inlaid and flat: if there is a decorative nailhead cut steel work on a fan it is generally kept to the guards. All the piqué techniques were used to enrich a fan in some way and to reflect the novelties in new methods of lighting—from new forms of candles (and looking glasses) in the eighteenth century to gaslight in the nineteenth century. Illustration Nos. XX, XXXVII, XXXVIII, 12, 22.

PLASTIC FANS

Plastics, in the modern meaning of the word, are synthetic materials that are capable of being formed into usable products by heating, milling, moulding etc: the term is derived from the Greek 'plastikos', 'to form'.

The first plastic was Parkesine, later called Xylonite, exhibited by the English chemist and inventor Alexander Parkes in 1862. Celluloid was first seen in 1869, invented by John W. Hyatt. Bakelite was the first completely synthetic plastic, commercially produced in 1910 by Leo Hendrik Baekeland, a Belgian-born American chemist. After that we have to consider the use of polymers. Many fans had sticks made from plastics in the nineteenth century: they were not especially cheap at the beginning but they were certainly valued for their novelty. The material was tough, with great tensile strength, resistance to water, oils and dilute acids and eventually capable of low-cost production in a variety of colours. Fan sticks (many were small and/or brisé) could be made to look like amber, tortoiseshell, ivory ('ivorine'), etc., the 'give-away' factor being its own even-ness in colour and patterning. Plastics were extremely easily destroyed by fire. See page 59, *The Book of Fans*.

PORNOGRAPHIC FANS (see FOUR SCENES FANS)

PRICKED WORK ON FANS (see DECOUPÉ FANS)

PUNKAH

In Hindi the generic term for a fan is 'pankha', from 'pankh'—a feather

XVI. German fan, with a double silk leaf painted with a family in a park, a canary, a finch and flowers, trimmed with braid and sequins. Sticks of blonde turtleshell, carved and pierced, applied with silver and two colours of gold. Guards backed with mother-of-pearl. Opens 160 degrees. 11″ : 28 cms. c 1775. Owned by Mrs Pamela Hudson.

XVII. Chinoiserie style fan (French), the leaf printed and painted with a cartoon lampooning the Chinese (the man on the left, selling grotesques and with a scroll notice 'Marchand de Magots') and the Europeans (the man with the Duke of Wellington's hat and smoking a meerschaum). 11½″ : 29 cms. c 1830. Owned by Mrs Pamela Hudson.

XVIII. Eighteenth century fan, probably French, the ivory satin leaf having an applied 'Teniers' scene surmounted by a heart, putti in the reserves. Oriental vases of flowers and the whole embellished with braid and spangles. The ivory sticks and guards are curved, pierced and overlaid with silver. c 1770. 11″ : 28 cms. Owned by Mrs Pamela Hudson.

XIX. Combination fan. The sticks are of silvered ivory, carved putti and trophies, very finely crafted. c 1770. The leaf was applied c 1845, of silk, embroidered with sequins and a small painting. Obviously someone considered the sticks too good to throw away when the leaf became damaged, possibly with candle-grease. Owned by Mrs Pamela Hudson.

XX. *Horne fan, brisé, with piqué-point decoration. c 1810–20. 6¼″ : 16 cms. Owned by Mrs Georgette Tilley.*

XXI. *Fontage fan, the leaf of printed silk, showing a swan, and signed A. T. Romasse; the sticks of blonde tortoiseshell, one guardstick marked 'Duvelleroy'. French. 10½″ : 26.75 cms. c 1900. Owned by Mrs Georgette Tilley.*

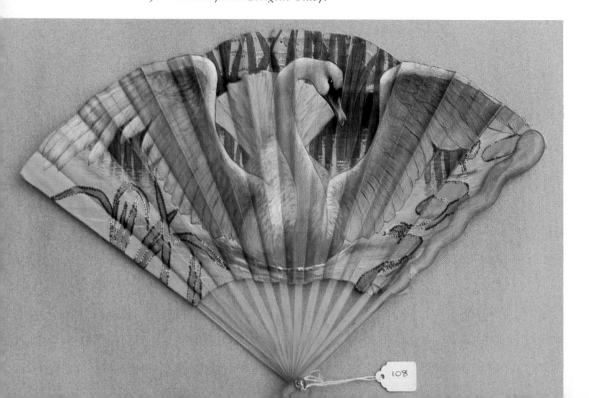

XXII. *Varnished fan, probably French. This is a brisé fan, of ivory sticks, the obverse painted with a scene of 'The Abduction of Helen' and then varnished. Erroneously called a 'Vernis Martin' fan in the past.* 8½" : 21.5 cms. c 1700. *Private Collection.*

XXIII. *Directoire fan, brisé, of alternating ivory and sandalwood; the central decoration is a coloured stipple engraving.* 10¼" : 26 cms. c 1790. *Private Collection.*

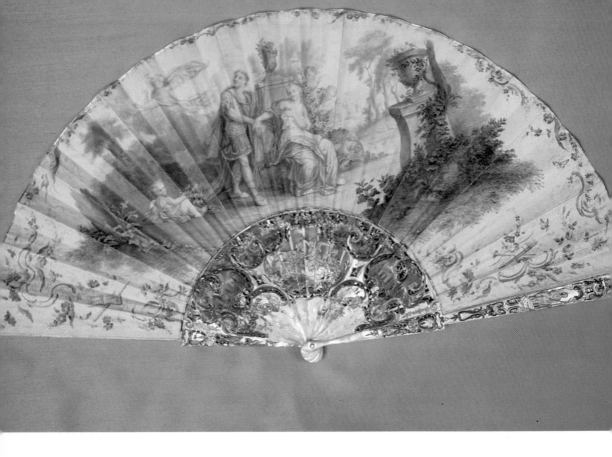

XXIV. Mother-of-pearl fan, the leaf
showing a painting of 'classical lovers', the
fine sticks, carved and gilt; has paintings
of 'palatial edifices' in the reserves.
$12\frac{1}{4}$" : 31.5 cms. c 1860. Private Collection.

XXV. Detail of same fan, showing one of
the 'palatial edifices' within gilt scrolls.

or bird's wing. The usage of this word is current in South-East Asia, which was strongly permeated with cultural and religious influences from the Indian sub-continent. On the whole people now feel the word refers to the large ceiling fans seen in the East, developed from the long flaglike ceiling fans of the past which were pulled by a rope.

PUZZLE FANS (see TRICK FANS)

QUIZZING FANS (see LORGNETTE FANS)

RESERVE (see CARTOUCHE)

REVERSED PAINTING FANS

This type were mainly made in the nineteenth century and chiefly in France. They were perfectly normal folding fans, generally of textile which was semi-transparent (such as a silk gauze), and they had a painted decoration (usually of gouache) of some scene where at least one person was seen 'face on' and another was seen with the back facing the viewer. On the reverse of the fan you saw exactly the same scene, but the person who was seen 'face on' was portrayed with his back to you, etc. The method was to attach an extra shaped piece of the textile on the reverse and paint upon that—but only over the area where the scene altered. There is one extant showing a gentleman leaning over a stone wall, speaking to a pretty lady: the reverse shows the other side of that wall, all of the gentleman, and only half of the lady because the wall obscures her. Another (Spanish) one shows on the obverse a gentleman of fashion with no less than three ladies on each arm. Reverse the fan and you see all their back views as they promenade. In some cases the fan is a straight reverse view painted onto a paper leaf (one is extant with back and front views of a scotty dog) and others are created from textiles with a double central section. The sticks and guards are made to complement the scene and many were made by Alexandre and Duvelleroy in Paris.

RIKIU OGI

The Japanese form of Tea Ceremony is accurately named *cha-no-yu*, and the fans used in these ceremonies are known as Rikiu ogi. The cult of the Tea Ceremony was a genuine instrument of culture with a lasting effect on the arts. Its allusive, restrained aesthetic is one of simplicity and elimination of the insignificant. Tea drinking, which originated in China, was first practised in Japan during the Kakamura period (1192–1333), by Zen monks trying to keep awake during meditation in their study halls. It later became an active part of Zen ritual and, in the fifteenth century, it came to mean a gathering of friends brought together in an isolated atmosphere to drink tea and discuss the aesthetic merits of painting, calligraphy and flower arrangements displayed in an alcove called the *toko-no-ma*, or quite often to discuss the merits of the tea utensils themselves. Fans were used at these ceremonies, not to fan oneself, but as plates on which to pass small cakes. These fans were composed of a very few sticks (three or four) and a simple leaf.

RIVETS

This is one of the most important parts of a fan as it holds it all together at the head. The rivet is self-explanatory: it is a piece of metal (sometimes known as a 'pin') round which pivot the sticks of both a brisé fan and a folding fan. Some of the early ones were known as 'barrel' rivets, in that they were composed of two pieces, one part screwing into another, often with a decorative tip such as a 'jewel' of paste. These have to be treated with immense care as they are made from a very thin metal and, after all these years, would easily split if one attempted to unscrew them. Later on the rivet turned into a simple piece of metal which was driven through the hole in the head and turned back upon itself. Very often there is a type of washer, or button (mother-of-pearl, tortoiseshell, etc.) which is added for strength and protection as well as decoration. In the nineteenth century a loop was added, attached to the rivet, through which ribbons might hang and be knotted. See also LOOPS, PARTS OF A FAN, and Chapter 5.

ROCOCO

This is a term in art describing a dainty and decorative style that originated chiefly in Paris in the early eighteenth century but was soon adopted throughout France and later in other countries, principally Germany and Austria. At the outset the style represented a reaction to the grand ponderousness of Louis XIV's Palais de Versailles and the official art of his reign. The noble and the wealthy bourgeoisie wished to reinstate Paris as the cultural centre of the country and built new residences, ordering them to be decorated in a lighter, more intimate style.

The proportions of the Rococo style are tall and slender. Mouldings are curved into 'C' scrolls, and asymmetry rather than symmetry is the rule. Light pastels, ivory-white and gold are the predominant colours and Rococo decorators made much use of mirrors. The decorative arts of the period *c* 1715 to 1745 admirably exemplified the Rococo tendencies, for it was a style better suited to them than to architecture.

Fans of the Rococo period are possibly the finest ever made in Europe, with their lightness of design, delicacy of carving, pastel shades (like the colours of the new porcelain) and foil-work within the guards to simulate the new mirrors. It is said that the word was made up from 'rocaille' and 'coquille' (pebbles and shells) because the style also featured elaborate stylised, shell-like, rock-like and scroll motifs, often in gold, gilt or gilded bronzes. Originally 'rocaille' was confined to the shellwork of artificial grottoes found in late-Renaissance gardens, but it broadened to mean more during the Rococo period.

Rococo fans exhibit fan making in its best period, when a leaf was 'married' to its sticks, all coming from the same 'stable' of craftsmen. They seem to be custom-made and the cleverest (and most expensive) show one scene painted upon the broad leaf and motifs from that scene painted or crafted into the sticks and guards. This is also the time when the sticks and guards were most wonderfully made, carved, pierced, engraved, embossed, repoussée, clouté and be-jewelled—and they are poems of decorative harmony.
Illustration Nos. XVI, XVIII, 8, 13, 14.

SANDALWOOD FANS
Fans have been made from sandalwood, which is the common name for semiparasitic plants of the genus Santalum and refers especially to the fragrant wood of the true, or white, sandalwood—*Santalum album*. Approximately 25 species of *Santalum* are distributed throughout south-eastern Asia and the islands of the South Pacific. Many other woods are used as substitutes for the true sandalwood, which grows to a height of about 33 feet (10 metres). Both tree and roots contain a yellow aromatic oil, called sandalwood oil, the odour of which persists for years in such articles as ornamental boxes, furniture and fans

made of the white sapwood. The oil is obtained by steam distillation of the wood and is used in perfumes, soaps, candles, incense, etc. Powdered sandalwood is used in the paste applied to make Brahmin caste marks and in sachets for scenting clothes. The wood itself is fine-grained and does not split when carved and pierced, which makes it perfect for creating fan sticks. It should not be confused with cedarwood, which is also aromatic but is red-tinged, decay-resistant and insect-repellant.

In the East, owners often dipped their sandalwood fans into a bowl of water to cool themselves down more efficiently, but they could not do this in the West as they generally decorated brisé sandalwood fans (they are all brisé) with engravings in a central cartouche (in the eighteenth and nineteenth centuries) or with cut steels piqué. They were mainly made in England and France and occasionally they were paired with a contrasting material such as ivory.

SCREEN FANS

For Oriental screen fans please see UCHIWA (for Japanese) or PIEN-MIEN (for Chinese). European screen fans will be found under HANDSCREENS.

SEQUINS AND SPANGLES

A sequin is always circular, a spangle is always shaped. The first known sequin was made in Venice: a gold coin there had been current (first minted in c 1280) named a zecchino, which was very small and circular. When, during the sixteenth century, these coins were suddenly withdrawn from usage, many people became extremely annoyed, especially one grand lady who had made a large collection of them 'for a rainy day'. In protest she had each of her coins pierced with a hole, sewed them all on to a spectacular dress and 'twinkled all over town'; she did not get the act rescinded but she did start a fashion in dress.

Spangles came along slightly later and, to differentiate between the two, the spangle came in a huge variety of shapes, leaving the sequin to its original coin shape. They were most popular during the eighteenth and nineteenth centuries. They did not always remain gold in colour but could also be silver, emerald green, red, blue, pink, etc. They were only used in the West, never in the Far East.

However, spangles and sequins are well-known in India and Pakistan: the maker of spangles was known as the *bindligar*, the word for

33. The black gauze leaf of this fan is decorated with the figure of an acrobat made from gold sequins, mounted on plain ebony sticks. French. 19th century. 9½" : 24 cms. By courtesy of Bonhams, Knightsbridge.

spangle being *bindli*. They were cut out of thin sheets of fine gold or silver known as *sitta*, and then worked with a small anvil (*ahran*), scissors (*mikruz*), forceps (*chumti*), parchment (*chamra charmi*) and small pincers (*sanni*). Many fans from this sub-continent were also decorated with gold thread (*kalabutun*), thin tinsel (*sulma*), tinsel-wire (*mukesh*) and gold ribbon (*ghota, kinara*). The people enriched their garments with silks, cloth-of-gold and sumptuous velvets; their side-mounted flag and other shaped fans lent themselves to all forms of decoration, from embroidery to spangles and innumerable small discs of mirror-glass. Illustration Nos. XIX, XXIII, XXXI, XXXV, XXXVII, XL, 33.

SHADOW FANS FROM JAVA
These are rigid fans from Java, quite small, which were made of buffalo-hide for the main section, strengthened by supports and with a handle of carved buffalo-horn. On the surface of the hide would be painted their traditional Wayang shadow-puppets, often in solid col-

ours of red with gold, and sometimes stylised peacocks as well. They were made all over Indonesia, especially during the nineteenth and twentieth centuries. See also PARCHMENT.
Illustration No. XII.

SHAPED-FABRIC FANS

These were made as cheap brisé fans with a simple piece of fabric cut out in scallops to imitate feathers and backed by a simple wooden stick, held together by a thin cord or thick thread. They were fashionable in Europe in the early 1870s. Their use continued into the twentieth century, some with scalloped paper instead of textile. A catalogue of Sears, Roebuck & Company of 1902 quotes a price of 26 cents. It is said that Jenny Lind used a fan such as this when on tour in the United States and in that country these fans are known as 'Jenny Linds'.

SHELL-SHAPED FANS

These small European folding fans were made *c* 1890–1935. The shape is shell-like with a scalloped edge. One noted collector has one made of silver sequins on silver net, with mother-of-pearl sticks, in a perfect scallop-shell shape. They were decorated in the prevailing styles. See also FONTAGE FANS, PALMETTO FANS.

SLATE FANS

There are still some slate quarries in Wales where the apprentice is expected, as his 'Master's Piece', to make a fan from one thick slab of black slate. He would have to place a screw at one end, around which the sticks would doubly revolve. The slate would then be most minutely divided and sub-divided into equal sections, showing his skill as a worker, and then all the sticks would be pulled out equally and a double fan would emerge, the points of the outer guards arranged to touch the surface on which it stood. It is a remarkable exercise in both mathematics and the worker's skill as a slate-worker. These fans can still be bought at places like slate quarries in Wales and big agricultural fairs such as the Royal Bath and West Show.

SPANGLES (See SEQUINS)

STAMPED OR PUNCHED WORK ON FANS (See DECOUPÉ FANS)

102

STRAW

This is the residue remaining after cereals are threshed to remove the grains. It consists of dried stalks, leaves and husks of such grains and it was quite often used in Germany, France and possibly the Low Countries for decorating fans, some having first been dyed. Straw was only ever used in Europe as a form of decoration in very small reserves, rather than being a full type of fan, and often in conjunction with other applied materials, such as feathers, on silk or fine rag-paper. As the fan had to fold, only very small pieces of straw could be used, often less than $\frac{3}{4}''$ (2 cm) long, or there would have been a risk of splitting or flaking, but longer pieces are known to have been laid lengthwise along a pleat. Some of the prettiest 'straw' fans show a tiny birdcage made of only eight pieces of very fine straw, with an even tinier bird inside, made of applied feathers. So fine is this work that the owner of such a fan may mistake the decoration for embroidery. See also VEGETABLE FIBRES FOR FANS.
Illustration No. 34.

34. The English version of the Chinese Applied Faces fan, pre-dating their great vogue. The vellum leaf is painted in watercolours showing three figures all with clothes of silk applied onto the leaf and faces of applied ivory; also in the decoration is straw, and stamped-paper flowers. In the centre is a hand-coloured aquatint of 'The Arts' after Angelica Kaufmann. The sticks are of carved and pierced ivory with blue and white Staffordshire ceramic medallions set in the guards. c 1790–1800. Private Collection.

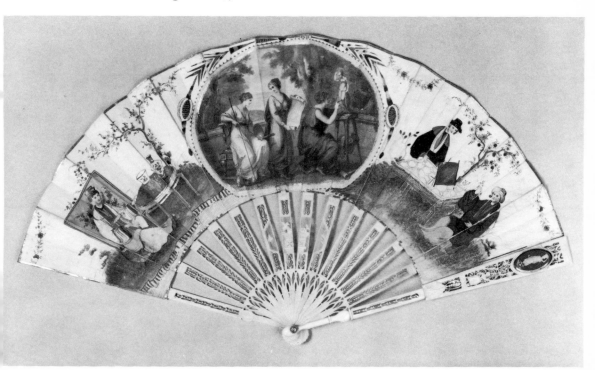

SUEHIRO

One author spells this word 'Suehiro' and another spells it 'Suyehiro': one never knows whether to follow the discipline of an academic or the everyday experience of an author/collector in these matters . . . let us hope it does not signify. The word is Japanese and means 'wide-ended'—a new type of fan for the Japanese after they had first seen fans from China which had a double leaf—the Japanese traditionally only used one. These new double leaves were introduced during the Muromachi period (1392–1568) and, in order to deal with the problem of a thicker leaf, the guards were designed to bend outwards from the middle. This means that when the fan is closed the leaf section looks as if it is half-open, even though the lower sticks are firmly shut.

TEA CEREMONY FANS (See RIKIU OGI)

TELESCOPIC FANS

Another word could be 'expanding'; it is quite extraordinary how often a new owner is slightly puzzled to own a thick, squat fan and is unaware that it pulls out to a 'proper' shape. This type appears perfectly normal as a folding fan but with short, stocky, straight sticks and guards. However, if the mount is gently pulled away from the gorge area when the fan is closed, the sticks seem to expand to twice their length: when the fan is opened out again it still appears the same fan but with the sticks twice as long and half as thick. The reason for this was entirely practical and novel: to save space. During the eighteenth century many telescopic fans were made of paper and during the nineteenth they were made from textiles. There are always exceptions to this rule, and there were also other types of telescopic fan which had sticks jointed in two sections.
Illustration Nos. I, II, III.

TOPOGRAPHICAL FANS

It is said that topographical fans, especially English examples, are rare. Topography is the collective term for all the physical features of an area, and in fans it generally includes figures as well. As an example, there is an illustration on page 69 of *A Collector's History of Fans* which shows a scene whose caption, at the time of publication, was vague and eventually found to be totally incorrect. Following help from the

35. Topographical fan, the chicken-skin leaf painted with a trompe l'oeil of three Italian views, La Grotta de Pozzuoli duputazione de la salute di Napoli *and also* La Grotta del Cana : *the bone sticks pierced and the guards carved with figures and foliage. Italian. $11\frac{1}{2}$" : 29 cms. (Fetched £150 in November 1982.) By courtesy of Christies, South Kensington.*

Royal Institute of British Architects (initiated by Anthony Vaughan) the fan has now been identified as being by Thomas Robins, showing Ralph Allen of Bath, together with John Wood the Elder, examining huge building blocks of Bath stone which were destined for Prior Park, Ralph Allen's 'country' house (on the hill just outside the City), lying ready in Ralph Allen's Stone Mason's Yard. The buildings in the background are now found to have been built for the stone masons and wharf-workers, the first 'real' commission of John Wood the Elder, and the River Avon lies on the right. It has taken much time to discover all these facts and, much to my delight and by pure coincidence, two years ago, I managed to buy the first of these cottages (on the left of the painting) for myself. They were built in 1727 and were due to be knocked down for road-widening some years ago, but fortunately the conservationists of Bath fought tooth and nail to keep them. Illustration No. 35.

TORTOISESHELL

The tortoise is a land-dwelling turtle, while turtles are aquatic or semi-aquatic creatures. Although tortoiseshell used for decorative purposes is really the shell taken from the hawk's-bill turtle (*Eretmochelys imbricata*), other forms of tortoiseshell are taken from other types of tortoise and turtle, and the use of the word 'tortoiseshell' (although not always completely accurate) is better understood than 'turtle shell'.

The marbled, varicoloured pattern and deep translucence of the plates (shells) of the creature have long been valued. Tortoiseshell was imported to Rome from Egypt, and in seventeenth century France the work attained a high level of artistry.

Basically, the turtle is a reptile which has not changed its appearance since the Triassic Period. It is toothless, generally slow moving and completely unaggressive—which makes it all the more unsavoury to learn that turtles' shells (plates) are ripped from their bodies whilst they are still alive in order to keep the translucency (I have watched this being done in Sri Lanka). Just recently a new technique has been developed so that the animal may be killed humanely first (in the past the shell went opaque after the animal was dead) and this technique has

36. French fan, the leaf painted with three groups of elegant figures in a park, with five circular portrait miniatures suspended at intervals around the border, four of an elegant couple and their children, and one of a European dressed as a tartar; the tortoiseshell sticks carved with putti, pierced, painted with vignettes, silver and gilt, the guardsticks set with painted mother-of-pearl plaques. 10″ : 25.5 cms. c 1760. (Fetched £520 in July 1982.) By courtesy of Christies, South Kensington.

coincided with new conservation laws which forbid the importation of tortoiseshell into some countries (notably Britain). The shell is light, strong, easily worked and most attractive and rich-looking. It was used for both sticks and guards and sometimes as both an inlay in other materials and as a strengthener by the head of a fan. Imitation tortoiseshell was used also: one type was made from stained horn and another was a dyed plastic. It was effectively used with piqué-work.
Illustration Nos. XVI, XXI, 27, 36, 47.

TRICK FANS

In order to startle your companions, a certain type of fan was made whereby you picked it up (or you invited them to do so) and it appeared to fall into nine broken pieces. After the initial cries of horror and shock you then picked it up yourself and it immediately appeared 'mended'. The 'trick' is the method by which the fan is either ribboned or mounted, and this is highly elaborate. Some are made all of ribbons, others of ribbons and lace alternately, and some are brisé. Conjurors used these in the last quarter of the nineteenth century but, because

37 a&b Trick fan, the ribbons of chine silk with flowers, the sticks being of decorated bone. The owner opens it up one way and it appears perfectly normal, opened the other way it falls apart into sections. Almost all fans only open from left to right apart from the Four Scenes fans, a few dance fans and this third category of Trick fans. Late 19th century c., English, 10″ : 25.5 cms. Owned by Mrs Georgette Tilley.

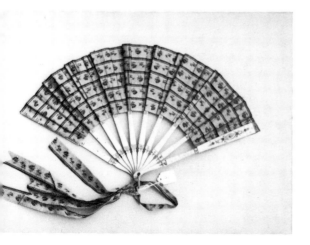 

they had to be seen from the stage, they were enormous in size. Everything depends on whether you open the fan up from left to right or right to left and, on careful examination, you will find that the sticks are arranged in pairs and the ribboning highly complicated.
Illustration No. 37.

T'UAN-SHAN

This is the Chinese name for a ceremonial fan. It was a screen fan but larger and mounted on a long handle. It was initially used in the ceremonial entourage of high officials (according to Julia Hutt) and, subsequently, at any important function or procession, together with the ceremonial umbrella and banner. Julia Hutt goes on to say (in *Fans from the East*) that the distinction between the ceremonial fan and banner is a difficult one to make for they often served a dual purpose. They go back for centuries.

UCHIWA

This Japanese word means a rigid screen fan: these could be mounted or left as a painting. As early as 930 there was a Japanese dictionary which listed both the 'ogi' (folding fan) and the 'uchiwa' (screen fan).

VARNISHED FANS

The general overall term is often 'Vernis Martin' but since the production of Hans Huth's book *Lacquer in the West: the History of a Craft and an Industry 1550–1950* and the author's own full chapter on 'Western European Varnished or Japanned Fans' in *The Book of Fans*, it seems agreed by collectors that the term 'varnished' is the most accurate. However, old habits die hard; auction houses set out to please the collectors and so keep to the old term of 'Vernis Martin', so we must consider them all together.

These fans were made in Holland, England, Germany and France *c* 1650–*c* 1730 and then again in the nineteenth century in admiration of past styles and techniques. Some were painted onto imported Chinese ivory sticks, very small and wedge-shaped and which, in the 1720s, became known as 'Lilliputians'. Some were created from scratch on tiny ivory brisé fans, wedge-shaped and keeping the Chinese style of having a 'different' decoration on guards and gorge. The date most associated with this type of fan is *c* 1700 (some were made as early as *c* 1680, some up to 1730), and these fans are rare. A great deal more research is needed on these fans, especially as they are immensely expensive and, since by now the paint and varnish tends to flick off when handled, they are becoming very delicate.

They were painted on prepared ivory with oil paints and then coated with a varnish to protect the paint; it should be mentioned that on no account should these fans be cleaned . . . the decoration merely washes off. The subjects most seen are either theatrical or mythological, or from the classics of Racine and Corneille. Some of the fans then display a mirror image on the reverse, which came from working in the Chinese manner of placing the fan upon a thin sheet of glass and positioning a candle underneath; the artist could then trace the design. Sometimes only the outline of the design is done and sometimes there is a complete repainting of the scene.

To hold the fan together there is either a tough, thin cord or knots of fine silk, or a fine silk ribbon about $\frac{3}{4}''$ (2 cm) wide. This ribbon is also known to have been made of fine skin. The ribbon is then hand-painted (not woven) with a design. Sometimes the design is in miniature, differing for every pleat; sometimes it is geometric; often it is of delicate gold lines.

On other fans of this type the reverse painting can be just as accomplished as the obverse but exhibiting either a landscape or a seascape. One noted collector feels that the way one can tell that a fan was made in France is to look for a wide cartouche in which there is a painting, irregular in shape, with heavy gilding on its outline and with some pierced work through the surrounding ivory leaves. Otherwise one can only rely upon one's knowledge of the prevailing styles of painting in various countries for a fan's place of manufacture.

It is also of interest to examine the manufacture of these fans: some, if taken apart for some reason, show that they numbered the sticks as they numbered good furniture parts. On others you can see how the artist would paint each stick in such a way that, when the fan was held up and opened, the scene did not abruptly stop at the edge of each stick but was painted a certain amount across, underlying the overlapping leaf. These fans appear to be of northern European manufacture and show deep tones of colour.

Illustration Nos. XIV, XXII.

VEGETABLE FIBRES FOR FANS

Fans, especially ethnographical ones, have been made from a variety of vegetable fibres all over the world from the beginning of time. They have also been made from reeds, *dib*; dry flags, *Typha angustifolia*; bagar grass, *Eriophorum cannabinum*; the inner bark of the dhaman (*Grewia oppositifolia*), *Fothergilla involucrata*; nettle-bark tree (*Celtis*), *Crotolaria, Saccharum officinaram*—and a huge variety of palms. Some of these materials are plaited, some woven, and some treated in the style of Indian 'chicks', a form of meshed bamboo for screening windows and verandahs. Many have been dyed, or have dyed fibres interwoven which make up some form of patterning. They are, on the whole, cheap local crafts which cost nothing (except time) to make.
Illustration No. 38.

VERNIS MARTIN (See VARNISHED FANS, LILLIPUTIAN FANS)

VIGNETTE (See CARTOUCHE)

WEDDING FANS (See MARRIAGE FANS)

ZŌGE OGI

During the mid-nineteenth century the Japanese made some very fine ivory brisé fans which were completely different from the ivory brisé fans of China. The Chinese pierced and carved the ivory, the Japanese applied both gold and semi-precious stones on to the ivory—exactly the opposite in technique. The Chinese divided the whole fan into three separate sections (above the ribbon, below the ribbon, and the gorge area) whereas the Japanese treated the fan as a complete canvas. They used rather thick ivory sticks and even thicker ivory guards, all with shaped finials (never the wedge-shape you see in some Chinese ivory brisé fans) and then created some exquisite scenes in *takamaki-e* or *hira-maki-e*, complicated layers of gold and lacquer which take a very long time to complete to such sophistication. On occasion the guard is similarly decorated and becomes a continuation of the scene; on other occasions shibayama inlay is used in another design (tiny insects, flowers and so on of jade, coral, or mother-of-pearl). These fans appear to have been made only from *c* 1860–*c* 1890 and some are signed.
Illustration No. XXXIV.

38. *Australian fans. Top left: a woven fan made by aboriginal women from Elcho Island, off the Northern Territory, taught by Fijian missionaries. Centre top: a fly-whisk made by aboriginals of emu feathers stuck onto a stick with native beeswax. Top right: woven fan made by aboriginals at the Mapoon mission station (now closed). Centre bottom: brisé fan made of Queensland woods by servicemen during the 1939-45 war in North Queensland. Owned by Mrs Audrey North.*

4 Identifying Illustrative Techniques

DRESS IN PORTRAITURE

Man's physical appearance throughout pictorial history, if recorded by a professional (artist in the past, photographer today), has always been a deliberate statement.

Details have always been accurately recorded, but the essence behind the presentation has generally been more of an oblique lie, because this recording might have been a 'once-in-a-lifetime' event. Even today, when a professional photographer is brought in to record an event of note, men and women still appear in 'fancy dress'.

No baby wears a lace christening gown more than once, any more than a bride would wear her wedding gown to a supermarket—yet posterity may only see us in these special clothes. The cheap but realistic home snapshot is now an honest assessment of our clothes and surroundings but is only a phenomenon of the twentieth century; if one is going to the expense of engaging a professional artist or photographer, one naturally wants to end up with something extra-special . . . and so it has been for the past 500 years. We should therefore look at paintings of the past (including, in miniature, on fans) with a carefully discerning eye.

The monarchs and courts of the sixteenth century were widely painted but portraits of the bourgeoisie were rare. This was partly because of the expense and partly because of a completely different critical attitude towards portraiture and dress at that time, which continued for several centuries.

Why was a portrait painted at all? To record a special event. When recording this event, how much could legitimately be the truth and how much was manipulated as a public relations exercise? A classic example was the vast painting of the Coronation of Napoleon, which included quite a few people who were not present on the day, left out some incidents and showed others that never occurred.

Paintings were propaganda, and an artist worked from an extremely carefully drawn up contract which specified every detail, from how many people should be portrayed, to the exact positioning of a family jewel, and how many colours were to be employed. Paintings were 'modern', showing both society's newest attitudes and the family's latest acquisitions, but they were also planned to last and not 'date'. This convention continued until mid-Victorian times; so, when examining a painted fan, one should heed the prevailing tastes in painting as a whole when attempting to date it and not go by clothes alone.

A number of later Elizabethan and early Jacobean paintings have survived in which the sitters are depicted wearing dress markedly different from their normal fashionable clothes. Their 'strange fantastick habit' would have been worn at a masque, an entertainment which had been introduced from Italy into the court of Henry VIII and had become a very popular feature of Elizabethan court life. Design of masque dress was governed by certain conventions, the most important being that it should not resemble 'examples of known attires' (Francis Bacon, *Of Masques and Triumphs*, 1597), an attitude which persisted for many years afterwards. This search for exotic costume led the designer to consult illustrations of the national dress of faraway countries, a fairly easy task as many costume books were published in the latter half of the century; by 1600 it is apparent from visual and documentary evidence that the garments worn at the English masque were influenced by Renaissance theatre costume.

Certain types of historical costume, mainly sixteenth and seventeenth century, appear frequently in eighteenth-century English and French portraiture, reflecting not only a nostalgia for the idealised past, but also the popularity of such costumes as worn at masquerades. When seen on painted fan-leaves this tends to confuse the new collector and shows how important it is to consider the entire fan with its sticks, guards and rivet, when attempting to date it. I have a fan, for instance, where all the gentlemen are dressed in Roman armour, the ladies in 'nightdresses' and the central lady in a fashionable dress of the 1730s, together with the contemporary jewels: all the other details date the fan to c 1740.

Seventeenth century Baroque artists were so worried about their pictures looking out of date (because of the costume becoming dated) that they tried to find clothes that would not date. They first tried

39. The leaf of this fan is painted with the 'Departure of a Hero', after a picture by a follower of De Troy signed Parmentier, the mother-of-pearl sticks carved with shepherds and shepherdesses, pierced, gilt and backed with mother-of-pearl. $11\frac{1}{4}''$: 28.5 cms. c 1880. (Fetched £180 in March 1982.) By courtesy of Christies, South Kensington.

the 'Arcadian' vogue, as can be seen in the works of Van Dyck and Rembrandt, but this, too, was a fashion, so another form was sought.

The middle of the seventeenth century promoted the 'Roman look', as it was an unchanged type of clothing which they thought would last. Van Dyck, Lely, and many others used it, but were not aware that the style dated as much as the wigs and pearls the sitters wore. That brings us to status: no matter how dateless the picture was meant to be, the sitters were not prepared to leave out those signals of their rank, the wigs, jewels and lace, which their contemporaries understood. For men the 'Roman costume' was mainly armour, but a way had to be found to paint non-military people, like writers and ladies. The answer was to use undress, either Indian gowns or shifts with a fabric over them (such as my fan with the 'nightdresses'). This was shocking, to show people in undress in public, but it was another form of status, for those at the top of society can ignore the rules and get away with it, while the lower orders cannot. Undress was allowed in court art, but was not approved by the Protestant middle class. Hence my fan must have been painted for a lady at court to use, since no lady down the social scale would have displayed it, for fear (and very genuine at that) of the disapproval of her contemporaries.

During the eighteenth century there was a growing appreciation of the glories of English history during the Tudor and Stuart periods and a gradual development of accuracy in historical costume on the stage and as used by the painter of history. The years 1730–1789 showed a lack of moderation in painting with an exaggerated cult of the aristocracy and of the military, both ladies and gentlemen using make-up to contrast with the vogue for powdered hair. During the Rococo period fashions spread quickly over the whole of Europe. The French ideas penetrated even into such artistically independent places as Venice, Rome, Vienna and Berlin, so that everywhere the salons and their frequenters were identical in appearance—for the first time paintings became truly international in depicting the sitter and fashions in dress.

The year 1792 in France (with the fall of the monarchy and the establishment of a people's commune) marked a decisive date in the evolution of costume for men. Jacques-Louis David, the leading painter of his day, was invited to present his ideas for official costumes for men in order to distinguish people in authority (they were not adopted), and the best proof that contemporaries themselves saw a connection between official dress and political outlook is furnished by a delightful little work entitled *Caricatures Politiques*, by Beauvart, dated 1798. It is important, therefore, to remember to look at the clothes a *man* wore at this time on European fan leaves, and to note also that 1792 is a fairly reliable cut-off point for French fans.

During the Empire period (c 1804–14) Napoleon was in charge of official dress. He possessed a real flair for its psychological import and instructed artists in the way he wanted himself and his court to be represented.

In Britain between 1820–1850, there was a great interest in national history, and public imagination was particularly captured by historical costume through which the past could come alive in a unique way. Many articles on costume history appeared in popular women's magazines—even in *Punch*—and the favourite form of activity in some circles was a 'fancy dress ball'. Some new collectors feel that early nineteenth-century fans are fakes because they show scenes of former centuries, but this is completely wrong: they did not try to fake earlier styles, or even techniques; they were attempting to show how learned they were in accurately representing the past. It is easy enough to see the difference; two guidelines are that powdered hair in nineteenth-century scenes is shown as white, whereas in the eighteenth century it would have been grey, and gilding is quite different and far more brassy.

During the nineteenth century, as many middle-class values took a downward trend, all the social classes began to participate in the public display of grief. Nineteenth century mourning dress is, in part, a manifestation of the new standards of respectability to which the middle classes laid claim—revelling in 'the luxury of woe'.

Black clothing was not, however, confined to mourning during this century; it was also the colour associated with the church, the business world of men and domestic service for women. It appealed to artists and poets of a romantic persuasion; it was flattering to a fair skin; it gave the illusion of slimness; it was dramatic as a contrast or foil to other colours and, not least, it was a practical choice for daily wear in polluted cities. All these uses of black can make distinguishing clothing problematic, especially for mourning. Relatives and friends were mourned in descending order and with a different shade and grade appropriate to each category, with much conflicting advice being poured out to their readers by women's magazines. As Henry Mayhew commented in 1865, 'our grief goes for nothing if not fashionable'. The fan collector must therefore beware of labelling a fan depicting ladies and gentlemen wearing black clothing as 'a mourning fan', for it may be nothing of the sort.

Not until the late nineteenth century did pictures of real peasants in working dress become popular, especially painted by the French and the Americans, but by that time owners of fine fans usually preferred satin, silks or feathers and not reproductions of contemporary art.

In general, therefore, European painted fans of the seventeenth, eighteenth and nineteenth centuries very often showed people in what we would consider 'fancy dress', and it is a *detail* rather than the costume which might give a clue to date. Not only do we owe a debt to art historians but also to costume historians: from David, Grasset de Saint Saveur, J. R. Planché and F. W. Fairholt in the past, to the famous academics of today.

Illustrations on fans have been executed in a large variety of media, some of which it may be helpful to explain.

WATERCOLOURS

Watercolours are pigments ground with gum arabic and thinned with water in use. Sable and squirrel ('camel') hair brushes are used on white and tinted paper. In the 'pure' technique, often referred to as 'the English method', no white or other opaque pigment is applied, colour intensity and tonal depth being built up by successive, transparent washes on damp paper. Patches of white paper are left unpainted to represent white objects and to create effects of reflected light. These flecks of bare paper produce the sparkle characteristic of 'pure' watercolour. Tonal gradations and soft, atmospheric qualities are rendered by staining the paper when it is very wet with varying proportions of pigment. Sharp accents, lines and coarse textures are introduced when the paper has dried. Some fans have been coloured by watercolour paints, but you find no opacity in the colouring and, because of the

40. Italian fan, the parchment leaf finely painted with fisherfolk in a landscape, mounted on pierced and carved ivory sticks. First quarter of the 18th century. 11″ : 28 cms. By courtesy of Bonhams, Knightsbridge.

nature of various pigments, the paint sometimes tends to flake in tiny shards. Printed fans which were hand-tinted had watercolours used on them.

GOUACHE

Gouache is opaque watercolour. It is thinned with water for applying, with sable and hog-hair brushes, to white or tinted paper, card, or silk. Honey or starch is sometimes added to retard its quick-drying property. Liquid glue is preferred as a thinner by painters wishing to retain the tonality of colours (which otherwise dry slightly lighter in key) and to prevent thick paint from flaking. Gouache paints have the advantage that they dry out almost immediately to a matt finish and, if required, without visible brushmarks. These qualities, combined with a wide colour range and the capacity to be washed thinly or applied in thick impasto, make the medium particularly suitable for painting on fabrics. It is the medium that produces the suede finish and crisp lines characteristic of many Indian and Islamic miniatures, as well as Western screen and fan decoration. Because of its elasticity, the colour does not flake from a fan which is continually being folded and unfolded. Creamy gouache shades were used on all fan surfaces, including parchment (vellum, chicken skin), paper and textiles.

INKS

Ink is the traditional painting medium of China and Japan, where it has been used with long-haired brushes of wolf, goat or badger on silk or absorbent paper. Oriental black ink is a gum-bound carbon stick that is ground on rough stone and mixed with varying amounts of water to create a wide range of modulated tones, or applied almost dry, with lightly brushed strokes, to produce coarser textures. The calligraphic brush technique is expressive of Zen Buddhist and Confucian philosophies, brushstroke formulas for the spiritual interpretation of nature in painting dictating the use of the lifted brush tip for the 'bone', or 'lean', structure of things, and the spreading belly of the hairs for their 'flesh', or 'fat', volumes. The Far Eastern artist poises the brush vertically above the paper and controls its rhythmic movements from the shoulder. Distant forms represented in landscapes painted on silk were sometimes brushed on from the reverse side in order to create a mysterious illusion of depth. Oriental fans very often featured inks on both paper and textile surfaces, sometimes alone and sometimes with added colours.

IVORY PAINTING

Ivory painting was practised in the eighteenth and nineteenth centuries in Europe and America for portrait miniatures or for fans. The decoration was often oval in form, especially if a professional artist or miniaturist was asked to decorate a fan. They were painted under a magnifying glass in fairly dry water colours or tempera stippling, with sable or marten-hair brushes; corrections were made with a needle. The velvet quality of the colours was enhanced, on the thinner ivories, by the glow produced by gold-leaf or a tinted backing.

TEMPERA

A tempera medium is dry pigment tempered with an emulsion and thinned with water. True tempera (one of the most ancient of painting techniques) is made by mixing the pigment with the yolk of fresh eggs, although a manuscript illuminator often used egg white and some easel painters used the whole egg. This egg tempera is the most durable form of the medium, being generally unaffected by humidity and temperature. It dries quickly to form a tough film that acts as a protective skin to the support. In handling, in its diversity of transparent and opaque effects, and in the satin sheen of its finish, it resembles the modern acrylic emulsion paints. When seen on an ivory fan you can enjoy the satin sheen if you tip the fan from side to side to catch the light.

PRINTING

Printing has traditionally been defined as a technique for applying under pressure a certain quantity of colouring agent onto a specified surface to form a body of text or an illustration. By the end of the second century the Chinese had apparently discovered, empirically, a means of printing texts; certainly they then had at their disposal the three elements necessary for printing: (1) paper, the technique for the manufacture of which they had known for several decades; (2) ink, whose basic formula they had known for 25 centuries; and (3) surfaces bearing texts carved in relief.

Paper, the production of which was known only to the Chinese,

41. Printed fan, the paper leaf decorated with hand-coloured satirical prints and slogans after the French Revolution of 1789; the reverse with the words of the song 'Le Trompe de L'Abbé Maury'; on wooden sticks. French. c 1790. 12½" : 31.5 cms. By courtesy of Bonhams, Knightsbridge.

followed the caravan routes of Central Asia to the markets of Samarkand, whence it was distributed as a commodity across the entire Arab world. The transmission of the techniques of paper-making appears to have followed the same route: Chinese taken prisoner at the Battle of Talas, near Samarkand, in 751, gave the secret to the Arabs. Paper mills proliferated from the end of the eighth century to the thirteenth, from Baghdad and on to Spain, then under Arab domination. Paper first penetrated Europe as a commodity from the twelfth century onward, through Italian ports that had active relations with the Arab world and also, doubtless, by the overland route from Spain to France; quite possibly fans were brought over at the same time.

Paper-making techniques were apparently rediscovered by Europeans through an examination of the material from which the imported commodity was made; possibly the secret was brought back in the mid-thirteenth century by returning crusaders or merchants on the Eastern trade routes. Paper-making centres grew up in Italy after 1275 and in France and Germany in the course of the fourteenth century. Thus the essential elements of the printing process collected slowly in Western Europe, where a favourable cultural and economic climate had formed.

Wood-block printing began in the sixth century in China and movable type was invented about 1041–48 by a Chinese alchemist named Pi Sheng. Xylography, the art of printing from wood carving, appeared in Europe no earlier than the last quarter of the fourteenth century, spontaneously and presumably as a result of the use of paper. Metallographic printing appears to have been practised in Holland around 1430, while Gutenberg's invention of typography (the concept of the printing press itself had never been conceived in the Far East) is generally credited with the date c 1450, and the first all-metal press was constructed in England in about 1795—from then on the techniques fairly galloped ahead.

Before the invention of photography, prints were the only means of conveying visual information to people in quantity. It is important to note, however, that the information conveyed by prints is not necessarily accurate. Sometimes this is due to the process of printmaking itself. With most engravings, for example, the engraver and the artist were different people. The artist might go to a certain place (Venice, for instance) and sketch on the spot; later he 'worked up' that sketch to make it more picturesque. Then the drawing went to the engraver, where it might be re-drawn by an intermediary to the size of the plate on which it was to be engraved in reverse. Eventually proofs were taken and the plate amended as required; unless the artist was there to check everything, the end result might be almost unrecognisable.

With etching and lithography this was less likely to happen as in these techniques the artist was often responsible for the work on the plate or stone.

In Europe during the seventeenth and eighteenth centuries, most prints carried all the relevant information on their margins. There was no legal obligation for a publisher to copyright a design for a fan, for instance, but many did and, as long as there is one remaining fan leaf (mounted or not) with all the relevant information on it, all other fans from that date can be correctly dated. Below is a short list of some of the abbreviations commonly found on prints:

Del, delt, delin = drew (from *delineavit*).
Descripsit = drew.
Desig, designavit = designed.
Inv, invenit = designed.

Pinx, pinxit, ping, pingebat = painted.
(The above words are usually bottom left, referring to the original artist or draughtsman.)
Aqua, aquaforti = etched.
Aquatinta = engraved in aquatint by.
F, fecit, fac, faciebat = made by.
Imp (impresset) = he printed it.
Inc, incidit, incidebat = engraved.
Lith, lithog = lithographed by.
Sc, sculp, sculpsit, sculpebat = engraved.

It was William Hogarth who was mainly instrumental in bringing about the English Copyright Act of 1735, which made the copying of prints illegal for a period of 14 years after issue and ensured that the original artist and printmaker were not robbed of their profits—as had happened to Hogarth himself with *The Harlot's Progress*, published in 1732 and copied wholesale.

Some fan leaves have been decorated with woodcuts, hand-coloured: they are early and crude. A great many are *line-engraved*: this means a burin or graver pushed across the surface of a copper plate. This technique virtually came to an end about 1821; after 1850 the copper was coated with a thin layer of steel which, if it ever wore out, could be replaced. How can one tell the difference between the two techniques? With copper, the design looks 'heavier' and the parallel lines are spaced further apart; *steel engravings* have a lighter, 'silvery' feel, and the parallel and cross-hatched lines are fine and close together.

With *aquatints* the outline of the design is usually etched onto the plate at the start. This technique was developed in England in the 1770s, notably by Paul Sandby; the effect was designed to produce tonal variations, the finished prints resembling wash drawings or water colours. *Aquatints* could be printed in one- or two-coloured inks with further colours added by hand.

Mezzotints were developed in the mid-seventeenth century, became an English speciality and towards the end of the eighteenth century were used for animal studies and prints after the paintings of George Morland.

Stipple engraving is created by a pointed instrument being used to build up the image by dotting the etching ground. It was popular in

Britain in the late eighteenth century and there are many fans known to have been stipple engraved by Francesco Bartolozzi.

Lithography was discovered as a technique in 1798 and marked the first important development in printmaking in several centuries. It was invented by Alois Senefelder of Munich, but not much used in Britain until Charles Joseph Hullmandel set up his lithographic printing press in London in 1818. It soon overtook aquatint for topographical illustration but attracted commercial printers rather than artists of note. In 1851 the Post Office listed some 135 lithographic printers in London.

Printing was an ideal technique for some fans, especially when they became cheap and topical. The saying 'Off with the old, on with the new' applied very much to the stripping off of passé printed fan-leaves and the application of new ones. The greatest collector of printed fans and fan-leaves was Lady Charlotte Schrieber whose collection was given to the British Museum in 1891; the catalogue by Lionel Cust (which may often be seen in good libraries) is used as a yardstick by collectors, and is referred to by auction houses in sales catalogues.

THE LANGUAGE OF FANS

One may look at a pretty fan and one may also look at the pretty girl who owns that fan—and carry on an animated conversation with her when, to comply with convention, no real speech is permitted.

42. An embossed paper leaf fan decorated with a coloured lithograph, mounted on pierced and painted wooden sticks. Made for the Spanish market or actually in Spain. c 1860. 10½″ : 26.5 cms. By courtesy of Bonhams, Knightsbridge.

123

In the past there have been several ways of using the fan for silent conversations; the first real satire on the way that ladies behaved behind their fans was published in *The Spectator* of 1711, when Joseph Addison (1672–1719) wrote a splendid essay describing a mythical academy for the training of young ladies and gentlemen in 'The Excerci/e of the Fan'.

In 1740 there was a reference to a conversation fan in *The Gentleman's Magazine* and, to avoid mistakes, I shall quote Wooliscroft Rhead (page 253, *History of the Fan*):

> Five signals are given, corresponding to the five divisions of the alphabet, the different letters, omitting the 'J', being capable of division into five, the movements 1 2 3 4 5 corresponding to each letter in each division. 1 By moving the fan with the left hand to right arm. 2 The same movement but with right hand to left arm. 3 Placing against bosom. 4 Raising it to the mouth. 5 To forehead.
>
> Example—Suppose *Dear* to be the word to be expressed. 'D' belongs to the first division, the fan must be moved to the right: then, as the number underwritten is 4, the fan is raised to the mouth. 'E' belonging to the same division, the fan is likewise moved to the right, and, as the number underwritten is 5, the fan is lifted to the head, and so forth. The termination of the word is distinguished by a full display of the fan, and as the whole directions with illustrations are displayed on the fan, this language is more simple than at first might appear.

It seems generally accepted that the first person to organise a 'language of the fan' was a Spaniard by the name of Fenella, who published (in Spanish) fifty directions on how to converse with the fan. Later on it was translated into German by Frau Bartholomaus and, finally, Duvelleroy of Paris translated it into English and made it available on small cards. The directions are refined into 33 actions and they 'speak' for themselves:

> Carrying in right hand in front of face: *Follow me*
> Carrying in left hand in front of face: *Desirous of acquaintance*
> Placing it on left ear: *I wish to get rid of you*
> Drawing across the forehead: *You have changed*

Twirling in the left hand: *We are watched*
Carrying in the right hand: *You are too willing*
Drawing through the hand: *I hate you*
Twirling in the right hand: *I love another*
Drawing across the cheek: *I love you*
Presented shut: *Do you love me?*
Drawing across the eyes: *I am sorry*
Touching tip with finger: *I wish to speak to you*
Letting it rest on right cheek: *Yes*
Letting it rest on left cheek: *No*
Open and shut: *You are cruel*
Dropping it: *We will be friends*
Fanning slowly: *I am married*
Fanning quickly: *I am engaged*
With handle to lips: *Kiss me*
Open wide: *Wait for me*
Carrying in left hand, open: *Come and talk to me*
Placed behind head: *Don't forget me*
With little finger extended: *Good-bye*
The shut fan held to the heart: *You have won my love*
The shut fan resting on the right eye: *When may I be allowed to see you?*
Presenting a number of sticks, fan part opened: *At what hour?*
Touching the unfolded fan in the act of waving: *I long always to be near thee*
Threaten with the shut fan: *Do not be so imprudent*
Gazing pensively at the shut fan: *Why do you misunderstand me?*
Pressing the half-opened fan to the lips: *You may kiss me*
Clasping the hands under the open fan: *Forgive me I pray you*
Cover the left ear with the open fan: *Do not betray our secret*
Shut the fully opened fan very slowly: *I promise to marry you*

During the nineteenth century the 'language of the fan' appears to have been enthusiastically taken up by the Spanish (whose social rules were stricter) and by some other European countries, notably France and England. It was a harmless diversion that must have passed away many a tedious evening, and it could be used at a distance with some eloquence.

5 Making and Repairing Fans

MAKING FANS

In appearance fans seem very fragile, like colourful butterflies which crush in the hand, and many new collectors wish to know how they are made.

In the late 1970s I was fortunate to be sent 19 colour transparencies showing a well-respected Japanese fan maker at work, together with a brief explanation of his techniques. Previous books have (nearly) all shown illustrations from Diderot's *Recueil de Planches sur les Sciences, les Arts Libéraux et les Arts Méchaniques* dated 1765 (to illustrate his encyclopaedia) but I feel it may be of interest to know how a modern Japanese fan master makes a folding fan today.

It seems that fan makers in eighteenth century Europe were generally women, whereas in the Orient they were generally men; in Europe they worked standing at trestle tables, while in Japan they were seated upon the floor. Mr Nakamura Kiyoe works on a shaped tree-trunk about 18 inches off the ground and about 18 inches across the roughly hewn surface, with all his materials spread around him in colourful disarray. His procedure for making a simple folding fan is as follows:

Two thin pieces of paper are glued together, after which they are painted with a design. The painting is often done with a blue dye, called *Gungyo*. Then the fan shape is cut out, and this basic shape of double paper is called *Washi*.

Two pieces of tanned, heavy-duty, pleated paper are then put to use; they are called *Kataji*, one side being called *Ogata*, the other *Megata*. The painted fan leaf (*washi*) is placed between the *kataji*, with the leaf being pleated between them, the fingers nipping the leaf home into each pleat. Then everything is separated and the fan leaf is re-pleated more firmly by itself, making knife edges.

As the *washi* is made from two thin pieces of paper glued together, it is necessary to part them in places for the sticks to be inserted within the pleats and evenly distanced. So a thin stick is inserted, up to a certain distance (in France this stick, or probe, was known as a *sonde* and was made of copper).

The next action is to cut along the edges of the folded paper leaf in order to neaten it, and to make a rice-paste glue (*Himenori*) for the bamboo sticks. These would have been supplied ready-made by other craftsmen, complete with a small metal rivet. When the glue is sufficiently kneaded it is rapidly brushed onto the upper part of the sticks, then the maker blows hard along the opened-up edge of the fan leaf and, with one swift, sure movement, the sticks are thrust into the fan leaf, one stick up each aperture. The fan is then left open to dry for a short while and is finally folded, ready for sale.

In Paris, during the nineteenth and early twentieth centuries, firms such as Lachelin and Duvelleroy used much the same process, except that the *kataji* were made from strong cardboard. In Japan all the interest was, and is, concentrated on the leaf of a fan; in Europe, including Spain, the interest was as much on the sticks and guards.

Spanish names for the parts of a fan are as follows: the leaf is *paise*, the sticks are *varetas*, the guards are *caberas*, the whole framework is *paquete*, the pin or rivet is *aboleta* and the area from the pin or head of the fan to the leaf is *fuente*. A good fan is an *abanico*, a cheap fan is a *chumbo* and brisé fans are called *baraja*.

Most people today associate fans with Spain (and bullfights) or Italy (and the opera). There is a tiny, isolated fanmaking industry in Italy and a very large one in Spain where, apart from a few innovations in the form of modern machinery, the flourishing fan industry has altered little in the past 150 years.

It is reported that the mounting of the leaf in Spain was left in the hands of nimble-fingered women: one group would pleat the paper or textile into a cardboard mould; another group would cut with precision along the upper edge of the pleated leaf; another would glue the upper section of the sticks and rapidly insert them among the pleats of the leaf. Then the folded fan would be tied together with a fine cord and left to dry for a day—after which the edging was applied.

It was only then that the artist would decorate the fan. He might copy an established painting by a famous artist (using the old cartoon techniques of pricking the outline of a tracing with a pin and shaking fine black powder through the holes) or he might paint as he wished.

During the twentieth century it became established practice for the 'background flowers' to be painted in first, followed by the main decoration.

Most of the fans made in Spain during the earlier part of the nineteenth century had carved wooden sticks; pine, brought from the Province of Cuenca, being used for the most expensive fans, poplar for the cheaper ones. It is reported that the wood was soaked in water for several days to soften it, after which the shaped sticks were covered with a roughly painted paper leaf. Later on, lithographs and colour prints were mounted on both paper and silk, and as time went by, there were introduced into Spanish fans sticks and guards made from tortoiseshell, mother-of-pearl, horn, bone and ivory, all of which were worked by machine, with a fretsaw (*serreta*) which was foot-controlled, using a traced design and working on three sticks at a time. In the twentieth century the types of wood used in Spain widened to beach, banana, medlar, apple, pear, birch, ebony and sandalwood.

Working as a fan painter in the twentieth century was no sinecure and was very competitive. An original design might take up to a week to complete, being painted on kid or silk and bringing in up to 500 pesetas (in 1957). Bench-workers, on piecework, working all day with hardly a break, might earn themselves up to 150 pesetas a day, and the 'in-between' workers, who produced a medium-price quality, received a moderate but regular income. Top-quality work was very nerve-racking in spite of the prestige, while the cheapest work was boring in its repetitiveness, so the medium-price quality was the most favoured.

The making of extremely fine fans has been well-documented in previous books, but no one has written very much about fans made during the past 100 years. It must be obvious from the above that techniques have stabilised, especially as fans became cheaper, and it may be of interest to consider relative prices about a hundred years ago. In *c* 1880 it was quite possible to pay out as much as £100 for a fine 'dress fan' made in France or Germany. 'Common fans' made by the French in 1880 were priced at five pence a dozen; cockade fans were six pence each, telescopic fans could be bought for $2\frac{1}{2}$ pence. Japanese *uchiwa* were six pence each and Chinese painted gauze or silk fixed fans were one shilling and sixpence. But the cheapest fans of all were sold in Spain, where some might be bought for a farthing each.

XXVI. Spanish fan, the paper
leaf showing a charming scene of
the dance; the sticks are of bone
overlaid with very small areas of
gold leaf. $10\frac{3}{4}''$: 27.5 cms. Mid-
19th century. Private Collection.

XXVII. Spanish fan, with a very
colourful scene of bull-fighting, etc.,
probably sold as a souvenir; wooden sticks.
$13\frac{3}{4}''$: 35 cms. Mid-19th century. Owned
by Mrs Margaret Little.

XXVIII. Spanish fan, the paper
leaf having a decoration on it of the
entrance of the toreadors; wooden
sticks. $13\frac{3}{4}''$: 35 cms. c 1850.
Owned by Mrs Margaret Little.

XXIX. Large folding fan: thin rust silk
gauze mount, hand-painted with
nasturtiums, buds and leaves; serpentine
sticks and guards of wood. Signed
'Daillard'. $14''$: 35.75 cms. Probably
French. c 1890–1900. Owned by Mrs
Grace Grayson.

XXX. Mother-of-
pearl fan with a leaf of
silk gauze most
delicately painted and
inset with panels of
Brussels needlepoint
lace. $13\frac{3}{4}''$: 35 cms.
c 1860. Private
Collection.

XXXI. Small
sequinned and
spangled fan which is
very effective when
carried at a dance.
8'' : 20.5 cms. Late 19th
century. Owned by
Mrs Margaret Little.

DISPLAYING FANS

The choice for fan collectors is either to display their fans or to put them away; this choice is entirely personal and there is no 'must' attached to either approach.

When displaying a fan the collector may mount it on a stand or may prefer to frame it. Putting it on a stand should only be a *very* temporary amusement—it would gather dust, dulling the materials, as well as being a magnet for interested fingers. If placed upon a stand (several shaped types are available), then a backing plate is absolutely essential for the fan to lean against—clear plastic is very suitable.

It is wisest to have a fan framed by a professional, for although it sounds easy enough to do, the project has many hidden pitfalls. Fans can be permanently damaged, drastically reducing their aesthetic and investment value, by a sloppy or unscrupulous framing job. The best way to protect your collection is to choose your framer with care; try hard to find a conscientious craftsman who can be trusted to use

43. The paper leaf is painted with a lover crowning his mistress: mounted on pierced, carved and painted ivory sticks. This would be magnificent displayed in a frame with a coloured background. Second half of the 18th century. Possibly German. $10\frac{1}{2}''$: 26.5 cms. By courtesy of Bonhams, Knightsbridge.

reliable materials.

Acidic materials are the greatest worry, but art must also be protected from light (especially sunlight), moisture, heat (never hang a framed fan over a fireplace or a radiator), air pollution, insects, handling and transport.

Be very careful about the cardboard borders used within a frame. Two kinds are generally available, a regular board and a rag board, and while the regular is sold in many enticing colours, it is very acidic and can do much harm to fan leaves of the past. Some form of cardboard, however, is essential, for it keeps the fan or fan leaf away from the glass which may contain injurious impurities; the board also creates a controlled air space without which you might get condensation, leading to water-spotting, mould and rot. There is also the danger that the illustration might actually stick to the glass.

Acid causes discolouration, brittleness and deterioration of paper and textiles, sometimes in a few months, sometimes in a few years, depending upon climatic conditions.

On the other hand rag board (or museum board, as it is also known) can be virtually free of acid. It is more expensive and the way to tell the difference is that, while rag board has a colouring which goes right the way through, regular board often has a sandwich of a different colour in the middle. Refuse the latter if you wish to care for your fan leaf.

The backing (the stiff board which holds the fan leaf) should, of course, be acid-free: it is always advisable to have a fan leaf mounted on rag board, treated wood or acid-free fabric. Also, when the whole fan or fan leaf is finally framed, make sure that no corrugated paper is used to seal the back; that, too, is filled with acid and would eventually show on the fan as brown stripes.

Light, especially sunlight, can be damaging to fan leaves or fans, so the type of glass used can be important. Good framers carry a wide choice, best of all being ultraviolet plexiglass which brings the work up to museum standards. It is very light in weight, looks like clear

44. Top: an ivory brisé fan with central painted vignette of Venus and Cupid: the whole fan finely pierced and carved. This technique would be almost impossible to repair. French. c 1820. 10″ : 25.5 cms. Bottom: a combination or repaired fan, the leaf painted in the 19th century, showing lovers in a landscape, the sticks of the 18th century, of carved, pierced and painted ivory. 11½″ : 29 cms. By courtesy of Bonhams, Knightsbridge.

45. Chinese goose-feather fan tipped with maribou and painted with typical Canton School butterfly and flower scene, the sticks and guards are of well-carved ivory. It is accompanied by its box decorated with fine two-colour gold painting on a black lacquer background. Very great care has to be taken with these fans, for the paint can easily chip off – this is in a perfect condition. $11\frac{1}{4}''$: 28.5 cms. Canton. c 1820. From Fans of Imperial China by Neville Iröns, by courtesy of the House of Fans Limited.

glass and is expensive, but offers the greatest protection because it filters out harmful rays which cause fading and discolouration. Ordinary plexiglass, also light in weight, does not have the filtering power of UV but is good for very large areas. Both kinds of plexiglass have the disadvantage of attracting dust and being easy to scratch, so special cleaners are necessary. Non-glare glass (a recent fad) is also expensive but does not actually offer any extra protection and tends to obscure the image.

Mouldings are now available in an enormous variety of styles, widths, shapes and prices. It is always wise to go to a framer where the work is done on the premises and where the primary interest is in the preservation of fans and fan leaves. Most good framers believe that the frame should enhance the fan and be chosen 'from the fan out', rather than 'from the room (where it is to be hung) out'.

It is wisest to go to some specialist fan framer rather than to a local firm dealing mainly with prints and photographs. The specialist knows which backing materials would harmonise and be correct for the age of the fan, and can also deal with such problems as the width of the rivet and the weight of the guards, so that the fan or fan leaf may be withdrawn from the frame at a later date, for exhibition or for sale, in the same condition as when you acquired it. Your framer will also advise on whether it would be better to have a rectangular-shaped frame or a fan-shaped frame, in order to blend in with all the other framed works of art in your home.

When discussing with a framer or repairer the work to be done, it is better to supply too many details than too few. Give the measurements, a description, the colouring (an instant photograph is most useful) and, when writing, enclose a self-addressed stamped envelope; do not be afraid to enquire about prices for, as you can see from the above, they would vary a good deal, depending upon the quality of the materials required.

There are several people in Britain who frame fans and it would be sensible to pick the one nearest to yourself; it is never wise to send anything through the regular post, far better to travel with your precious fan and speak to your framer yourself. In that way there can be no confusion over backing fabrics, colours, frame mouldings and prices; for both your sakes it is also a good idea to have all these details enumerated on paper.

For both making and repairing fans (other than through the Fan Museum) consult:

John Brooker,
Flint Studio, East Rudham,
King's Lynn, Norfolk PE31 8RB.
Tel: 048 522 303

I would write to him in the first instance and then, should it be convenient to you both, arrangements might be made to meet. Don't hurry the repair or framing of a fan: it has, after all, been in existence for many, many years and it would be a false economy to expect a deadline now. Once your fan is repaired or framed it is obviously going to enhance its value and give it many more years of life, so it is worth being patient. In this way you will find a charming relationship building up between yourself and the specialist craftsman, for a repairer of fans, with the multitude of materials involved, is often a repairer of most small antiques and therefore extremely useful to know.

STORING FANS

When you store a fan it is as well to remember the danger points raised above: light, moisture, heat, insects and handling. Firstly you should carefully fold the fan, seeing that none of the ribbons have doubled back upon themselves, and then wrap it gently but firmly in a double sheet of acid-free white tissue paper. Use a large sheet, so that both ends of the fan are covered and the paper is folded back over the fan. It is not wise to use a rubber band which, over the months, would put a strain on some part—the tissue paper should hold it if you use enough. Don't worry about the inevitable creases, but be careful to keep the paper clean because dirt usually comes from fingermarks and there is little grime more acid than the perspiration on the fingers.

The container in which you plan to store your fans must then be prepared. Should you be fortunate enough to have a specialist fan cabinet you will find there is depth for only one fan to be placed flat in each compartment, rather than fans lying on top of each other in an ordinary drawer. But first you must ensure that the drawer, wherever it is, is free of insects or fungus. Treat the drawer with a fungicide/bactericide in any case, for some bacteria or mites are hardly visible and you would be amazed if you knew how much animal life you are entertaining in your home, however clean. I suggest either *SOPP* or *Mystox LPL*, both available from *Picreator Enterprises Ltd, 44 Park View Gardens, London NW4 2PN*; or *Talas, 213 West 35th Street, New York, NY 10001–1 966*; or *Conservation Materials Ltd., 240 Freeport Boulevard, PO Box 2884, Sparks, Nevada 89431, USA.*

Some museum experts suggest that you then line your drawer with velvet, holding it down with an adhesive, so that the tissue-paper-wrapped fans do not slide up and down the drawer each time it is opened or shut. Lastly, you should guard against damp in the drawer. In order to find out if any damp is there, you can make up some small gauze or net bags of *Silica Gel* and place them permanently in a corner of the drawer. *Silica Gel* (ask for the special self-indicating type at a chemist or photographers) is a crystalline substance which absorbs atmospheric moisture in a closed container, changing colour from blue to pink as it reaches its saturation point. Once it has turned pink you can re-use it by warming it in a very cool oven, which drives off the moisture and restores the original blue tint. You can also buy *Silica Gel* from the specialist firm mentioned above which makes conservation materials for most of the museums of the world.

REPAIRING FANS

Many collectors have to decide whether they wish to repair a damaged fan, whether it should be conserved (conservation is virtually the museum technique of a reversible repair and, obviously, although extremely costly, the best choice) or whether merely to clean it.

I have given a complete chapter on 'The Repair of Fans' in *The Book of Fans* which has, I understand, helped many amateurs to set up a small workshop. However, if a new collector wishes to tidy up a recent purchase on a strictly limited scale, the following may be of assistance.

Fans need to be cleaned when bought, and care taken over both leaf and sticks. Each material should be considered separately, and a decision made as to whether to leave it alone or not. Unhappily, many owners in the past used stamp hinges to hold a fan leaf together, or, since the last war, an impact adhesive; this must first be completely removed (*Dissolvex* is good) with infinite patience, and then the damage assessed.

Most dirt is a strange mixture of dust, fluff, food and perspiration

XXXII. *Japanese Export fan, rigid and asymetrical, made from bamboo covered with soft paper, embossed with 'ribs'. The flowers are cunningly made from silk with no stitching at all. The handle is solid and there is a signature of the artist. Approx. 12″ × 11″ (30.5 cms × 28 cms). c 1890–1903. Owned by Mrs Grace Grayson.*

XXXIII. *Two Japanese ogi (folding fans). This illustration shows the obverse of one fan (on the left) and the reverse of another. They are delicate paintings in watercolours and gold leaf on a leaf made from a silk and paper mixture. The sticks are of plain, polished, 'tea-stick' bamboo, serrated along the edges; the guards are of ivory with shibayama inlay and cut off sharply and squarely – both the serrations and the 'squared-off' look are typically Japanese. 10¾″ : 27.5 cms. c 1875. From* Fans of Imperial Japan *by Neville Irons, by courtesy of The House of Fans Limited.*

XXXIV. *Zōge ogi, decorated in varying shades of gold (takamaki-e and hiramaki-e), the guards having shibayama inlay; there is a long cord with a double tassel. These fans were only made between 1860–1885. Japanese, for the Export market. 9½″ : 24 cms. Owned by Mrs Geraldine Pember.*

XXXV. *Empire fan leaf. The subject, painted upon silk, is that of Orpheus (seated) with his lyre, accompanied by Eurydice, seen in a Neo-classical interior with columns of foil, statues, vases, etc., embellished with different sizes of gilt sequins and gilt embroidery. c 1800. Author's Collection.*

XXXVI. Marriage fans in action! The bride is Wendy Alves, seen recently with her attendants in California, all carrying flowers and ribbons with their fans. The flowers, fans and design were by Mrs Geraldine Pember, the photograph by Juliette Ohleyer in Orinda, California.

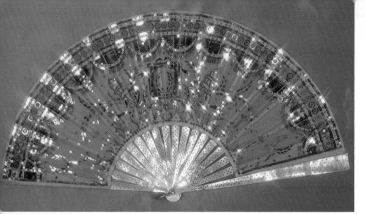

XXXVII. Spangled fan, embroidered with silver spangles and sequins on net, with mother-of-pearl sticks and guards decorated with cut-steels 'piqué-point'. English or French. 19th century. $9\frac{1}{2}''$: 24.25 cms. Owned by Mrs Margaret Little.

XXXVIII. Spanish fan, the paper leaf decorated with bull-fighting scenes. The sticks of pierced aromatic wood and cut-steels 'piqué-point'. $10\frac{1}{2}''$: 26.75 cms. 19th century. Owned by Mrs Margaret Little.

XXXIX. Articulated fan, the leaf printed with a 'Watteau-esque' design, the sticks and guards of bone. A tiny pin, half-way down the guard, pushes upwards and a small mirror emerges from the top of the guard – not so much to check on the lady's appearance, but more to discover if a gentleman is hovering behind her. $8\frac{1}{2}''$: 21.5 cms. Late 19th century. Private Collection.

XL. Edwardian fan, the leaf being backed with netting, embellished with gilt spangles and sequins; the sticks and guards are of mother-of-pearl. $8\frac{1}{2}''$: 21.5 cms. Private Collection.

all bonded together over the years; in many cases it is actually holding the fan together, in some it can come off in a solid piece, in others it has to be removed by stages. When it has all gone the underlying material may be found to be too fragile without new support.

I would suggest to the new collector that, on the whole, the fan leaf should be left alone, apart from carefully brushing off surface dust with a clean, soft brush. The specialist repairer can work miracles (and there are many techniques) but the new owner is wise to leave well alone.

Fan sticks could, in some cases, be cleaned by the amateur, using a magnifying glass and a strong light. If the sticks are made from ivory there are two basic methods to follow: either knead a substance such as *Groom/stick* into all the crevices (available at *Picreator*, above) or clean with a minute amount of distilled water on a cotton-wool-covered orange-stick. *Groom/stick* looks a little like putty when warmed in the hand and, if sufficiently supple from the warmth, it can be gently pushed into every crevice of the carving and then peeled off, taking the dirt with it. It can be used again and again. Otherwise the ivory sticks may be cleaned, one section at a time, with distilled water (never water from the tap). Both these techniques apply as well to tortoise-shell, bone, horn and mother-of-pearl.

Having cleaned the sticks and allowed them to rest and dry out completely (moisture is the greatest danger) it is wise to preserve them with a little *Mystox* solution as a fungicide/bactericide/insecticide, followed by *Renaissance* wax polish to give the sticks a faint sheen and protection for about ten years. (Both solutions are available from *Picreators* and the wax polish is on sale in many good stores, too.)

If any of the sticks happen to be broken, a new collector should ask the advice of a professional before embarking on any repairs. Only after years of actually handling fans do owners feel competent to try to repair their own fans, not just because of the techniques but also because of the stress points on the fan; an inexperienced collector could break a stick while working on the leaf, purely through ignorance of the crucial balance and stress areas on a certain type of fan.

On the whole it is acceptable to collectors to remove grime but not to add anything, such as touching up a painted decoration, because today's paints are rather different from those originally employed. The scene might look much better to begin with but, after a short time, it would be obvious where the new paints had been used.

The same applies to the use of new textiles, lace and so on: if a textile is to be repaired, then a textile of the same period should be used from another fan which is past repair.

It cannot be stressed too much that a new collector should try to avoid buying a fan which needs repairing; if she has done so (and paid a lot for it) she should seek out a specialist repairer instead of embarking on the work herself. There are quite a few in most countries and the Fan Societies generally have some names on their books and can advise. If, on the other hand, the new owner is absolutely determined to carry out repairs herself, there are two basic rules: make an appointment with the conservation department of the best local museum to get specialist advice and then, if in any doubt at all about her capabilities—DON'T.

THE BACKGROUND TO AN INDUSTRY

It is curious that the countries which made fans in the past, and to which we give the loudest praise, are those which have no fan industries today; the one country that fan collectors have rather denigrated, and whose fans fetch the lowest prices—because of collectors' general ignorance on the subject—now has the major production ... Spain. Fans from most other European countries have been studied in depth, as well as fans from the Orient, but fans of Spain have never been written about until very recently (my book, *Fans and Crafts of the Hispanic Empire*, first published by the FCI *Bulletin* 1990).

The position of the craftsman in Spain has always been difficult, however creative or brilliant he was. In fact it is not so long ago that the expression *viles artesanos* (vile artisans) was banished from legal phraseology. Spaniards, throughout the history of their development, have always preferred the calling of the priest or the soldier, believing that the 'arts of peace' were venal, despicable, and effeminate—and definitely unworthy of a gentleman. 'The Spaniards,' wrote Fernandez de Navarrete, 'are so proud-hearted that they do not accommodate themselves to servile labour.' Craftsmen, therefore, came very low in the social hierarchy, and the crafts were neither considered of real worth, nor were they written about as subjects in their own right.

Individual fans were made in Spain during the thousand-year period of the ninth to nineteenth centuries, and fortunately we have portraits showing the styles, and records which document the prices paid and the names of some, at least, of the individual artists, makers or suppliers.

Spain was, for a long time, the richest empire in Europe, and ladies of rank reflected this happy state by owning the finest fans available. The Spanish were also amongst the greatest traders around the world, which accounted for the huge variety of materials they used in the fans, much being brought into the country by the Manila Galleon: gold, in which they traded all over the world; silver from their mines at Potosi in South America, together with mica (flicking with light) from other mines in the area; brilliant, iridescent feathers from the rare birds of Mexico and Spanish South America; glowing tortoiseshell and gleaming mother-of-pearl from Yucatan and Mexico; gems of every hue from India and the East, together with oriental fans and styles; ivory from Africa; shimmering textiles through their Moorish connections in the Near East (who taught the Spaniards how to weave them), and the supple gilded leathers which they developed in their own country through Moorish help. Fragile lace was made in Spain, often of either gold or silver, to 'go with' the magnificent embroidery in bullion on everything from both gentlemen's and ladies' garments to horses' harness, and Spain was the first European country to develop the craft of paper-making . . . it becomes obvious that they had every-thing for making fans of every type.

From earliest times fans were used in that country for the simplest reason—to cool people down. Even today, at a bull-fight, or along the street cafés, fans are still wielded and fluttered for the same purpose. They are also manipulated for the other purpose of 'attention-getting' as a lady opens her fan with a roaring *snap*! just as her opponent is reaching the climax of a story or fluttering long eyelashes a little too much at her husband; or the fan is used as a cordless phone across a large room, gesticulating messages of assignation, disapproval, boredom or flirtation, far more expressive than an extra hand.

In the past fans were also used as banners/flags for the military, for ceremonial parades and for the guilds. The huge and fascinating Army Museum in Madrid shows an astonishing array of military banners, not only Spanish but from many other countries (especially those which they captured in their long history). In Manuel Rocamora's book on fans the frontispiece illustrates a magnificent early fourteenth-century ceremonial banner (or flag) fan, embroidered with gold thread and sequins, showing the coat of arms of Barcelona. This was originally owned by the Marqués dell Valle de Ribas (General Llander) who was Capitán General of Cataluña, and is only one of many to be seen in the rich museums of Spain. And in the Museo Mares, Barcelona, for instance, there are several glass cases filled with flag-shaped fans which had been carried by guild members in the past, made from a strange variety of materials and showing highly personalised symbols, tassels, straw and cut-leather-work.

However, one cannot stress too highly the foreign influences on Spanish fashion, which the collector must be careful to take into account when viewing Spanish fans of any era; after the sixteenth century fans were largely associated with ladies' dress and fashions, although, to this day, you still see men naturally carrying them around for comfort's sake:

—every queen between Isabel I (1451–1504) and Isabel II (1830–1904) was a foreigner (and so were all since), and they probably had more influence on fashion than anyone else;

—there were two dynastic changes, or rather one and a half: Philip V in 1700, totally French, and Carlos III in 1759, coming to Spain with all his courtiers after being King of Naples for years;

—even under Isabel II, the prime influence was the France of Napoleon II, which was aped in almost every way, finance, fashion, foreign policy included.

Gradually the Spaniards lost confidence in their own fan-making (as well as many other crafts) as the queens imported foreign styles; the *Companion Guide to the Museum of History and Costume* at Aranjuez states that, in 1792, imports of fans from France alone numbered 652,720. This concerned the King and his government to such an extent that, in 1788, a report was compiled by D. Eugenia Larruga on the state of the industry: he suggested that proper factory production might be introduced.

The industry took some time to persuade, but eventually came into being in the nineteenth century (a real renaissance of the fan), mostly in and around Valencia—where the main factories are today. They were not run as a nationalised concern, but as individual factories; they were a homogeneous group of like-minded owners who were (and are) in great competition yet loosely linked through friendships, rather than completely controlled by their guilds.

A Royal Fan Factory is known to have existed in Valencia in 1802, in the Plaza de Cajeros; during that year, for the visit of Carlos IV and Maria Luisa, the firm made some outstanding illuminated addresses in their honour, as well as some interesting fans: sadly that factory no longer exists, although some of the fans are known. This was the beginning of true factory production, but the individual fan-maker still existed (and exists), making one-off fans for the discerning lady with both taste and money.

Through both financial and trade ties with France (and at a time when Spain's finances were at their lowest ebb in history), the earliest 'real' factories in Valencia were started around 1830—M. Coustellier from Paris being one of the first owners. In 1840 D. José Colomina, an industrialist from Jijona in Alicante, founded another factory of note in Valencia, importing his silks from France, which were woven by the Valencian *vellutera*; he was reported to have made sufficient really artistic fans 'to satisfy the market', and was eventually elevated to the rank of Marqués.

Many more fan factories opened during the long period of female rule (Isabel II 1833–1868, the Regent from 1833–1843 being her mother, Maria Cristina) and during the general period of stability from 1875–1923. But the factory owners made it absolutely clear that the industry was a Spanish one—so no completely foreign fans were sold through them. They might easily import French or English designs or prints for the leaves, for instance, but then they would mount them on sticks crafted in Spain; or the other way about: the final fan would always be sold as Spanish. Because labour was so incredibly cheap in Spain, a very great many fans were exported to European countries, the USA and to Spanish South American countries, too. Now, in the 1990s, Spain has the only serious factory production for fans in Europe, and they export millions all over the world, including to Japan.

Because so little is known in Spain about fans in general, and their own fans in particular, it is a glorious place to search for them. As there is no real market, the collector will be surprised over the prices asked. Nineteenth-century painted Spanish fans, with mother-of-pearl sticks and guards (called *Isabelinas*), sell for very high prices: most Europeans don't care for them, but many Americans and Germans love them. But you can pick up early French fans, light eighteenth-century

English fans, and rare oriental fans for a song—because most Spaniards simply don't know what they are. Nor do they care. But you must bargain—hard.

Pre-factory-produced Spanish fans never show themes from the Renaissance, the French Revolution, Art Nouveau or anything which is sexually explicit, for all are either politically or morally dangerous and no husband would care to have his wife brandishing them about. Instead most Spanish fans highlight Spain's historical exploits and try to revive the nation's pride in its past—the exploits of Christopher Columbus, for instance, and Ferdinand and Isabel; battles, special occasions in their dominions, topographical scenes, musical events, plays, national disasters or triumphs, and so on.

On the whole the Spanish look at their fans (continually in use) with a different eye from the rest of Europe. Firstly, they have to be practical, opening and shutting at the rivet with ease, and being sure to give a really cool breeze. Then they have to be of the newest fashion, for the ladies change their fans as we would change shoes. Then they have to be one of three types: for everyday use, for Sunday use and 'for the vitrine'. What everyone examines is the balance of a fan, believing (as they have done for centuries) that really heavy sticks and guards of imported mother-of-pearl, tortoiseshell, ivory, etc., finely crafted, and heavily gilded, are really worth paying for. (To satisfy the animal conservationists today they also produce *nacarina*, a very superior plastic, which cannot be moulded but has to be crafted like mother-of-pearl.) Lastly, they consider the painting on the leaf, which, to many, is of minimal interest; 'never mind the painting,' they believe, 'but, if you want quality, feel the weight.' Too quickly all this will change, so buy antique fans in Spain while you can, avoiding modern, pavement-sold factory-made ones—unless for everyday use!

46. *This nineteenth century fan with a printed leaf shows four albumen print portrait photographs and three view photographs, believed to be related to a Paraguayan Revolution, mounted on pierced bone sticks. Probably made in Spain. c 1850/60. 10″ : 25.5 cms. By courtesy of Bonhams, Knightsbridge.*

47. Nineteenth-century 'Cabriolet' fan of hand-painted silk, the lower leaf signed Y. Serand. Sticks and guards of tortoiseshell. Possibly French. 9½″: 24 cms. The owner dates this c 1830. Owned by Mrs Geraldine Pember. As this has neither a cabriolet painted upon this unusual fan, nor any other form of transport, it should technically be termed a 'double-leafed' fan as it is of the 19th century.

6 Guilds

European cities, in medieval days, were the natural habitat of the bourgeoisie, merchants and specialised craftsmen; an oligarchy of competence, they became forced to organise their agglomerations. Out of ignorance and chaos they created a system of municipal administration for free men living together—and thus, in time, helped to end the ancient feudal systems.

They elected their own town officials headed by their greatest man, their 'mair'—from the Latin 'major' or 'maior', meaning 'greater'—a word which eventually became 'mayor'. To assist him they elected the elder statesmen of the city, the 'elders' or, later, 'aldermen'; and they all met to discuss business sitting round a slab of wood which nowadays we call a table but which, in those days, was merely called 'the board' ... resulting in the phrase 'The Mayor and Board of Aldermen'.

Eventually the educated bourgeoisie infiltrated the office-holding class, providing many notaries, lawyers and accountants; they acquired such a standing that they were often entertained by kings. The bourgeoisie had a very strong civic sense and this could expand, in time, to become a national patriotism. Some countries (such as modern Germany or Italy) have come late to this; they did not acquire a national identity until fairly recently and, at times of stress, some of their national leaders still think with a regional spirit. But amongst themselves it was generally agreed that, on the basis of a very strong moral background, 'if you worked hard and long hours and wisely weighed up your decisions, then you would become wealthy and honoured by your fellow citizens; the poor were merely contemptuous layabouts.'

The backbone of medieval economy was the guild (the word first appears in Charlemagne's decrees) which had strong religious overtones. In England the guilds, religious associations of men with similar mercantile interests, were established to provide mutual aid, protection, a moral standard and better times. The same applied in France until they rejected their faith.

At first there was one guild to a town, but as the population grew and interests were diverted into differing channels, the guilds divided: vertically into the merchant-owners and the workers, employers and employees, rich and poor; horizontally into crafts or trade guilds and sometimes separated by distinctions as narrow as some of the union branches of Britain today. The obvious purpose was to promote the economic welfare of each member of each guild and to guarantee him full employment at high wages by restricting membership. The guild regulated work procedures and hours of labour, it set maximum wages (not minimum) and standardised quality, it promoted discipline and solidarity and set out to preserve the status quo. But it also restricted its members in many ways: it forbade price-cutting, overtime work, public advertising and the introduction of new tools . . . its aim, therefore, was in fact control. (One of the most brilliant word pictures of mercantile life in late-medieval times is *The Merchant of Prato* by Iris Origo.)

Guilds extracted dues from their members and some became very rich, owning property, having their own chapels in great churches and cathedrals, looking after the stricken living (widows, children or invalids) and contributing to the arts through gifts to churches or by producing the 'Mystery Plays' (from the Latin 'mysterium', meaning 'full of or wrapt in mystery').

These plays were about the miracles of Christ and in medieval times were traditionally acted out only by members of guilds. 'The Art or Mistery of Fanmaking' comes from another Latin word 'ministerium', which is quite different and means 'service, occupation or handicraft'.

In France the making of fans became of such importance during the reign of Henry the Great (who came to the throne in 1598 and was assassinated in 1610) that in 1594 several bodies of craftsmen were granted certain concessions, others being added in 1664. In 1673 the master fan makers of the City of Paris presented a petition to King Louis XIV and they were constituted a corporate body in that year. Sixty masters became the nucleus, fighting for their privileges, which became further strengthened by new edicts in 1676 and 1678, decreeing that no one could become a master without first serving a four-year apprenticeship and then producing his 'master's piece' which must pass the test of craftsmanship. The company was ruled by four jurors, two of whom were re-nominated each year by an assembly in which every master could participate. The entrance fee to the company was 400 livres and widows were permitted to continue their late husband's businesses as long as they remained single, as well as being granted various other privileges. By the middle of the eighteenth century, when fanmaking reached a peak in France, 150 Master Fan Makers were recorded in the City of Paris alone, protected and assisted by their guild regulations.

On 27th August, 1789, the Constituent Assembly of France adopted the Declaration of the Rights of Man and of the Citizen. The great desideratum of the bourgeoisie was 'freedom' in its public and political aspects; with 'freedom', the Declaration closely associated 'equality', demanded by the bourgeoisie in opposition to the aristocracy and by the peasants in the face of the feudal lords. The Declaration held that the law was to be the same for everyone and all citizens were equal in its eyes. The entire country went through a political and administrative upheaval and, in March 1791, the Allarde Law abolished journeymen's associations, guilds, secret societies and privileged manufacturers as well. The national market was unified by the abolition of customs dues and tolls. Finally there was freedom of work, with every individual free to create and produce, to pursue profit and to employ it as he desired. To a certain extent the fanmaking industry was shattered in France and it took some years to re-stabilise; sadly, for historians, so many records carefully kept by the many guilds were then lost or deliberately destroyed in the face of this new freedom.

Unhappily there were no fan guilds in the German States, which deprives us of much essential information.

The guilds of the City of London (that is, the part of London which is within the ancient boundaries, not the whole area which is called 'London' today), under the jurisdiction of the Lord Mayor and Corporation, had existed for many years before Edward III came to the throne in 1327; during his reign he made their powers and privileges much more definite and he himself became a member of the Merchant Taylors Company.

It was at that time that some of the guilds chose to call themselves 'companies' to differentiate themselves from other guilds, after which they began to wear a distinctive dress or 'livery'; as a result, they came to be called 'Livery Companies'. To this day the Mercers appear in dark red edged with fur, the Haberdashers in dark blue edged with fur and the Drapers in blue and yellow.

Nowadays there are about 84 Livery Companies in the City of London, although in some cases members have drifted away from being directly concerned with a certain type of trade; many men are Liverymen of various Companies either through business or family connections, treating them like social clubs with a strong charitable bias.

The 'Great Twelve' are the Mercers, Grocers, Drapers, Fishmongers, Goldsmiths, Skinners, Merchant Taylors, Haberdashers, Salters, Ironmongers, Vintners and Clothworkers . . . food and clothing taking pre-eminence.

In the past these Livery Companies generally had their own Halls in which they met or gave banquets; before the last World War there were 36 important examples, showing extremely interesting architecture over the decades, but 19 Halls were destroyed and a further 15 badly damaged by enemy bombing.

For the greater part of its history the British Worshipful Company of Fan-Makers had no fixed habitation but held its meetings in sundry taverns in the City of London. Until the outbreak of the Second World War it received hospitality from one or other of the old Livery Companies possessing their own halls.

The Worshipful Company of Fan-Makers were granted their Charter during the reign of Her Majesty Queen Anne. It is dated 19th April, 1709, and was enrolled in the Chamber of Guildhall of the City of London on 5th October, 1710, by the then Lord Mayor, Sir Samuel Garrard, Baronet, and the Court of Aldermen. The Fan-Makers Company is thus the youngest of the 'old' City Guilds, engaging in its craft of 'The Art or Mistery of Fanmaking'.

In 1941 the Court met for the first time in the Upper Room of the reconstructed St Dionis Hall, Lime Street, and dined in the hall itself. In 1952 the Company was accorded certain rights for the use of the parish hall of St Botolph's Church, Bishopsgate. As a result the Company extensively restored the hall; it was rededicated by the Bishop of Willesden and re-opened on 23rd October, 1952, by Her Royal Highness the Princess Alice, Duchess of Gloucester. This parish church hall is now known also as the Hall of the Worshipful Company of Fan-Makers.

The furnishing of the hall is in keeping with the history of the Company. The oak panelling dates back to 1726, the curtains being of a very old Tudor design against the rich contrasting colours of the silk banners of Arms belonging to certain Past Masters of the Company (many of whom had served the high office of Lord Mayor of London).

The emblem of their ancient craft of the fan is encased in a frame made from the timbers of the Guildhall destroyed by enemy action in 1940 and set in the panelling above the marble fireplace, surmounted by a carved Royal Coat of Arms.

The fan so portrayed is a fine copy of the Ostrich Fan presented to Her Majesty Queen Elizabeth, The Queen Mother, at the time of her Coronation. Below this, on a small autograph fan, are the signatures and autographs (dating from the time of Queen Victoria) of those members of the Royal Family to whom the Company has presented a fan to commemorate some historic or special occasion. This fan has now had every blade signed, so a new autograph fan was commissioned by the Fan-Makers in order to start afresh. It has been made by a firm in Madrid from a set of undecorated, overlapping nineteenth century ivory sticks with a simple, blank skin leaf of approximately the same age. The Arms of the Worshipful Company of Fan-Makers have been carved on a separate piece of ivory, lightly engraved, and then applied near the top of the guardstick. Members of the Royal Family who sign it do so with an antique quill-pen owned by the Company: the first signature on this new autograph fan is yet to be written—perhaps on the occasion of the next Coronation?

At the south end of the hall, over the entrance, is a stained-glass window depicting the arms of the Company. On either side of the entrance, on the panelling, are inscribed the names of the Masters since the Company's inception. For reasons of security the original Charter of the Company cannot be displayed, but a photocopy, suitably framed, is on view on the oak screen in front of the entrance and behind the chair in which the Master sits during Court meetings. Above the Charter is the coat of arms of Queen Anne, the Company's Charter Queen.

Although about 275 years does not sound a long time, the Company has distinguished itself with many Royal occasions. In 1897 HM Queen Victoria was presented with a fan to mark the occasion of her Diamond Jubilee; coronations were similarly marked in 1902 for Queen Alexandra, in 1911 for Queen Mary, in 1937 for Queen Elizabeth and in 1953 for our present Queen Elizabeth. Weddings, too, were prettily expressed with fans for HRH the Princess Mary in 1922, HRH the Princess Elizabeth in 1947, HRH the Princess Margaret in 1960, HRH the Princess Alexandra in 1963, HRH the Princess Richard of Gloucester in 1972, HRH the Princess Royal in 1973, and finally Diana, Princess of Wales in 1981.

Royalty must, by tradition, ask permission to enter into the City of London which is very jealous of its ancient rights and prerogatives. The greatest person in the City of London is the Lord Mayor and no less than six Masters of the Worshipful Company of Fan-Makers have been Lords Mayor since 1888. These are: Sir James Whitehead, Bart (Master 1884, Sheriff 1884 and Lord Mayor in 1888), Sir Alfred James Newton, Bart (Sheriff 1888, and having the twin honour of being both Master and Lord Mayor in 1899), Sir John Pound, Bart (Master in 1891, Sheriff 1895 and Lord Mayor in 1904), Sir John Bell, Bart (Master 1897, Sheriff 1901 and Lord Mayor in 1907), Sir Stephen Killick (Master 1917, Sheriff 1922 and Lord Mayor in 1934) and finally Colonel Sir Charles Davis, Bart (Sheriff 1942, Lord Mayor 1945 and Master in 1946).

The Company have not only played their part socially but have also acted within the framework of City Livery Companies. They have their main role, however, as the authorititive body of the Fan-Makers. Their list of bye-laws (which are still in use) was formed in 1741; most unfortunately their earliest Minutes only date from 1775, but it must have been an enthralling moment when, in 1951, one of the Company's chests was found complete with the original Charter of 1709, the bye-laws of 1710 and 1741 and an old Bible of 1726.

The Company's motto is 'Arts and Trade United' and this has genuinely been their aim throughout their history, especially their object of protecting the English Fan-Maker in the eighteenth century when so many of the French Fan-Makers came over to London, either for religious reasons (the Huguenots were nearly always the finest craftsmen in France and the 1689 Revocation of the Edict of Nantes drove out many of them) or merely to satisfy the burgeoning English market for fine fans. The Company's historic Minutes make fascinating reading but they still keep their traditions with the trade by providing three bursaries or prizes.

48. *Original Pump Room, Interior, Bath. 1737. Copper-engraving 187 × 428 mm, attributed to George Speren. Both Speren and Pinchbeck produced fan views of Bath, the former at*

the Fan and Crown in the Grove, Bath: the latter at the Fan and Crown in the New Round Court in the Strand, London. By courtesy of the Victoria Art Gallery, Bath City Council.

To encourage the arts there is the Latchford Prize, Bronze Medal and Money Award: this is open to students of the Royal Academy School of Art, City of London Schools and other recognised bodies, and given once every three years for 'A Design for a Painted Fan or Monochrome'. A Member of the Fan Circle International, Peter Greenhalgh, won this Prize in 1981 and subsequently mounted the painted design on to suitable sticks for the Fan-Makers.

To encourage the rather more prosaic and technical 'machine to agitate the air' there is a Silver Medal and money prize now awarded to the best student of the year of the Fan Engineering section of the National College of Heating, Ventilating, Refrigeration and Fan Engineering.

Finally there is a Bursary or Scholarship awarded in connection with wind-tunnel or other aeronautical research work at the Cranfield Institute of Technology . . . which is about as up to date as one could go.

Many of the names mentioned above are disembodied people, distanced from us by time and by stature, so how can we relate to them and clothe them with flesh and blood? I have been fortunate in my friendship with Mr and Mrs Anthony Vaughan to whom I am enormously grateful for permission to reproduce some material which Anthony Vaughan had researched for a book, which may help bring to life an ordinary citizen of London.

Anthony Vaughan is, in many ways, a great link with the past. He is a Fan-Maker (although a Solicitor by occupation) and also a Member of the Fan Circle International, and he is within a long and continuing line of Vaughans who have been Fan-Makers since its Charter. Tony wrote a most fascinating book on the Georgian actress, Hannah Pritchard, also an ancestor of his, and her Fan-Maker brother (Edward Vaughan) who was well-known in his time; his account places in context the role of the fan and the actress during the eighteenth century when European fanmaking was at its peak. (*Born to Please: Hannah Pritchard, Actress, 1711–1768—A Critical Biography* by Anthony Vaughan, 1979). He wrote:

Of Hannah's three brothers Edward, the eldest, was born in or about 1704/5. In 1717 his father apprenticed him to a Japanner, Edward Wootton of St Martin's in the Fields, at a premium of £15, and on 21st December, 1725, he was admitted to the Fan-Makers Company (Admission Number 682).

He first set up business in Playhouse Yard, Drury Lane, in premises adjoining the Theatre, but eight years later (in 1733) he moved to Russell Court, Drury Lane. It was from the Golden Fan near the Chapel in Russell Court that Edward advertised his Necromantic Fan in the *Craftsman* for Saturday, 3rd August, 1734:

By Eo, Meo, & Areo,
On Monday last was published.
The Necromantic Fan, or Magick Glass.
Being a new-invented Machine Fan, that by a
slight Touch unseen a Lady in the Fan changes her
Dressing-Glass according to the following invitations:

If anyone himself would see,
Pray send the gentleman to me;
For in my Magick Glass I show
The Pedant, Poet, Cit or Beau;
Likewise a Statesman wisely dull,
Whose plodding Head's with Treaties full.
Etc.

Made and sold by Edward Vaughan,
Fanmaker, at the Golden Fan near the Chapel in Russell Court,
Drury Lane.

In July 1736 he obtained the Freedom of the City by redemption and moved again to premises adjoining the Royal Exchange, Cornhill, being the second house east from Sweetings Alley. A contemporary print of the Royal Exchange dated 1741 (after a drawing by Maurer) shows Edward Vaughan's shop in great detail in the foreground. It is represented as a tall, narrow five-storey building, the ground floor occupied by a double-fronted shop with bow windows. The fans can be seen clearly displayed for sale behind the small panes and over the entrance is a large carved wooden or plaster fan in a decorative cartouche. Two ladies have just left the shop and are proudly displaying the fans they have purchased.

Watches can also be seen hanging in the window of Mr Creake the clockmaker next door. Edward Vaughan or one of his assistants is leaning from a first floor window. There is another view taken some fifteen years later and published by Bowles which shows in addition an elaborate sign painted with a fan.

An insurance policy issued by the Hand in Hand in 1746 further complements and confirms this description. The house measured twelve feet six inches (frontage) by thirty-four feet (depth). It was five storeys in height with four rooms wainscotted and four rooms wainscotted half-way. It has one portland stone chimney piece (only those of portland stone or marble were mentioned). The building, having been damaged in the disastrous fire of March 1748, was destroyed in the fire of 1759 which swept Cornhill, a detailed description of which can be found in the *Gentleman's Magazine* for that year. Edward Vaughan then moved with his family to number 6, St Michael's Alley, next to St Michael's Churchyard. The new premises formed the southern end of the Jamaica Coffee House and adjoined on the other side the George and Vulture. The deeds still survive and these show a frontage of seventeen feet five inches and a depth of thirty-two feet nine inches.

It is difficult to know what Edward Vaughan was like as a person. There is a note in the front of the Fan-Makers Company's Stamp Book that he was serving on the Court of Assistants in 1749, the date the book was commenced, so that it is almost certain he went on to serve as Warden and Master if he was not already a Past Master by this date (unfortunately the Minute Books and other Company records for this period which could have established this are lost).

A letter in the Heal Collection in the British Museum refers to a fine trade card of his dating from *c* 1740 formerly pasted in a Hogarth tome in the Dyson Perring Collection at Malvern, but it has proved impossible to trace.

He had two recorded apprentices, Elizabeth Ebbett, daughter of Samuel Ebbett who paid a premium of £6 in 1740, and Mary Kitchin, £10.10.0 in 1755. It would appear from a biographical account in the *Hibernian Magazine*, October 1804, that William Vaughan was also brought up in his elder brother's business of fan painting before deciding to go on the stage. It is known that Edward was in the habit of selling tickets each year for Hannah Pritchard's Benefits as the name 'Mr Vaughan Fanmaker at the Golden Fan next the Royal Exchange Cornhill' often appears on her playbills advertising these. His name and that of his widow Amy Ann annually recur in the Drury Lane Account Books so that it is highly likely he supplied the Theatre with costume fans.

One imagines he would not have been slow to take advantage of his stage connections and no doubt he did a lavish trade—theatrical fans showing scenes from the popular plays of the day, particularly those in which his famous sister was best known. Many such fans have survived, but as they are rarely, if ever, signed it is almost impossible to identify them as the works of a particular maker.

James Lynch in his book *Box, Pit and Gallery* makes the interesting observation that because of the moral stigma attached to the stage and its players, ladies in the later seventeenth century were expected to attend the theatre wearing masks. Some of this attitude remained well into the next century, and indeed until the 1760s, in spite of the claims of Collier, Cibber and Steele to have reformed the stage 'so that fashionable accoutrements that could represent ritualistic moral objection without hindering the enjoyment of the drama were still necessary.' The fan simply took the place of the mask—and 'had the advantage of being able to disguise the blush (or its absence) without concealing its owner's identity.'

Edward's name constantly recurs also in the Vestry Minutes and Church Wardens' Accounts for St Michael, Cornhill, where he served as Church Warden, sidesman, auditor of accounts and, for very many years, overseer of the poor. He was also a collector of land tax, for Thomas Lennard in his will mentions having stood surety for him.

He married Amy Ann Gilbert. They had two sons, Thomas Lennard (1743–78) and Edward (1746–c 1814). Both boys were scholars of St Paul's School, Thomas being admitted in 1754 and Edward in 1755. Thomas was commissioned in the Royal Artillery, having entered the Royal Military Academy, Woolwich, as a cadet in 1760, and was killed in action in the war of American Independence at the Battle of the Court House, Monmouth, New Jersey, during the British retreat from Philadelphia on 28th June, 1778. He died unmarried and is mentioned in Major Duncan's *History of the Royal Artillery*.

Edward, the younger son, was a miniature painter and exhibited regularly at the Society of Artists and later the Royal Academy over a period of some forty years. He married Sarah King, a Huguenot girl from Christchurch, Spitalfields, at St Michael, Cornhill, on 29th May, 1773. Her uncle was William Jourdain the Silk Mercer, whose shop in Artillery Row, just off Bishopsgate, is said to have the finest mid-Georgian shop front still surviving in London.

After Edward the Fanmaker's death on the morning of Friday 21st March, 1766, 'of an apoplectick fit' according to the contemporary newspapers, his widow Amy Ann kept on the fanmaking business, assisted by her two spinster daughters Amy Ann (1741–1826) and Henrietta (1739–98). For the remainder of her long life—she died in 1799 at the age of 95—she also held the appointments of Sextoness and Organ Blower to the Church of St Michael, Cornhill. On her death, her surviving daughter Amy Ann succeeded to the appointments in her place and continued as Sextoness and Organ Blower until her death in 1826. She continued to live at 6, St Michael's Alley and apparently to practise as a fanmaker—she was certainly still in business there in 1820.

This meticulously researched account of the lives of one fan-maker's family is invaluable in helping to piece together the working lives of fanmakers in the eighteenth and early nineteenth centuries, and shows how they took part in their local community of church and theatre. It is also of interest to follow the continuity of fanmaking and the protection they must have been accorded by their Guild, the powerful Worshipful Company of Fan-Makers.

7 Present-Day Collectors

A most especial focus for fan collectors in the future will be The Fan Museum, 10/12 Croom's Hill, Greenwich, London SE10. The information given to me by the Fan Museum Trust is as follows:

It will be the first and only museum in the world devoted in its entirety to all aspects of the ancient art and craft of fan-making. The superb Hélène Alexander fan collection of over 2,000 items is to be gifted to the nation, and will be housed in two listed Georgian townhouses being beautifully restored for this purpose in historic Greenwich.

Exhibitions illustrating a variety of themes such as Children or Flowers in fans will be mounted and changed about three times a year, and there will be a permanent display of the history, materials used and types and sources of fans.

The Museum will have study and research facilities including comprehensive microfiche and reference libraries. Seminars, lectures, courses and visits for special interest groups will also be organised.

The craft workshop, open to visitors, will have demonstrations of fan-making and related crafts. Restoration of fans under the supervision of a trained museum conservator will be undertaken. It is hoped to provide youth training/employment schemes and opportunities for the disabled. The workshop opened in 1989.

The Museum will be staffed by a nucleus of professional full-time and part-time staff augmented by a team of volunteers acting as host guides.

A delightful feature will be the recreation of a Georgian garden overlooked by an Orangery which will be used for the lectures, seminars, and social events. There will be special facilities for the disabled including a lift.

On the whole there was very little interest in fans during the years 1930 to 1970. No books were written about them in English and, because there was simply no market for them, some fans changed hands for a few pence. A fine fan might be sold at a famous auction house sale but within the category 'toys' or 'costume', never in a category of its own.

Some well-known collections of fine fans were made during the nineteenth century: Robert Walker's collection was, sadly, sold at auction, but a good catalogue of them was made at their exhibition. Lady Charlotte Schrieber gave the majority of her fans to the British Museum; the De Witt Clinton Cohen Collection became the nucleus of the Esther Oldham Collection (now at the Museum of Fine Arts, Boston) and the Leonard Messel Collection is now at the Fitzwilliam Museum, Cambridge.

In 1974 Mr Martin Willcocks suggested to the author the idea of a society for fan collectors and they both invited Mrs Hélène Alexander to join them. For almost a year the groundwork for such a club was explored, opinions asked, affiliations tentatively suggested and feelers put out into both the museum and collectors' worlds. Was the fan art or craft? Should we 'tag on' to an established organisation or branch out into the unknown?

Eventually it was agreed that our aim was to establish a society based on a serious pursuit of academic knowledge, yet we should never lose interest in the fact that we were collectors first and foremost and that any society should be fun, too! It seemed clear that there was a need for some authoritative body which would work at a very high level through museums, art galleries, textile and costume societies and the like and, especially, should learn from the age-old Worshipful Company of Fan-Makers—the only fan City and Craft Guild in the world still in existence. Therefore a wide spectrum was envisaged in order to bring in established as well as would-be collectors, staff of museums, art historians, those interested in ethnography, Orientalists and those working in the conservation field.

In 1975 the Fan Circle was born. At a later date, by request of the author, the name was altered to the Fan Circle International (because so many members joined from all over the world), and in 1982 the FCI was registered as a Charity, mainly for educational purposes. The Patrons, past and present, have presented a roll-call of famous names;

and, as a 'badge' for their initiative the three innovators were, in 1982, made honorary members of the FCI as well.

The magnet which attracts members to any society is the written word. For FCI members that is the *FCI Bulletin*, made up of at least 38 printed pages (A4 size), published three times a year. With hindsight it is noticeable how carefully the balance has been controlled to provide original research, advertisements, illustrations, advance news of auction sales (London and occasionally elsewhere) followed by an analysis of each sale—including (fearless) comments on both prices and quality—letters and news from members, articles, advance notice of events and analytical reports on them afterwards.

Another important function of the FCI is its mounting and promotion of exhibitions. On each occasion the FCI has worked in harmonious friendship with the staff of the museum involved, with co-operation all along the line. The FCI has solicited the fans from a variety of sources, together with the captions for the catalogues. There have been exhibitions entitled 'The World of the Fan', 'Fans from the East', 'Fans and the Grand Tour', 'Fans of the Belle Epoque' and 'Royal Fans'. Each exhibition had a catalogue, and certainly Debretts, who published *Fans from the East*, achieved worldwide sales of both hard and soft-backed versions.

The purposes of the FCI are eminently worthy and the list of its achievements quite astonishing for such a short period. What is also remarkable about the organisation is the spectrum of its members: many men amongst the women, both established collectors and absolute beginners with only a handful of fans, but, in every case, apparently fascinated with the subject.

Interested readers may make contact through the following address:

The Hon. Secretary,
Fan Circle International,
79A Falcondale Road,
Westbury on Trym,
Near Bristol BS9 3JW, England.

In the USA there is another such society, known as The Fan Association of North America (FANA), which began in 1982. Because of their vast distances they concentrate greatly on their annual 'Assemblage', which takes place in a variety of different venues, to cater for all members. They also have the *FANA Quarterly*, which covers many subjects and is well illustrated. Contact:

FANA Membership Chairman,
201 Palmetto Ct,
St Simons,
GA 31522
USA

Understandably there are many who are members of both organisations, enjoying to the full all the benefits of each, and all of whom will gain much from the future Fan Museum at Greenwich, which plans to be fully operational in 1990.

Bibliography

ALEXANDER, HÉLÈNE. *Fans*, Batsford, London, 1984.

ALEXANDER, HÉLÈNE. *Fans*, Shire Publications, 1989.

ALEXANDER, HÉLÈNE. 'German Fan Fair', article in *Art & Antiques Weekly*, May 1980.

ALEXANDER, HÉLÈNE. 'Some Facets of Fan Collecting, Part One: The Finer Examples', article in *Antique Collecting*, Dec. 1979.

ALEXANDER, HÉLÈNE. 'The Pleasures of Fans', article in *Apollo*, 1977.

ARMSTRONG, NANCY. *Abanicos*, (translated by Juan Costa) Castell Ediciones, S.A., Barcelona, 1979.

ARMSTRONG, NANCY. *A Collector's History of Fans*, Studio Vista, London, and Clarkson N. Potter, Inc., New York, 1974.

ARMSTRONG, NANCY. *Fans and Crafts of the Hispanic Empire*, FCI Bulletin, 1990.

ARMSTRONG, NANCY. *Fans from the Fitzwilliam*, Fitzwilliam Museum, Cambridge, 1985.

ARMSTRONG, NANCY. 'Fans from the Seychelles to the Philippines', article in *Country Life*, 1978.

ARMSTRONG, NANCY. *Jewellery: An Historical Survey of British Styles and Jewels*, Lutterworth Press, Guildford, 1973.

ARMSTRONG NANCY. *Los Abanicos del Museo Lázaro Galdiano*, Goya, Revista de Arte, Madrid, 1986.

ARMSTRONG, NANCY. Part-author of *Otros Abanicos*, Fundación Banco Exterior de España, Madrid, 1985.

ARMSTRONG, NANCY. 'Regency Horn Fans', article in *The Antique Collector*, 1978.

ARMSTRONG, NANCY. *The Book of Fans*, Colour Library International, New Malden, and Mayflower Books, New York, 1978.

ARMSTRONG, NANCY. *Victorian Jewellery*, Studio Vista, London, and Macmillan, New York, 1976.

Art Journal. *Catalogue of the 1851 Exhibition.*

Arundel Society. *Fans of All Countries*, 1871.

Baden-Powell, B. H. *Handbook of the Manufactures and Arts of the Punjab*, 1872.

Bapst, Germain. *Deux Éventails du Musée de Louvre*, Paris, 1882.

Baro, Carlos M., and Escoda, Juan. *Éventails Anciens*, Payot, Lausanne, 1957. (Also under *Alte Fächer*, showing collection from Barcelona).

Bennett, Anna. *Unfolding Beauty*, Museum of Fine Arts, Boston, 1988.

Bennett, Anna G., and Berson, Ruth. *Fans in Fashion*, Catalogue of the Exhibition, San Francisco, 1981.

Berkhout, J. G. *Waaierweelde in Beeckestijn keuze uit het waaierkabinet Felix Tal*, Exhibition Catalogue, 1979.

Blondel, M. S. *History of Fans*, Librairie Renouard, Paris, 1875.

Blondel, M. S. *Histoire des Éventails chez tous les Peuples et à toutes les Epoques*, Librairie Renouard, Paris, 1875.

Boehn, Max von. *Accessorias de la Moda*, Salvar Editores S. A., Barcelona–Buenos Aires, 1944.

Boger, H. Baterson. *The Traditional Arts of Japan*, Doubleday, New York, 1964.

Bordeilles, Pierre de, Seigneur de Brantome. *Memoires des dames illustrée de France*.

Bouchot, Henri. 'L'Histoire par les Éventails Populaires', two articles in *Les Lettres et Les Arts*, Paris, 1883.

Bowie, Henry P. *On the Laws of Japanese Painting*, Paul Elder, San Francisco, 1941.

Bush, George. *Der Fächer*, Dusseldorf, 1904.

Catalini, Carla. *Waaiers*, Van Dishoeck, Bussom, Holland, 1966.

Catalogue of the Celebrated Collection of Fans of Mr. Robert Walker— exhibited at the Fine Art Society's, 148 New Bond Street, London, 1882.

Catholic Encyclopaedia, The. Vol. 6, article on flabelli, Caxton, London & New York 1909–1912.

Chiba, Reiko. *Painted Fans of Japan: 15 Noh Drama Masterpieces*, Tuttle & Co., Rutland, Vermont, and Tokyo, Japan, 1962.

Collins, Bernard Ross. *A Short Account of the Worshipful Company of Fan-Makers*, Favel Press, London, 1950.

Commoner, Lucy. Folding fans in the collection of the Cooper-Hewitt Museum, New York, 1987.

Coomaraswamy, A. K. *Arts and Crafts of India and Ceylon*, 1913.

Cosway, M. 'English Fans', article in *The Concise Encyclopaedia of Antiques IV*, 1959.

Croft-Murray, Edward. 'Watteau's Design for a Fan Leaf', article in *Apollo*, 1974.

Crossman, Carl L. *The China Trade*, Princeton, 1972.

Cunnington, C. W. and R. E., and Beard, Charles. *A Dictionary of English Costume 900–1900*, A. & C. Black, London, 1960.

Cust, Lionel. *Catalogue of the Collection of Fans and Fan Leaves presented to the Trustees of the British Museum by Lady Charlotte Schrieber*, Longmans, London, 1893.

Dawes, Leonard. 'The Nicely Calculated Flutter of the Fan', article in *Antique Dealer and Collectors Guide*, March, 1974.

Dunn, D. 'On Fans', article in *The Connoisseur*, 1902.

Durian-Ress, Saskia, and Heller-Winter, Elisabeth. *Fächer, Kunst und Mode aus fünf Jahrhunderten*, Bayerisches Nationalmuseum, Munich, 1987.

Duval, E. *Les éventails*, Paris, 1885.

Duvelleroy. 'Exposition Universelle, Paris 1867', in *Rapports du Jury International Vol. IV*.

Eeghen, Dr. I. H. van. *De Amsterdamse Waaierindustrie, ae XVIIIe eeuw*, Amstelodamum, 1953.

Eeghen, Dr. I. H. van. *Tijdschrift voor Geschiedenis*, Amsterdam, 1961.

Eitner, Lorenz E. A. *The Flabellum of Tournus*, College of Art Association of America, sponsored by the Archeological Institute of America, 1941.

Enciclopedia Universal Illustrada—Europeo Americana, Madrid.

Erler, M. *Der Moderne Fächer*, Kunstgewerbeblatt, 1904.

Falluel, F. *Éventail Miroir de la Belle Époque*, Paris Musées et Societé de l'Histoire du Costume, Paris, 1985.

Fan Circle International, The, and Brighton Museum. *Fans and the Grand Tour*, Catalogue of the Exhibition, 1982/3.

Fan Circle International, The, and the Harris Museum and Art Gallery, Preston. *The World of the Fan*, Catalogue of the Exhibition, 1976.

Fan Circle International publications (including *Bulletins*) 1975–1983.

Fans from the East, various authors, Debrett's Peerage in association with the Fan Circle International and the Victoria and Albert Museum, London, 1978.

Fan Leaves, published by The Fan Guild, Boston, Mass., U.S.A., 1961.

FLORY, M. A. *A Book About Fans*, Macmillan & Co., New York, 1895.

FOWLES, W. A. *The Revised History of the Worshipful Company of Fan-Makers 1709–1975*, Lund Humphries, Bradford and London, 1977.

GALTER, JUAN SUBIAS. *El Arte Popular en España*, Editorial Seix Barral, S.A., Barcelona, 1948.

GIBSON, EUGENIE. 'Queen Mary's Collection', article in *The Connoisseur*, 1927.

GIBSON, EUGENIE. 'The Golden Age of the Fan', article in *The Connoisseur*, 1920.

GILCHRIST, JAMES. *Anglican Church Plate*, The Connoisseur and Michael Joseph, London, 1967.

GILES, H. A. 'Chinese Fans', article in *Fraser's Magazine*, London, May, 1879.

GINSBURG, MADELEINE. *Victorian Dress in Photography*, Batsford, London, 1983.

GOSSON, STEPHEN. *Pleasant Quippes for Upstart Newfangled Gentlewomen*, London, 1596.

GOSTELOW, MARY. *The Fan*, Gill & Macmillan, Dublin, 1976.

Great Exhibition, The, Official Catalogue of, London, 1851.

GREEN, BERTHA DE VERE. *A Collector's Guide to Fans over the Ages*, Muller, London, 1975.

GROS, GABRIELLA. 'The Art of the Fanmaker,' article in *Apollo*, 1957.

HAMMAR, BRITTA. (Swedish) *Fans of the 18th century*, Kulturen 1976, translated by Marion Maule for the *FCI Newsletter/Bulletin*.

HEATH, RICHARD. 'Politics in dress', article in *The Woman's World*, June, 1889.

HENDERSON, MILNE. Catalogue of the Exhibition *The Art of Chinese Fan Painting*, London, 1974.

HENDERSON, MILNE. Catalogue of the Exhibition *Nanga Fan Painting*, London, 1975.

HIRSHORN, A. A. 'Mourning Fans', article in *Antiques*, 1973.

HOLME, C. 'Modern Design in Jewellery and Fans', article in *Studio*, 1902.

HOLT, T. H. 'On Fans, their use and antiquity', *Journal of the British Archaeological Association*, 1870.

HONOUR, HUGH. *Chinoiserie: The Vision of Cathay*, John Murray, London, 1961.

Household Guide, The, Vol. 1. Cassells, London, 1880.

HUGHES, THERLE. 'A Flutter of Fans', article in *Discovering Antiques*, London, 1971.

HUGHES, THERLE. 'Fans from the Leonard Messel Collection', two articles in *Country Life*, June, 1972.

HUGHES, THERLE. *More Small Decorative Antiques*, Lutterworth Press, London, 1962.

HUGHES, THERLE. 'Storm Dragons and Plum Blossom', article in *Country Life*, 1972.

HUTH, HANS. *Lacquer of the West: The History of a Craft and an Industry, 1550–1950*, Chicago, 1971.

IMPEY, O. *Chinoiserie: The Impact of Oriental Styles on Western Art and Decoration*, London, 1977.

IRÖNS, NEVILLE J. *Fans of Imperial China*, Kaiserreich Kunst (Hong Kong) and The House of Fans, London, 1982.

IRÖNS, NEVILLE J. *Fans of Imperial Japan*, Kaiserreich Kunst (Hong Kong) and The House of Fans, London, 1982.

JACKSON, MRS F. NEVILL. 'The Montgolfiers', article in *The Connoisseur*, 1909.

JENYNS, SOANE. *A Background to Chinese Painting*, London, 1935.

JOURDAIN, M., AND JENYNS, S. *Chinese Export Art in the Eighteenth Century*, London, 1950.

KAMMERL, CHRISTL. *Der Fächer; Kunstobjeckt und Billetdoux*, Badisches Landesmuseum, Karlsruhe, 1989.

KENDALL, B. 'CONCERNING FANS', article in *The Connoisseur*, 1903.

KIYOE, NAKAMURA. *Nihon no Ogi (Fans of Japan)*, Oyashima Shuppan, Kyoto, 1942.

KIYOE, NAKAMURA. *Ogi to Ogie (Fans and Fan Painting)*, Kawara Shoten, Kyoto, 1969.

LEARY, E. *Fans in Fashion*, Catalogue of the Exhibition, Temple Newsam, Leeds, 1975.

Leisure Hour, The, London, 1882.

L'ESTOILE, PIERRE DE. *The Isle of the Hermaphrodites*, 1588.

Liverpool Arts Club, *Exhibition Catalogue*, 1877.

MARCEL, GABRIEL. *En Éventail Historique du dix-huitieme Siècle*, Paris, 1901.

MARGARY, IVAN D. 'Militia Camps in Sussex, 1793, and a Lady's Fan', Sussex Archaeological Records, Vd 107, 1969.

MAYOR, SUSAN. *Collecting Fans*, Studio Vista, London, 1980.

MELLING, JOHN K. *Discovering London's Guilds and Liveries*, Shire Publications Ltd., Aylesbury, 1981.

'Milady's Fan—500 years of a Coy History', article in *Majorca Daily Bulletin*, 1970.

MONGOT, VINCENTO ALMELA. *Los Abanicos (Fans of Valencia)*, Spain.

MONTGOMERY, MARY C. 'Fan Histories and Fashions', article in *The Cosmopolitan*, 1890.

MOTOI, OI. *Instructions in Sumi Painting*, Tokyo, 1958.

MOUREY, GABRIEL (with others). *Art Nouveau Jewellery and Fans*, Dover Publications, New York, 1973.

MUNSTERBERG, HUGO. *The Landscape Painting of China and Japan*, Tuttle & Co., Rutland, Vermont, 1955.

New Encyclopaedia Britannica, The (30 vols), 1974.

NEWTON, STELLA M. *Renaissance Theatre Costume*, Rapp and Whiting, 1975.

NIVEN, T. *The Fan in Art*, New York, 1911.

NORITAKE, TSUDA. *Ideals of Japanese Painting*, Tokyo, 1958.

NORTH AUDREY. Australia's Fan Heritage, Brisbane, 1985.

OHM, DR. ANNALIESE. *Fächer, Reallexikon zur Deutschen Kunstgeschichte*, Stuttgart, 1972.

OLDHAM, ESTHER. 'Fans of the Paper Stainers: Dominotier and Imagier', article in *Hobbies*, December, 1959.

OLDHAM, ESTHER. 'Jenny Lind', article in *Antiques Journal*, November, 1961.

OLDHAM, ESTHER. 'Mrs Jack's Fans', article in *Spinning Wheel*, May, 1967.

OLDHAM, ESTHER. 'The Fan. A Gentleman's Accessory', article in *The Connoisseur* 125:14–20.

PALLISER, MRS BURY. *History of Lace*, 1865.

PARR, LOUISA. 'The Fan', article in *Harper's Magazine*, London, August, 1889.

PERCIVAL, MacIVER. 'Some Old English Printed Paper Fans', article in *The Connoisseur* 44, p 141.

PERCIVAL, MacIVER. *The Fan Book*, Fisher Unwin, London, 1920.

PERIS-MENCHETA, JUAN. *Libros y Abanicos*, Barcelona, 1946.

PETIT, EDOUARD. *Etudes, Souvenirs et Considérations sur le fabrication de l'éventail*, Versailles, 1859.

REDGRAVE, S. *Catalogue of the Loan Exhibition of Fans*, South Kensington

Museum, 1870.

RHEAD, GEORGE WOOLISCROFT. *History of the Fan*, Kegan Paul, Trench, Trubner & Co., London, 1910.

REIG Y FLORES. *La Industria Abaniquera en Valencia*, Tipografía de Archivos, Madrid, 1933.

ROBINSON, F. MABEL. 'Fans', article in *The Woman's World*, London, January, 1889.

ROCAMORA, MANUEL. *Abanicos Históricos y Anecdóticos*, Tobella, Barcelona, 1956.

ROSENBERG, MARC. *Alte und Neue Fächer aus dem Wettbewerbung und Ausstellung zu Karlsruhe*, Vienna, 1891.

RUSSELL, RONALD. *Discovering Antique Prints*, Shire Publications Ltd., Aylesbury, 1982.

SALWEY, CHARLOTTE MARIA (née Birch). *Fans of Japan*, Kegan, Paul, Trench, Trubner & Co., London, 1894. And her private book of Press Cuttings lent to me by her grand-daughter, Mrs Anne Wright.

SCHAFER, EDWARD H. *The Golden Peaches of Samarkand*, California, 1963.

SCHRIEBER, LADY CHARLOTTE. *Fans and Fan Leaves—English*, John Murray, London, 1888.

SCHRIEBER, LADY CHARLOTTE. *Fans and Fan Leaves—Foreign*, John Murray, London, 1890.

SHEPPARD, MUBIN. *Taman Indera* (Malay Decorative Arts and Pastimes), 1971.

Sociedad Española de Amigos del Arte. *El Abanico en España,* Madrid, June, 1920.

SPIELMANN, HEINZ. *Oskar Kokoscha: die Fächer für Alma Mahler*, Verlag Hans Christians, Hamburg, 1969.

STANDEN, EDITH A. 'Instruments for Agitating the Air', article in the *Metropolitan Museum of Art*, New York, 1965.

STRANGE, EDWARD F. *The Colour-Prints of Hiroshige*, Cassell & Co., London, 1925.

TAIPEI, TAIWAN. *Masterpieces of Chinese Album Painting in the National Palace Museum*, 1971.

TAL, FELIX. *De Waaier Collectie Felix Tal*, (Exhibition in Utrecht, 1967).

THORNTON, PETER. 'Fans', article in *Antiques International*, London, 1966.

University of Kansas. *Chinese Fan Paintings from the Collection of Mr Chan Yee-Pong*, Lawrence, Kansas, 1971.

UZANNE, OCTAVE. *The Fan*, Nimmo and Bain, London, 1884.

VAN BRIESSEN, FRITZ. *The Way of the Brush*, Tuttle & Co., Rutland, Vermont and Tokyo.

VAUGHAN, ANTHONY. *Born to Please. Hannah Pritchard, Actress, 1711–1768, A Critical Biography*, The Society for Theatre Research, London, 1979.

Viften—The Fan, Catalogue of the Exhibition in Copenhagen, 1957.

VOLET, MARYSE. *L'imagination au service de l'éventail. Les brevets déposées en France au 19e siècle*. Vésenaz, 1986.

VOLET, MARYSE, and BEENTJES, ANNETTE, *Éventails. Collection du Musée d'art d'histoire de Genève*, Genf, 1987.

WADDELL, MADELEINE C. 'The Rise and Fall of the Fan', article in *The Antique Collector*, December, 1966.

WARDLE, PATRICIA. 'Two Late Nineteenth Century Lace Fans', article in *Embroidery* 1970.

WHEATLEY, LOUIS and IVISON. *The indispensable fan: the story of the fan in society*, Edinburgh, 1984.

WHITE, MARGARET E. 'Collecting Handscreens', article in *Antiques*, April, 1941.

Woman's World, article on fans, London, 1889.

YEE, CHIANG. *The Chinese Eye*, London, 1935.

YETTS, W. P. *Symbolism in Chinese Art*, Leyden, 1912.

Zauber des Fächers: Fächer aus dem Besitz des Museums, Altonaer Museum, Hamburg, 1974.

Index

172

A Russian Journal

Also by John Steinbeck

THE WAYWARD BUS

CANNERY ROW

BOMBS AWAY

THE MOON IS DOWN *(novel)*

THE MOON IS DOWN *(play)*

SEA OF CORTEZ
(In collaboration with Edward F. Ricketts)

THE GRAPES OF WRATH

THE FORGOTTEN VILLAGE

THE LONG VALLEY

THE RED PONY

OF MICE AND MEN *(play)*

OF MICE AND MEN *(novel)*

SAINT KATY THE VIRGIN

IN DUBIOUS BATTLE

TORTILLA FLAT

TO A GOD UNKNOWN

THE PASTURES OF HEAVEN

CUP OF GOLD

John Steinbeck

A RUSSIAN
JOURNAL

WITH PICTURES BY *Robert Capa*

1948

The Viking Press • NEW YORK

DK
28
S8

28729

Parts of this book appeared in the *New York Herald Tribune*
and other newspapers.

Photos on pp. 75, 84, 99, 157, copyright 1948
by The Curtis Publishing Company.

A Russian Journal

Chapter 1

IT WILL be necessary to say first how this story and how this trip started, and what its intention was. In late March, I, and the pronoun is used by special arrangement with John Gunther, was sitting in the bar of the Bedford Hotel on East Fortieth Street. A play I had written four times had melted and run out between my fingers. I sat on the bar stool wondering what to do next. At that moment Robert Capa came into the bar looking a little disconsolate. A poker game he had been nursing for several months had finally passed away. His book had gone to press and he found himself with nothing to do. Willy, the bartender, who is always sympathetic, suggested a Suissesse, a drink which Willy makes better than anybody else in the world. We were depressed, not so much by the news but by the handling of it. For news is no longer news, at least that part of it which draws the most attention. News has become a matter of punditry. A man sitting at a desk in Washington or New York reads the cables and rearranges them to fit his own mental pattern and his by-line. What we often read as news now is not news at all but the opinion of one of half a dozen pundits as to what that news means.

Willy set the two pale green Suissesses in front of us and we began to discuss what there was left in the world that an honest and liberal man could do. In the papers every day there were thousands of words about Russia. What Stalin was thinking about, the plans of the Russian General Staff, the disposition of troops, experiments with atomic weapons and guided missiles, all of this by people who had not been there, and whose sources were not above reproach. And it occurred to us that there were some things that nobody wrote about Russia, and they were the things that interested us most of all. What do the people wear there? What do they serve at dinner? Do they have parties? What food is there? How do they make love, and how do they die? What do they talk about? Do they dance, and sing, and play? Do the children go to school? It seemed to us that it might be a good thing to find out these things, to photograph them, and to write about them. Russian politics are important just as ours are, but there must be the great other side there, just as there is here. There must be a private life of the Russian people, and that we could not read about because no one wrote about it, and no one photographed it.

Willy mixed another Suissesse, and he agreed with us that he might be interested in such things too, and that this was the kind of thing that he would like to read. And so we decided to try it—to do a simple reporting job backed up with photographs. We would work together. We would avoid politics and the larger issues. We would stay away from the Kremlin, from military men and from military plans. We wanted to get to the Russian people if we could. It must be admitted that we did not know whether we could or not, and when we spoke to friends about it they were quite sure we couldn't.

We made our plans in this way: If we could do it, it would be good, and a good story. And if we couldn't do it, we would have a story too, the story of not being able to do it. With this in mind we called George Cornish at the *Herald Tribune,* had lunch with him, and told him our project. He agreed that it would be a good thing to do and offered to help us in any way.

Together we decided on several things: We should not go in with chips on our shoulders and we should try to be neither critical nor favorable. We would try to do honest reporting, to set down what we saw and heard without editorial comment, without drawing conclusions about things we didn't know sufficiently, and without becoming angry at the delays of bureaucracy. We knew there would be many things we couldn't understand, many things we wouldn't like, many things that would make us uncomfortable. This is always true of a foreign country. But we determined that if there should be criticism, it would be criticism of the thing after seeing it, not before.

In due time our application for visas went to Moscow, and within a reasonable time mine came through. I went over to the Russian Consulate in New York, and the Consul General said, "We agree that this is a good thing to do, but why do you have to take a cameraman? We have lots of cameramen in the Soviet Union."

And I replied, "But you have no Capas. If the thing is to be done at all, it must be done as a whole, as a collaboration."

There was some reluctance about letting a cameraman into the Soviet Union, and none about letting me in, and this seemed strange to us, for censorship can control film, but it cannot control the mind of an observer. Here we must explain something that we found to be true during our whole trip. The camera is one of the most frightening of modern weapons, particularly to people who have been in warfare, who have been bombed and shelled, for at the back of a bombing run is invariably a photograph. In back of ruined towns, and cities, and factories, there is aerial mapping, or spy mapping, usually with a camera. Therefore the camera is a feared instrument, and a man with a camera is suspected and watched wherever he goes. And if you do not believe this, try to take your Brownie No. 4 anywhere near Oak Ridge, or the Panama Canal, or near any one of a hundred of our experimental areas. In the minds of most people today the camera is the forerunner of destruction, and it is suspected, and rightly so.

I don't think Capa and I really ever thought that we would be able to do the job we wanted to do. That we were able to do it is as much a surprise to us as to anyone else. We were surprised when our visas came through, and we held a mild celebration with Willy behind the bar when they did. At that point I had an accident and broke my leg and was laid up for two months. But Capa went about assembling his equipment.

There had been no camera coverage of the Soviet Union by an American for many years, so Capa provided the very best of photographic equipment and duplicated all of it in case some of it might be lost. He took the Contax and Rolleiflex that he had used during the war, of course, but he took extras also. He took so many extras, and so much film, and so many lights, that his overweight charge on the overseas airline was something like three hundred dollars.

The moment it became known we were going to the Soviet Union we were bombarded with advice, with admonitions and with warnings, it must be said, mostly from people who had never been there.

An elderly woman told us in accents of dread, "Why, you'll disappear, you'll disappear as soon as you cross the border!"

And we replied, in the interest of accurate reporting, "Do you know anyone who has disappeared?"

"No," she said, "I don't personally know anyone, but plenty of people have disappeared."

And we said, "That might very well be true, we don't know, but can you give us the name of anyone who has disappeared? Do you know anyone who knows anyone who has disappeared?"

And she replied, "Thousands have disappeared."

And a man with knowing eyebrows and a quizzical look, the same man, in fact, who two years before had given the total battle plans for the invasion of Normandy in the Stork Club, said to us, "Well you must stand in pretty good with the Kremlin or they wouldn't let you in. They must have bought you."

We said, "No, not as far as we know, they haven't bought us. We just would like to do a job of reporting."

He raised his eyes and squinted at us. And he believes what he believes, and the man who knew Eisenhower's mind two years ago knows Stalin's mind now.

An elderly gentleman nodded his head at us and said, "They'll torture you, that's what they'll do; they'll just take you into a black prison and they'll torture you. They'll twist your arms and they'll starve you until you're ready to say anything they want you to say."

We asked, "Why? What for? What purpose could it serve?"

"They do that to everybody," he said. "Why I was reading a book the other day—"

A businessman of considerable importance said to us, "Going to Moscow, huh? Take a few bombs and drop them on the Red sons-of-bitches."

We were smothered in advice. We were told the food to take, otherwise we would starve; what lines of communications to leave open;

secret methods of getting our stuff out. And the hardest thing in the world to explain was that all we wanted to do was to report what Russian people were like, and what they wore, and how they acted, what the farmers talked about, and what they were doing about rebuilding the destroyed parts of their country. This was the hardest thing in the world to explain. We found that thousands of people were suffering from acute Moscowitis—a state which permits the belief of any absurdity and the shoving away of any facts. Eventually, of course, we found that the Russians are suffering from Washingtonitis, the same disease. We discovered that just as we are growing horns and tails on the Russians, so the Russians are growing horns and tails on us.

A cab driver said, "Them Russians, they bathe together, men and women, without no clothes on."

"Do they?"

"Sure they do," he said. "That ain't moral."

It developed on questioning that he had read an account of a Finnish steam bath. But he was pretty upset at the Russians about it.

After listening to all this information we came to the conclusion that the world of Sir John Mandeville has by no means disappeared, that the world of two-headed men and flying serpents has not disappeared. And, indeed, while we were away the flying saucers appeared, which do nothing to overturn our thesis. And it seems to us now the most dangerous tendency in the world is the desire to believe a rumor rather than to pin down a fact.

We went to the Soviet Union with the finest equipment of rumors that has ever been assembled in one place. And in this piece we insist on one thing: if we set down a rumor, it will be called a rumor.

We had a final Suissesse with Willy at the Bedford bar. Willy had become a full-time partner in our project, and meanwhile his Suissesses got better and better. He gave us advice, some of the best advice we had from anyone. Willy would have liked to come with us. And it might have been a good thing if he had. He made us a super Suissesse, had one himself, and we were finally ready to go.

Willy said, "Behind the bar you learn to listen a lot and not talk very much."

We thought about Willy and his Suissesses a lot during the next few months.

That was the way it started. Capa came back with about four thousand negatives, and I with several hundred pages of notes. We have wondered how to set this trip down and, after much discussion, have decided to write it as it happened, day by day, experience by experience, and sight by sight, without departmentalizing. We shall write what we saw and heard. I know that this is contrary to a large part of modern journalism, but for that very reason it might be a relief.

This is just what happened to us. It is not the Russian story, but simply *a* Russian story.

Chapter 2

Fʀᴏᴍ Stockholm we cabled Joseph Newman, head of the *Herald Tribune* bureau in Moscow, our estimated time of arrival and settled back content that he would have a car to meet us and a hotel room to receive us. Our route was Stockholm to Helsinki, to Leningrad, to Moscow. We would have to pick up a Russian plane at Helsinki, since no foreign airline enters the Soviet Union. The Swedish airliner, polished, immaculate, and shining, took us across the Baltic and up the Gulf of Finland to Helsinki. And a very pretty Swedish stewardess gave us very nice little Swedish things to eat.

After a smooth and comfortable trip we landed in the new airport of Helsinki, the buildings recently completed and very grand. And there, in the restaurant, we sat down to wait for the arrival of the Russian plane. After about two hours the Russian plane came in, an old C-47, flying very low. Her brown war paint was still on. She hit the ground, her tail-wheel exploded, and she came leaping like a grasshopper up the runway on a flat tail-wheel. It was the only accident we saw during our trip, but, coming at this time, it did little to arouse our confidence. And her scarred and scratched brown paint, and her general appearance of unkemptness, did not contrast well with the brightly shining planes of the Finnish and Swedish airlines.

She bumped and bumbled up to the line, and out of her boiled a collection of American fur-buyers recently come from the auctions in Russia. A depressed and quiet group, who claimed the plane had flown not over a hundred meters high all the way from Moscow. One of the Russian crew climbed down, kicked the flat tail-wheel, and sauntered to the airport terminal. And very soon we were told that we would not take off that afternoon. We would have to go to Helsinki to spend the night.

Capa marshaled his ten pieces of luggage and clucked around them like a mother hen. He saw them into a locked room. He warned the airport officials again and again that they must mount guard over them. And he was never satisfied for a moment while he was away from them. Normally lighthearted and gay, Capa becomes a tyrant and a worrier where his cameras are concerned.

Helsinki seemed a sad, pleasureless city to us, not badly bombed, but considerably shot up. Its hotels mournful, its restaurants rather silent, and in its square a band playing not merry music. In the streets soldiers seemed like little boys, so young, and pale, and countrified. Our impression was of a bloodless place, and a place of little joy. It seemed as though, after two wars and six years of fighting and struggle, Helsinki just couldn't get started again. Whether all of this is true economically we do not know, but that is the impression it gives.

Up in the town we found Atwood and Hill, the *Herald Tribune* team which was making a social and economic study of the countries behind the so-called iron curtain. They lived together in a hotel room surrounded by reports and pamphlets and surveys and photographs, and they had one lone bottle of Scotch whisky which they had been saving for some unimaginable celebration. It turned out we were it, and the whisky didn't last very long. Capa played a little sad and unprofitable gin rummy, and we went to bed.

In the morning, at ten, we were at the airport again. The tail-wheel of the Russian plane had been changed, but some work was still being done on the number two engine.

During the next two months we flew a great deal in Russian transport planes, and there are points of likeness in all of them, so that this plane may as well be described as representative of all of them. All were C-47's, with brown war paint, remains of lend-lease stock. There are newer transport planes on the fields, a kind of Russian C-47 with a tricycle landing gear, but these we did not fly in. The C-47's are a little run down insofar as upholstery and carpeting go, but their engines are kept up and their pilots seem to be very fine. They carry a larger crew than our planes do, but since we did not get up into the control room we don't know what they do. When the door opened, there

· 10 ·

seemed to be six or seven people in there all the time, among them a stewardess. We don't know what the stewardess does either. She seems to have no relation to the passengers. No food is carried by the plane for the passengers, but the passengers make up for this by carrying great quantities of food for themselves.

The air vents in the planes we traveled in were invariably out of order, so that no fresh breeze came in. And if the odor of food and occasional nausea filled the plane, there was nothing to do about it. We were told that these old American planes will be used until they can be replaced by the newer Russian planes.

There are customs which seem a little strange to Americans used to our airlines. There are no safety belts. Smoking is prohibited while in the air, but once the plane lands, people light up cigarettes. There is no night flying, and if your plane cannot make its port before sundown, it sits down and waits until the following morning. Except in times of storm, the planes fly much lower than ours. And this is comparatively safe because most of Russia is completely level. An airplane can find a forced landing field almost anywhere.

The loading of the Russian planes also seemed peculiar to us. After the passengers are seated, luggage is piled in the aisle.

I suppose what worried us most on this first day was the appearance of the plane. She was such a scratched and disreputable-looking old monster. But her engines were in beautiful condition and she was flown magnificently, so we had nothing really to worry about. And I suppose the shining metal of our planes does not really make them fly any better. I once knew a man whose wife claimed that the car ran better whenever it had been washed, and maybe we have that feeling about many things. The first principle of an airplane is that it stay in the air and get where it is going. And the Russians seem to be as good at this as anyone else.

There were not many passengers on the Moscow run. A nice Icelandic diplomat and his wife and child, a French Embassy courier with his pouch, and four silent, unidentified men who never spoke. We don't know who they were.

Now Capa was out of his element, for Capa speaks all languages

· 11 ·

except Russian. He speaks each language with the accent of another. He talks Spanish with a Hungarian accent, French with a Spanish accent, German with a French accent, English with an accent that has never been identified. But Russian he does not speak. After a month he had picked up some words of Russian, with an accent which was generally considered to be Uzbek.

At eleven o'clock we took off and flew toward Leningrad. Once in the air, the scars of the long war were apparent on the ground—the trenches, the cut-up earth, the shell holes, now beginning to be overgrown with grass. And as we got nearer and nearer to Leningrad, the scars became deeper, the trenches more frequent. The burned farmhouses with black and standing walls littered the landscape. Some areas where strong fights had taken place were pitted and scabbed like the face of the moon. And close to Leningrad was the greatest destruction. Trenches and strong points and machine-gun nests were very visible.

On the way we were apprehensive about the customs we would have to go through at Leningrad. With our thirteen pieces of luggage, with our thousands of flash bulbs and hundreds of rolls of film, with the masses of cameras and the tangle of flashlight wires, we thought it might take several days to go through us. We thought also that we might be heavily assessed for all this new equipment.

At last we flew over Leningrad. The outskirts were shattered, but the inner part of the city seemed not very much hurt. The plane sat lightly down on the grass field of the airport and drew into the line. There were no airport buildings except maintenance buildings. Two young soldiers with big rifles and shining bayonets came and stood near our plane. Then the customs came aboard. The chief was a smiling, courteous little man with a glittering smile of steel teeth. He knew one word of English—"yes." And we knew one word of Russian—"da." So that when he said yes we countered with da, and we were right back where we started. Our passports and our money were checked, and then came the problem of our luggage. It had to be opened in the aisle of the plane. It could not be taken out. The customs man was very polite, and very kind, and extremely thorough. We opened every bag, and he went through everything. But, as he proceeded, it became clear to us that he was not looking for anything in particular, he was just interested. He turned over our shining equipment and fingered it lovingly. He lifted out every roll of film, but he did nothing about it and he questioned nothing. He just seemed to be interested in foreign things. And he also seemed to have almost unlimited time. At the end he thanked us, at least we think that's what he did.

Now a new problem arose, the stamping of our papers. From the pocket of his tunic he took a little parcel wrapped in newspaper and from it extracted a rubber stamp. But this was all he had, he did not have an inking pad. Apparently, however, he had never had an inking pad, because his technique was carefully designed. From another pocket of his tunic he brought out a lead pencil; then, after licking the rubber stamp, he rubbed the lead pencil on the rubber and tried it on our papers. Absolutely nothing happened. He tried it again. And nothing happened. The rubber stamp did not make even the suggestion of an imprint. To help him, we took out our leaking fountain-pens and dipped our fingers in the ink and rubbed it on his rubber stamp. And finally he got a beautiful impress. He wrapped his stamp up in his newspaper and put it back in his pocket, shook hands warmly with us, and climbed off the plane. We repacked our luggage and piled it up on one of the seats.

Now a truck backed up to the open door of the plane, a truck loaded with a hundred and fifty new microscopes in their boxes. A girl stevedore came aboard—the strongest girl I have ever seen, lean and stringy, with a broad Baltic face. She carried heavy bundles up forward, into the pilot's compartment. And when that was piled full, she stacked the microscopes in the aisle. She wore canvas sneakers and a blue coverall and a headcloth, and her arms were bunched with muscles. And she, like the customs man, had shining stainless steel teeth, which make the human mouth look so much like a piece of machinery.

I think we had expected unpleasantness; all customs are unpleasant anyway, a peculiar violation of privacy. And perhaps we had halfway believed our advisers who had never been here, and expected to be insulted or mistreated in some way. But it didn't happen.

· 13 ·

Eventually the baggage-laden plane got into the air again and started toward Moscow over the endless flat land, a land of forests and of cut-out farmlands, of little unpainted villages and bright yellow straw stacks. The plane flew quite low until a cloud came down and we had to rise above it. And the rain began to pour down on the windows of the plane.

Our stewardess was a big, blond, bosomy, motherly looking girl, whose sole duty seemed to be to carry bottles of pink soda water, over the piled-up microscopes, to the men in the pilot's compartment. Once she took a loaf of black bread up to them.

We were beginning to starve, for we had had no breakfast, and there seemed to be no possibility of eating again. If we could have spoken we would have begged a slice of bread from her. We couldn't even do that.

About four o'clock we came down through the rain cloud, and to the left of us saw the sprawling, gigantic city of Moscow, and the Moscow River running through it. The airport itself was very large. Some of it paved and some of it long grass runways. There were literally hundreds of planes standing about, old C-47's and many of the new Russian planes with their tricycle landing gear and their bright aluminum finish.

As we rolled up to the new large and impressive airport building, we looked out of the window for some face which looked familiar to us, for someone who might be waiting for us. It was raining. We got out of the plane and assembled our baggage in the rain, and a great loneliness fell on us. There wasn't one person there to meet us. There wasn't a familiar face. We couldn't ask a question. We didn't have any Russian money. We didn't know where to go.

From Helsinki we had cabled Joe Newman that we would be one day late. But there was no Joe Newman. There was nobody for us. Some very husky porters carried our luggage to the front of the airport and waited expectantly to be paid, and we couldn't pay them. Busses went by, and we realized we couldn't even read their destinations, and besides they were so crowded with people inside, and were so hung with people on the outside, that we and our thirteen pieces of luggage

· 14 ·

could not possibly have got in. And the porters, very husky porters, waited for their money. We were hungry, and wet, and frightened, and we felt completely deserted.

Just then the courier for the French Embassy came out with his pouch, and he loaned us money to pay the porters, and he put our baggage in the car which had come to meet him. He was a very nice man. We had been close to suicide and he saved us. And if he should ever see this, we want to thank him again. He drove us to the Hotel Metropole, where Joe Newman supposedly was staying.

I don't know why airports are so far from the cities they supposedly service, but they are, and Moscow is no exception. The airport is miles and miles from the city, and the road goes through pine forests, through farms, and through endless potato and cabbage patches. There were rough roads and smooth roads. The French courier had anticipated everything. He had sent his driver out for a little lunch, so that on the way in to Moscow we ate *piroschki,* and little meat balls, and ham. And by the time we reached the Hotel Metropole we were feeling much better.

The Hotel Metropole was a rather grand hotel, with marble staircases and red carpets, and a great gilded elevator that ran sometimes. And there was a woman behind the desk who spoke English. We asked for our rooms, and she had never heard of us. We had no rooms.

At that moment Alexander Kendrick of the *Chicago Sun,* and his wife, rescued us. Where, we asked, was Joe Newman?

"Oh, Joe! He hasn't been here for a week. He's in Leningrad, at the fur auction."

He had not received our cable, nothing had been prepared, and we had no rooms. And it was ridiculous to try to get rooms without preparation. We had supposed that Joe would get in touch with whatever Russian agency was responsible for it. But since he hadn't, and hadn't received the cable, the Russians hadn't known we were coming either. But the Kendricks took us to their room, and fed us smoked salmon and vodka, and made us welcome.

After a while we didn't feel lonely and lost any more. We decided to move into Joe Newman's room to punish him. We used his towels, and his soap, and his toilet paper. We drank his whisky. We slept on his couch and his bed. We thought that was the least he could do for us, to repay us for having been miserable. The fact that he didn't know we were coming, we argued, was no excuse for him, and he had to be punished. And so we drank his two bottles of Scotch whisky. It must be admitted that we didn't know at that time what a crime this was. There is considerable dishonesty and chicanery among American newspapermen in Moscow, but it has never reached the level to which we brought it. A man does not drink another man's whisky.

Chapter 3

WE DIDN'T know yet what our status was. In fact, we weren't quite sure how we had got there, who had invited us. But the American correspondents in Moscow rallied around, and helped us, and held our hands—Gilmore, and Stevens, and Kendrick, and the rest, all good and sympathetic men. They took us to dinner in a commercial restaurant at the Hotel Metropole. And we found that there are two kinds of restaurants in Moscow: the ration restaurant, where you use your ration tickets and the price is quite low; and the commercial restaurant, where the price is fantastically high for much the same food.

The commercial restaurant in the Metropole is magnificent. A great fountain plays in the center of the room. The ceiling is about three stories high. There is a dance floor and a raised place for a band. Russian officers and their ladies, and civilians in the upper brackets of income, dance around the fountain with great decorum.

The band, incidentally, played louder and worse American jazz music than any we had ever heard. The drummer, an obvious but distant student of Krupa, whipped himself into a furor and juggled his sticks in the air. The clarinet player had been listening to Benny Goodman records, so that here and there one could hear a faint resemblance to a Goodman trio. One of the piano players was a lover of boogie-woogie, which he played with considerable skill and great enthusiasm.

Dinner consisted of four hundred grams of vodka, a great bowl of black caviar, cabbage soup, steak and fried potatoes, cheese, and two bottles of wine. And it cost about a hundred and ten dollars for five people, at the Embassy rate of twelve roubles to the dollar. It also took about two hours and a half to serve, a thing that startled us a little bit, but which we found was invariable in Russian restaurants. And we also found out later why it takes so long.

Since everything in the Soviet Union, every transaction, is under the state, or under monopolies granted by the state, the bookkeeping system is enormous. Thus the waiter, when he takes an order, writes it very carefully in a book. But he doesn't go then and request the food. He goes to the bookkeeper, who makes another entry concerning the food which has been ordered, and issues a slip which goes to the kitchen. There another entry is made, and certain food is requested. When the food is finally issued, an entry of the food issued is also made out on a slip, which is given to the waiter. But he doesn't bring the food back to the table. He takes his slip to the bookkeeper, who makes another entry that such food as has been ordered has been issued, and gives another slip to the waiter, who then goes back to the kitchen and brings the food to the table, making a note in his book that the food which has been ordered, which has been entered, and which has been delivered, is now, finally, on the table. This bookkeeping takes considerable time. Far more time, in fact, than anything to do with the food. And it does no good to become impatient about getting your dinner, because nothing in the world can be done about it. The process is invariable.

Meanwhile the orchestra howled out "Roll Out the Barrel" and "In the Mood," and a tenor came to the microphone, which he did not need, for his voice was sufficient for the room, and he sang "Old Man River" and some of the Sinatra favorites, like "Old Black Magic" and "I'm in the Mood for Love," in Russian.

While we were waiting, the Moscow correspondents coached us on what to expect and how to conduct ourselves. And we were very fortunate that they were there to tell us. They pointed out that it would be desirable for us not to become accredited to the Foreign Office. They emphasized the rules which applied to men so accredited, the one of major importance to us being that then we could not leave the Moscow area. And we didn't want to stay in Moscow. We wanted to go into the country and see how people on the farms lived.

Since we had no intention of sending dispatches or entering cables which would come under the censorship bureau, we thought it might be possible to avoid this Foreign Office accreditation. But we still didn't know who was sponsoring us. It would be either the Writer's Union, we thought, or Voks, which is the cultural relations organization of the Soviet Union. And we liked to think of ourselves as a cultural relation. We had determined beforehand that the information we wanted was non-political, except insofar as the politics were local, and insofar as they directly affected the daily lives of people.

The next morning we telephoned Intourist, which is the organization that takes care of foreigners. And we found that as far as Intourist was concerned, we had no status, we didn't exist, and there were no rooms. And so we called Voks. Voks said that they knew we were coming, but they had no idea we had arrived. They would try to get us rooms. That was very difficult, because all of the hotels in Moscow are full all of the time. Then we went out and walked in the streets.

I had been there in 1936 for a few days, and the changes since then were tremendous. In the first place the city was much cleaner than it had been. The streets were washed and paved, where they had been muddy and dirty. And the building in the eleven years was enormous. Hundreds of tall new apartment houses, new bridges over the Moscow River, the streets widened, and statues every place. Whole sections of the narrow, dirty districts of the old Moscow had disappeared, and in their place were new living quarters and new public buildings.

Here and there there was some evidence of bomb damage, but not very much. Apparently the Germans did not get their planes over Moscow with any success. Some of the correspondents who had been there during the war told us that the anti-aircraft defense was so effective, and the fighter planes so numerous, that after a few trials with great losses the Germans more or less gave up aerial bombardment of Moscow. But a few bombs came through: one dropped on the Kremlin, and a few dropped on the outskirts. But by that time the Luftwaffe had taken its beating over London and was not willing to sacrifice the large number of planes necessary for the bombardment of a heavily protected city.

We noticed also the work that was being done to the face of the city. There were scaffoldings against all the buildings. They were being painted, and broken places were being repaired, for within a few weeks the city would have its eight-hundredth anniversary, and this was to be celebrated with a great deal of ceremony and decoration. And a few months afterwards there was to be the thirtieth anniversary of the November Revolution.

Electricians were stringing lights on the public buildings, and on the Kremlin, and on the bridges. And this work did not stop in the evening—it went on with floodlights all night, this painting and grooming of the city for its first non-war celebration in many years.

But in spite of the bustle and preparation the people in the streets seemed tired. The women used very little or no make-up, and the clothing was adequate but not very pretty. Great numbers of the men in the streets were in uniform, but they were not in the Army. They were demobilized, and their uniforms were the only clothes they had. The uniforms were without insignia and without shoulder boards.

Capa did not take his cameras out, for he had been told by the other correspondents that without permission in writing this is not a desirable thing to do, particularly for a foreigner. The first policeman picks you up and takes you in for questioning unless your permissions are written and in order.

We had begun to feel lonely again. Far from being watched and shadowed and followed, we could hardly get anyone to admit that we were there at all. And we knew that bureaus would move slowly in Moscow, just as they do in Washington. Now, skulking around in other people's rooms, surrounded by our hundreds of rolls of film and our camera equipment, we began to get worried.

We had heard of a Russian game—we prefer to call it the Russian gambit—which has rarely been beaten. It is played very simply. The man in the government bureau you want to see is not there, is sick, is in hospital, or is away on his vacation. This can go on for years. And if you should shift your attack to another man, he also is out of town, is in hospital, or is away on his vacation. One Hungarian commission, with some kind of petition which, I imagine, was not looked on with favor, had been waiting for three months, first to see a particular man, and finally just to see anyone. But they never did. And an American professor, with an idea for exchange students, a brilliant, intelligent, and good man, had been sitting in anterooms for weeks. And he too had never seen anyone. There is no way to oppose this gambit. There is no defense against it, except to relax.

Sitting in Joe Newman's room, we thought that this might well happen to us. Also, from having done a bit of telephoning, we had discovered another interesting thing about Russian offices. No one gets to an office before noon, no one. The office is closed until noon. But, from noon on, the office remains open, and people work, until midnight. The mornings are not used for work. There may be bureaus which do not follow this formula, but the ones we had to deal with in the following two months all kept this kind of hours. We knew that we must become neither impatient, nor angry, since if one does one loses five points in the game. It turned out that our fears were groundless, for the next day Voks swung into action. They got us a room in the Savoy Hotel, around the corner, and they invited us over to their office to discuss our plans.

The Savoy is a hotel which, like the Metropole, is assigned to foreigners. People living at the Metropole claim that the Savoy is the better hotel of the two, that its food and service are better. On the other hand, the people who live at the Savoy claim that the food and service at the Metropole are better. This mutually complimentary game has been going on for years.

We were assigned a room on the second floor of the Savoy. We walked up marble stairs lined with statuary, our favorite being a bust of Graziella, a famous beauty who had come in with Napoleon. She was dressed in an Empire costume, and wore a large picture hat, and by some mistake the sculptor had chiseled her name not as Graziella, but as Craziella, and Crazy Ella she became to us. At the top of the stairway was an enormous stuffed Russian bear in the position of charge. But some timid customer had removed the claws from his front paws, so that he attacked with no fingernails. In the semi-darkness of the upper hall he was a constant source of mild shock to new customers of the Savoy.

· 21 ·

Our room was large. We discovered later that it was a very desirable room in the eyes of people who lived in other rooms in the Savoy. The ceiling was twenty feet high. The walls were painted a doleful dark green. And it had an annex for the beds, with a curtain that drew across. Its best features were a huge combination in black oak of couch, mirror, and double closets, and a mural which ran around the top of the wall. That mural got into our dreams as time went on. If it can be described at all, it is thus: At the bottom and center of the picture is an acrobat lying on his stomach with his legs over his back. In front of him two identical cats are gliding under his hands. Across his back lie two green alligators, and resting on top of the alligators' heads is an insane monkey, with bat-wings, who wears an imperial crown. This monkey, who has long and sinewy arms, reaches through two portholes in his wings and grasps the horns of two goats which have the tails of fishes. Each of these goats wears a breastplate which terminates in a thorn on which there are pierced two violent-looking fishes. We didn't understand this mural. We didn't know what it meant, nor for what reason it was put in our hotel room. But we began to dream about it. And certainly it did have a quality of nightmare about it.

Three huge double windows overlooked the street. As time went on, Capa posted himself in the windows more and more, photographing little incidents that happened under our windows. Across the street, on the second floor, there was a man who ran a kind of camera repair shop. He worked long hours on equipment. And we discovered late in the game that while we were photographing him, he was photographing us.

Our bathroom, and we were the glory of Moscow for having a private one, had certain peculiarities. The entrance was difficult, for one could not open the door simply and go in, because the door was interfered with by the bathtub. One stepped inside, crouched back in the corner beside the washstand, closed the door, and then one was free to move about. The bathtub was not evenly set on its legs, so that once filled, if one moved suddenly, the whole thing swayed and water slopped out on the floor.

It was an old bathtub, probably pre-revolutionary, and its enamel

had been worn off on the bottom, leaving a surface a little like sand-paper. Capa, who is a delicate creature, found that he began to bleed after a bath, and he took to wearing shorts in the tub.

This bathroom had a peculiarity which was true of all the bathrooms we experienced in the Soviet Union. There may be other kinds, but we did not find them. Whereas all the taps leaked—the toilet, the basin, the bathtub faucets—all the drains were completely watertight. Consequently, if you filled the basin, the water stayed there, and when you pulled the plug out of the bathtub drain, it had no effect at all in allowing the water to escape. And in one hotel in Georgia the roar of water escaping from the taps was so great that we had to close the bathroom door to get any sleep. It was from this that I made my great invention, which I offered to turn over to heavy industry. It is very simple. Reverse the process: put the taps where the drains are, and the drains where the taps are, and the whole thing would be solved.

But our bathroom did have one very fine quality. There was always plenty of hot water in it, sometimes mostly on the floor, but it was there when we wanted it.

It was here that I discovered an unpleasant quality in Capa's nature, and I think it only right to set it down in case some young woman should ever listen to any suggestion of matrimony from him. He is a bathroom hog, and a very curious one. His method is as follows: He rises from his bed and disappears into the bathroom and draws a tub of water. He then lies in that tub of water and reads until he becomes sleepy, whereupon he goes to sleep. This may go on for two or three hours in the morning, and it can be readily seen that the bathroom is immobilized for any more serious purposes while he is in there. I offer this information about Capa as a public service. With two bathrooms, Capa is a charming, intelligent, good-tempered companion. With one bathroom, he is a ——

Already we had been subjected to the intricacies of Russian money. It had several values, official and non-official. The official rate was five roubles to one dollar. The American Embassy rate was twelve roubles to one dollar. But you could buy roubles on the black market for fifty roubles to one dollar, and certain South American legations bought

· 24 ·

roubles in other countries, like Poland or Czechoslovakia, for a hundred roubles to one dollar. The American Embassy, which maintained strict honesty in this matter of twelve to one, was criticized by some of its employees for making things very expensive. For example, if a member of our Embassy gave a party, it was vastly expensive at twelve to one, while a member of one of the aforementioned embassies could give a party at a hundred to one, and the party was incredibly cheap.

When we registered at the Savoy Hotel we were issued ration tickets, three for each day, for breakfast, lunch, and dinner. By using these tickets in the ration restaurant in the hotel we could eat quite reasonably. If we wanted to eat in a commercial restaurant, the food was very expensive, and not very much better. The beer was sour, and very expensive. It averaged about a dollar and a half a bottle.

In the afternoon Voks sent a car to take us to the main office for an interview. It was our impression that there had been some battle about who was to be responsible for us, the Writers' Union or Voks. And Voks had lost and got us. The Voks offices are in a beautiful little palace, which was once the home of a merchant prince. We were received by Mr. Karaganov in his office, which is oak-paneled to the ceiling and has a stained-glass skylight—a very pleasant place to work. Mr. Karaganov, a young blond, careful man, who spoke a precise, slow English, sat behind his desk and asked us many questions. He doodled on a pad with a pencil, one end of which was blue and the other red. And we explained our project, which was to avoid politics, but to try to talk to and to understand Russian farmers, and working people, and market people, to see how they lived, and to try to tell our people about it, so that some kind of common understanding might be reached. He listened quietly and made angular marks with his pencil.

Then he said, "There have been other people who wanted to do this." And he named a number of Americans who have since written books about the Soviet Union. "They have sat in this office," he said, "and have spoken in one way, and then they have gone home and have written in another way. And if we seem to have a mild distrust, it is because of this."

"You must not think that we came either favorably or unfavorably," we replied. "We came to do a job of reporting, if it is possible to do it. We intend to set down and to photograph exactly what we see and hear, with no editorial comment. If there is something we don't like, or don't understand, we will set that down too. But we came for a story. If we can do the story we came for, we will do it. If we can't do it, we still have a story."

He nodded very slowly and thoughtfully. "This we could trust," he said. "But we are very tired of people who come here and are violently pro-Russian, and who go back to the United States and become violently anti-Russian. We have had considerable experience with that kind.

"This office, Voks," he continued, "has not very much power, nor very much influence. But we will do what we can to let you do the work that you want to do." Then he asked us many questions about America. He said, "Many of your newspapers are speaking of war with the Soviet Union. Do the American people want war with the Soviet Union?

"We don't think so," we answered. "We don't think any people want war, but we don't know."

He said, "Apparently the only voice speaking loudly in America against war is that of Henry Wallace. Can you tell me what his following is? Has he any real backing among the people?"

We said, "We don't know. But this we do know, that in one speaking tour Henry Wallace collected in paid admissions an unprecedented amount of money. We do know that this is the first time we have ever heard of that people paid to go to political meetings. And we do know that many people were turned away from these meetings, because there was no place for them to sit or stand. Whether this has any emphasis on the coming elections we have no idea. We only know that we, who have seen a little bit of war, do not favor it. And we feel that there are a great many people like us. We feel that if war is the only answer our leaders can give us, then we indeed live in a poverty-stricken time." And then we asked, "Do the Russian people, or any section of them, or any section of the Russian government, want war?"

At that he straightened up, put down his pencil, and said, "I can answer that categorically. Neither the Russian people, nor any section of them, nor any section of the Russian government, wants war. I can go further than that—the Russian people would do almost anything to avoid war. Of this I am certain." And he took up his pencil again and made round doodles on his pad.

"Let us speak of American writing," he said. "It seems to us that your novelists don't believe in anything any more. Is this true?"

"I don't know," I said.

"Your own most recent work seems to us cynical," he said.

"It is not cynical," I answered. "I believe one job of a writer is to set down his time as nearly as he can understand it. And that is what I am doing."

Then he asked questions about American writers, about Caldwell, and Faulkner, and when would Hemingway have a new book. And he asked what young writers were coming up, what new people. We explained that a few young writers were beginning to emerge, but that it was too soon to expect them to come out. Young men who should have been practicing their trade of writing had spent the last four years in the service. Such an experience was likely to shake them very deeply, and it might take some time for them to comb out their experience and their lives, and to settle down to writing.

He seemed a little surprised that writers in America do not get together, do not associate with one another very much. In the Soviet Union writers are very important people. Stalin has said that writers are the architects of the human soul.

We explained to him that writers in America have quite a different standing, that they are considered just below acrobats and just above seals. And in our opinion this is a very good thing. We believe that a writer, particularly a young writer, too much appreciated, is as likely to turn as heady as a motion-picture actress with good notices in the trade journals. And we believe that the rough-and-tumble critical life an American writer is subject to is very healthy for him in the long run.

It seems to us that one of the deepest divisions between the Russians and the Americans or British, is in their feeling toward their governments. The Russians are taught, and trained, and encouraged to believe

· 27 ·

that their government is good, that every part of it is good, and that their job is to carry it forward, to back it up in all ways. On the other hand, the deep emotional feeling among Americans and British is that all government is somehow dangerous, that there should be as little government as possible, that any increase in the power of government is bad, and that existing government must be watched constantly, watched and criticized to keep it sharp and on its toes. And later, on the farms, when we sat at table with farming men, and they asked how our government operated, we would try to explain that such was our fear of power invested in one man, or in one group of men, that our government was made up of a series of checks and balances, designed to keep power from falling into any one person's hands. We tried to explain that the people who made our government, and those who continue it, are so in fear of power that they would willingly cut off a good leader rather than permit a precedent of leadership. I do not think we were thoroughly understood in this, since the training of the people of the Soviet Union is that the leader is good and the leadership is good. There is no successful argument here, it is just the failure of two systems to communicate one with the other.

Mr. Karaganov's pad was covered with red and blue symbols. He said finally, "If you will write down a list of things you want to do and see, and send it through to me, I will see whether it can be arranged."

We liked Karaganov very much. He was a man who spoke straight and unconfusedly. Later we were to hear many flowery speeches and many generalities. But this we never heard from Karaganov. We never pretended to him that we were anything but what we were. We had a certain outlook, an American viewpoint, and possibly to him certain prejudices. Far from disliking us, or distrusting us because of this, he seemed to trust us more. During our stay in the Soviet Union he was of great help to us. We saw him a number of times, and his one request of us was, "Just tell the truth, just tell what you see. Don't change it, put it down as it is, and we will be very glad. For we distrust flattery." He seemed to us an honest and a good man.

The silent fight was still going on concerning our trip. At the present time one can go to the Soviet Union only as a guest of some organization, or to do some particular job. We were not sure whether the Writers' Union or Voks was sponsoring us, and we were not sure that they knew either. It may be that each was trying to move this dubious honor on to the other. One thing we were sure of, we did not want to become accredited as regular correspondents, with correspondents' credentials, for in that case we should have been under the sponsorship and control of the Foreign Office. The Foreign Office rules are very strict regarding correspondents, and if we once became their babies, we could not have left Moscow without special permission, which is rarely granted. We could not have traveled with any freedom, and our material would have been subject to Foreign Office censorship. These things we did not want, for we had already talked to the American and British correspondents in Moscow, and we had found that their reporting activities were more or less limited to the translation of Russian daily papers and magazines, and the transmission of their translations, and even then censorship quite often cut large pieces out of their cables. And some of the censorship was completely ridiculous. Once, one American correspondent, in describing the city of Moscow, said that the Kremlin is triangular in shape. He found this piece of information cut out of his copy. Indeed, there were no censorship rules on which one could depend, but the older correspondents, the ones who had been in Moscow a long time, knew approximately what they could and could not get through. That eternal battle between correspondents and censor goes on.

There is a famous story of a new ground mole, and it goes like this: A civil engineer invented a ditch-digging, or tunnel-digging, machine called a ground mole. Pictures of it and specifications appeared in a Soviet scientific magazine. This was picked up by an American magazine and was printed. A British newspaper, seeing the article, wired its correspondent in Moscow to get a story on the ground mole. Whereupon the British correspondent went to the Soviet scientific journal, dug out the material, and sent it to its paper, only to find the whole story killed by censorship. This happened a number of months ago, and, as far as I know, the story is still held up in censorship.

The correspondents were further inhibited by a fairly new decree, which makes the divulgence of agricultural, industrial, or population figures equally treasonable with the divulgence of military information. The result is that one can get no figures at all concerning any Russian production. Everything is dealt with in percentages. Without a base figure, this leaves you about where you started. For example, you cannot be told how many units are turned out by a certain tractor factory, but you can be told that it is, say, ninety-five per cent of the 1939 level. If you know how many units were turned out in 1939, your figure is likely to be accurate, but if you have no other figure you are lost. In some cases this whole thing is ridiculous. If, for example, one asks what the present population of Stalingrad is, one would be told that it is eighty-seven per cent of the pre-war figure. The process then is to look up the population pre-war and compute the number of people now living in Stalingrad.

A constant double talk warfare goes on between the Moscow correspondents and the censorship office, and we did not want to become involved in it.

At this point Joe Newman returned from his junket to the fur auctions in Leningrad. In addition to being a good friend, Joe is a very effective man. He was trained in Japan and in Argentina, and this training makes him particularly fit for the Moscow scene. He has an easy quality from long experience in countries where directness is highly uncommon; he has grown sensitive to nuances and to suggestions. He can read the meaning behind meanings, and besides this he is a relaxed man. You have to be in this job, or you very soon go crazy. We are greatly indebted to him for the information and training he gave us.

We called at the American Embassy, and it is different from any I have ever seen. Whereas in most embassies the line of American tourists and visitors is interminable, at the Moscow Embassy practically no one calls. There is no one to call. There are no tourists. Very few Americans go to Moscow. And while we have a fairly large staff in Moscow, they are limited more or less to associating with one another and with members of other embassies. For the association of foreigners with Russians is rather limited. There is no question, in this period of tension, that Russians do not like to be seen with members of the American Embassy, and this is fairly understandable. One member of our Embassy explained it to me in this way. He said that he had been speaking with a State Department man who had come to Moscow and who complained that he was not able to get in touch with Russian people. The Embassy man said, "Well, let's suppose that in Washington you heard that one of your secretaries was going out with somebody from the Russian Embassy. What would you do?" And the State Department man replied, "Why, I'd fire her, immediately." And the Embassy man said, "Well, you see, maybe the Russians feel the same way."

General Smith, the American Ambassador, asked us to dinner, and we found him an intelligent and careful man, who desperately tried to do the best he could for the relations of the two countries. And it must be admitted that he is working under great difficulties. For the diplomatic services of foreign countries are under the same restrictions as the correspondents. They are not permitted to leave Moscow, they cannot travel about the country, and their access to the homes of Russians is highly limited. It is not that there is anything said, it is just that one is not invited. And if one invites a Russian something usually happens. He is ill, or he cannot come, or he is not in town. This is unfortunate, but true. And it is equally unfortunate that in America the same thing may be, to a certain extent, true.

It is our belief that the Russians are the worst propagandists, the worst public relations people, in the world. Let us take the example of the foreign correspondents. Usually a newspaperman goes to Moscow full of good will and a desire to understand what he sees. He promptly finds himself inhibited and not able to do the work of a newspaperman. Gradually he begins to turn in mood, and gradually he begins to hate the system, not as a system, but simply because it keeps him from doing his work. There is no quicker way of turning a man against anything. And this newspaperman usually ends up nervous and mean, because he has not been able to accomplish what he was sent to do. A man who is unable to function in his job usually detests the cause of his failure to function. The Embassy people and the correspondents feel alone, feel cut off; they are island people in the midst of Russia, and it is no wonder that they become lonely and bitter.

This section on Foreign Office accreditation is put in in justice to the regular Moscow correspondents. We were able to do many things they are not permitted to do. But if it had been part of our job to report news as they must, then we would have been taken under the Foreign Office, and we too could not have left Moscow.

Now Voks assigned an interpreter to us, and an interpreter was very necessary, for we could not even read a street sign. Our interpreter was a young, small, and quite pretty girl. Her English was excellent. She was a graduate student at the University of Moscow, in American history. She was quick and sharp and tough, and a daughter of a colonel in the Soviet Army. She was of great help to us, not only because she knew the city thoroughly and was able to get things done with great efficiency, but also because in conversation she gave us an idea of what the young people, at least of Moscow, were thinking and talking about. Her name was Svetlana Litvinova. Her first name was pronounced Sweet Lana, and this name so charmed us that we decided that it should be spread. We tried Sweet General Smith, and Sweet Harry Truman, and Sweet Carrie Chapman Catt, and none of them seemed to work. Finally we hit upon Sweet Joe Newman, and this seemed to be permanent. He is still known as Sweet Joe.

Sweet Lana was a dynamo of energy and efficiency. She got cars for us. She took us to see the things we wanted to see. She was a determined little girl, and her opinions were as determined as she was. She detested modern art of all kinds. The abstractionists were decadent Americans; the experimenters in painting were decadent too; Picasso nauseated her; the crazy mural in our bedroom she described as an example of decadent American art. The only painting she really liked was nineteenth-century representational photographic painting. We found that this was not her own personal view, but was general. We do not think that there is any actual pressure put upon a painter. But if he wants his pictures hung in the state galleries, and that is the only kind of gallery that exists, then he will paint photographic paintings. He will, publicly at least, not experiment with color and line, invent no new techniques, use no subjective approach to his job. Sweet Lana

· 32 ·

was vehement on this subject. And she was vehement on most subjects. It was through her that we learned of the wave of morality that is upon the young people of the Soviet Union. It is somewhat like the morality of an American small town a generation ago. Nice girls are not seen in night clubs. Nice girls do not smoke. Nice girls do not use lipstick or nail polish. Nice girls dress very conservatively. Nice girls do not drink. And nice girls are very circumspect with their boy friends. Sweet Lana was so moral that she made us, who had never thought of ourselves as being very immoral, feel rather bawdy. We like a well made-up woman, and we have a critical eye for a well-turned ankle. We lean toward mascara and eye-shadow. We like swing music and scat singing, and we love the pretty legs in a chorus line. These were all decadent things to Sweet Lana. These were the products of decadent capitalism. And this attitude was not limited to Sweet Lana. It was true of most of the young people we met. And it was interesting to us that the attitudes of our most conservative and old-fashioned groups are found in the attitudes of the young people of the Soviet Union.

Sweet Lana was very trim and neat, and her clothes were well made, simple and well fitting. And when occasionally she had to conduct us to a theater or to a ballet, she wore a little veil on her hat. During the time we were in the Soviet Union Sweet Lana grew a little less apprehensive of our decadence. And when finally we were leaving, on our last night, there was a little party, and Sweet Lana said, "I've conducted many people around, but I never had any fun before."

Her study of American history at the University had been exhaustive, and in the Soviet manner scientific. She knew things about American history that we had never heard of, but she knew it, of course, always in terms of Marxist criticism, so that events that we did know about had a strange and foreign sound when they came from her. It is very highly possible that our knowledge of Russian history would have the same sound to her ears. Slowly I think she came to like us a little, in spite of our decadence. For one thing, we were a little different from most tourists with whom she had come in contact. And once in a while the deep seriousness of Soviet young people tipped over in Sweet Lana and she had a little non-decadent fun too.

· 33 ·

We were anxious to know about this state of mind, and gradually it became a little clear to us. Soviet young people are trained to feel that there is so much work to be done, more work than they can ever accomplish, that there is not much time for play. The competition among them is constant. One takes examinations for schools, and the highest grade wins; the highest grade gets the scholarship. There are always more applicants for the universities than there are places, so that the competition is very keen. And everywhere the honors and the emoluments go to the most effective person. There is no such thing as reliance on past performance, or on the performance of your father or grandfather. One's position is entirely dependent on one's own intelligence and one's own effort. And if this method makes Soviet youngsters seem a little tense and humorless, it also makes them work very hard.

Sweet Lana took us out to the Lenin Hills, and we stood on that

eminence that overlooks the whole city and saw Moscow stretching to the horizon, a huge city. There were black piled clouds in the sky, but the sun shone underneath and glittered on the golden domes of the Kremlin. It is a city of great new buildings, and little old wooden houses with wooden lace around the windows, a curious, moody city, full of character. There are no figures as to its population now, but it is said to have between six and seven millions.

We drove slowly back into town. The ditches were full of growing cabbages, and the sides of the road were planted with potatoes. What we knew as victory gardens are continued now, and will continue. Everyone has his little plot of cabbages and potatoes, and the protection of these plots is ferocious. While we were in Moscow two women were sentenced to ten years of hard labor for stealing three pounds of potatoes from a private garden.

As we drove back toward Moscow a great black cloud turned over, and the rain began to fall on the city.

Probably the hardest thing in the world for a man is the simple observation and acceptance of what is. Always we warp our pictures with what we hoped, expected, or were afraid of. In Russia we saw many things that did not agree with what we had expected, and for this reason it is very good to have photographs, because a camera has no preconceptions, it simply sets down what it sees.

We had to wait about Moscow for our permits to leave the city and to travel through the country.

We went, on invitation, to see the temporary head of the press bureau. He was dressed in a gray uniform with the square shoulder boards of the Foreign Office. His eyes were bright blue, like turquoises.

Capa spoke fervently about taking pictures. So far he had not been able to. The chief of the press bureau assured us that he would do his best to get the permits for photography as soon as possible. Our meeting was formal and very courteous.

Later we went to visit the Lenin Museum. Room after room of the scraps of a man's life. I suppose there is no more documented life in history. Lenin must have thrown nothing away. Rooms and cases are full of bits of his writings, bills, diaries, manifestoes, pamphlets; his pens and pencils, his scarves, his clothing, everything is there. And around the walls are huge paintings of every incident of his life, from his boyhood on. Every incident of the Revolution in which he took part is recorded in monster paintings around the wall. His books are sunk in white marble frames, about the walls also, and the titles are in bronze. There are statues of Lenin in every possible pose, and later, in the pictures of his life, Stalin enters. But in the whole museum there is not one picture of Trotsky. Trotsky, as far as Russian history is concerned, has ceased to exist, and in fact never did exist. This is a kind of historical approach which we cannot understand. This is history as we wish it might have been rather than as it was. For there is no doubt that Trotsky exerted a great historical effect on the Russian Revolution. There is also no doubt that his removal and his banishment were of great historical importance. But to the young Russians he never existed. To the children who go into the Lenin Museum and see the history of the Revolution there is no Trotsky, good or bad.

The museum was crowded. There were groups of Soviet soldiers; there were children; there were tourists from the various republics, and each group had its lecturer, and each lecturer had a pointer, with which he or she indicated the various subjects under discussion.

While we were there a long line of war orphans came in, little boys and girls from about six to thirteen, scrubbed and dressed in their best clothes. And they too went through the museum and gazed with wide eyes at this documented life of the dead Lenin. They looked in wonder at his fur cap, and his fur-collared overcoat, at his shoes, the tables he wrote on, the chairs he sat in. Everything about this man is here, everything except humor. There is no evidence that he ever, in his whole life, had a light or a humorous thought, a moment of whole-hearted laughter, or an evening of fun. There can be no doubt that these things existed, but perhaps historically he is not permitted to have them.

In this museum one gets the idea that Lenin himself was aware of his place in history. Not only did he save every scrap of his thinking and his writing, but the photographs of him are there by the hundreds. He was photographed everywhere, in all conditions, and at every age, almost as though he had anticipated that there would someday be a museum called the Lenin Museum.

There is a hush over the place. People speak in whispers, and the lecturers with their pointers talk in a curious melodic litany. For this man has ceased to be a man in the Russian mind. He is no longer of flesh, but of stone, and bronze, and marble. The bald head and the pointed mustache are everywhere in the Soviet Union. The intent, squinting eyes look out of canvas and peep out of plaster.

In the evening we went to a party at the American club, a place where Embassy employees and soldiers and sailors from the Military and Naval Attachés' offices go for recreation. There was a viperine punch, made of vodka and grapefruit juice, a fine reminder of prohibition days. A little swing band was led by Ed Gilmore, who is a swing *aficionado*. He once called his organization the Kremlin Krows, but since this name was slightly frowned on it was changed to the Moscow River Rats.

After the solemnity of the afternoon in the Lenin Museum the slight violence and noise and laughter of this party were a pleasure to us.

Among the girls at this party were a number of the now-famous wives of Americans and Britons who are not permitted to leave the Soviet Union. Pretty and rather sad girls. They cannot join their husbands in England or America, and so they are employed by their embassies until some final decision is reached.

There are many things we cannot understand about the Soviet Union, and this is one of them. There are not more than fifty of these women. They are no good to the Soviet Union. They are suspected. Russians do not associate with them, and yet they are not permitted to leave. And on these fifty women, these fifty unimportant women, the Soviet Union has got itself more bad publicity than on any other single small item. Of course this situation cannot arise again, since by a new decree no Russian may marry a foreigner. But here they sit in Moscow, these sad women, no longer Russians, and they have not become British or American. And we cannot understand the reasoning which keeps them here. Perhaps it is just that the Russians do not intend to be told what to do about anything by anyone else. It might be as simple as that.

When Clement Attlee personally requested that they be sent out of Russia, he was told, in effect, to mind his own business. It is just one more of the international stupidities which seem to be on the increase in the world. Sometimes it seems that the leaders of nations are little boys with chips on their shoulders, daring each other to knock them off.

It was a good party at the American club, a good noisy party, and it made us feel a little homesick. All of the people there were homesick too, for Russia is not very kind to foreigners, particularly if they happen to be employees of foreign governments. And although we had not been long in the Soviet Union, the lipstick, the mascara, and the colored nails of the girls looked good to us.

The following afternoon we went to the air show. While there were some civilian events, most of the show was given by the Soviet Air Force. Different branches of the Soviet armed forces have their days. There is Tank Day, Infantry Day, and Navy Day, and this was the Air Force Day. Since it was semi-military, we were told that no cameras would be permitted. This seemed a little ridiculous to us, because every military attaché, from every embassy, would be there, people who really know about airplanes. We didn't know an airplane from a hole in the ground. It was very probable that every military attaché would be sketching and understanding what he saw, and we wouldn't.

A car came for us. We went out a long avenue lined with flags, miles of them, red flags and Air Force flags. The highway was bordered with large portraits of Stalin, and Marx, and Lenin. Hundreds of thousands of people moved toward the airfield on trains and on busses, and other hundreds of thousands went on foot.

Our places were in the grandstand, which was a mistake. We should have been on the great green field where literally millions of people stood to watch the show. It was a hot day, and there was no cover from the sun. On the flat green field were pavilions where soft drinks were sold, and little cakes. When we were seated, a low hum started, and it grew to a great roaring. It was all of the people standing there greeting Stalin, who had just arrived. We couldn't see him, we couldn't see his box, because we were on the wrong side of the grandstand. The response to his arrival was not a cheer but a buzz, like that of millions of bees.

The show started almost at once. It began with civilian pilots, some from factories, some from flying clubs, some groups of women. They flew formations, intricate formations, and did it superbly. Long lines of planes played follow-the-leader, and made loops, and turns, and dives, one behind the other.

Then the military ships came in, and flew tight formations, threes, and fives, and sevens, wing to wing, activated as one plane. It was really magnificent flying, but it wasn't what the crowd had come to see. They had come to see the new models, the jets and rocket-boosted planes. And eventually these came. Some of them climbed almost perpendicularly into the sky, at great speed, with the rockets on their wing tips putting out a trail of white. And finally the jet ships came. And I don't know whether it was to confuse the observers or not, but they flew only about three hundred feet above the earth, and by the time we heard them they were almost gone, they zipped past and were gone. There seemed to be three or four new models. We have no idea of how they compare with other jet planes, they seemed very fast to us. Of all the ships in the whole show there were only two large ones which might be considered bombers.

Next there was a mock battle in the sky. Enemy ships came in, and defensive ships went up to meet them, while on the ground, far in the distance, batteries of anti-aircraft flashed and roared, and the whole field trembled with the reverberation. It was very theatrical, for here and there a ship would spout black smoke and flame and would go into a spin, and then from over the edge of the hills there would come a flash of calcium light, as though the plane had crashed and burned. It was a very effective piece of drama.

The last item of the show was the most spectacular of all. A large group of transport planes came over the field and suddenly each one spat out parachutes. There were at least five hundred in the air at once, and the parachutes were red, and green, and blue. The sun made them look like flowers in the air. They floated down to the field, and just before they landed each parachute sprouted a second parachute, so that the men landed standing up, and they did not tumble or roll.

The air show must have been practiced for many weeks, because its timing was perfect, there were no delays. One event followed directly on the heels of the other. When it was over, the hum of the crowd arose again, and a soft clapping from hundreds of thousands of people. It was Stalin going away, and we still didn't see him.

There are definite disadvantages to having the best seats in the grandstand, and we wished we had been out on the field, where the people sat on the grass, in comfort, and watched the show, and saw more than we did. We never made the mistake again of going any place V. I. P. It may be flattering to the ego, but you don't see as much.

The next morning our permits to photograph came through. Capa was at last to be turned loose with his cameras, and his fingers were itching. We wanted photographs of the rebuilding of Moscow, and of the frantic painting and repairing of buildings in preparation for the anniversary of the city's founding. Sweet Lana was to go with us as guide and interpreter.

Almost immediately we ran afoul of the general suspicion toward foreign photographers. We were photographing children playing in a

pile of rubble. They were preoccupied with building, piling stones one on top of another, and moving dirt in little wagons, imitating what the adults were doing. Suddenly a policeman appeared. He was very polite. He wanted to see the permits to photograph. He read them but was not quite willing to go out on a limb for a little piece of paper. And so he took us to the nearest call box, where he called some kind of headquarters. Then we waited. We waited for half an hour until a car drove up, full of plain-clothes men. They read the letter of permission. Each one read it, and then they had a little conference; we don't know what they said, but then they telephoned again, and finally they all came back smiling, and they all touched their caps, and we were free to photograph in that neighborhood.

Then we moved to another part of the town, for we wanted photographs of the stores, the food shops, the clothing shops, the department stores. And again a very polite policeman approached, and read our permit, and he too went to a call box while we waited. And again a car with plain-clothes men came up, and they each read our permit, and they had a consultation, and they telephoned from the call box. It was the same thing. They came back smiling, and touched their caps, and we were free to photograph in that district.

This practice seems to be general in the Soviet Union. I suppose it is general any place where bureaus of the government operate. No one is willing to go out on any limb. No one is willing to say yes or no to a proposition. He must always go to someone higher. In this way he protects himself from criticism. Anyone who has had dealings with armies, or with governments, will recognize this story. The reaction to our cameras was invariably courteous, but very careful, and the camera did not click until the policeman was quite sure that everything was in order.

The food stores in Moscow are very large, and, as with the restaurants, there are two kinds: the ration stores, where food is very cheap if one has the ration tickets to get it; and the free stores, also operated by the government, where one can buy nearly anything in the way of food at very high prices. The canned goods are piled in mountains, the champagne and wine from Georgia are pyramided. We saw here some products which might have come from United States' stocks. There were cans of crab with Japanese marks still on them. There were German goods. And there were the luxury products of the Soviet Union itself—large cans of caviar, piles of sausages from the Ukraine, cheeses, salt fish, and even game, wild duck and woodcock, bustard and rabbits and hares, small birds and a white bird that looks like a ptarmigan. There were smoked meats of all kind.

But this food is all luxury food. To the average Russian the important thing is the price of bread and its quantity, and the price of cabbage and potatoes. In a good year, such as this one, the prices of bread, cabbage, and potatoes come down, and this is the index of the success or failure of the crops.

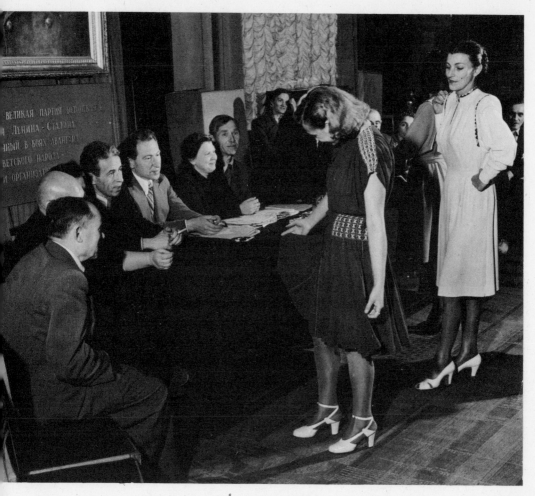

The windows of the food stores, both ration and commercial, are filled with wax figures of the food sold inside. There are wax hams and bacons and sausages, wax quarters of beef, even wax cans of caviar.

We went next to the department stores, where clothing, shoes and stockings, suits and dresses, are sold. The quality was not very good, and the tailoring was not very good either. It is the principle of the Soviet Union to make utility goods as long as they are necessary, and to make no luxuries until utility goods have taken up the slack of need. There were print dresses, some woolen suits, and the prices seemed very high to us. But here we come to the danger of making general statements, for even during the short time we were in the Soviet Union

· 43 ·

prices came down and quality seemed to be improving. It seems to us that a thing which is true one day is untrue the next.

We went on to the commercial shops where secondhand goods are sold. These are specialty shops. One handles china and lamps, another deals in jewelry—antique jewelry since there is very little modern jewelry made—garnets and emeralds, earrings, rings, and bracelets. A third sells photographic supplies and cameras, mostly German cameras that have come back from the war. A fourth carries secondhand clothes and shoes. There are shops where the semi-precious stones from the Ural mountains are sold, the beryls, topazes, aquamarines.

Outside of these shops there is another kind of trading. If you come out of a camera shop, two or three rather furtive men will approach you, and each one carries a package, and in the package is a camera, a Contax, or Leica, or Rolleiflex. These men will give you a glimpse of the camera and tell you the price. The same thing happens outside jewelry shops. There is a man with a squib of newspaper. He opens it quickly, shows you a diamond ring, and mentions a price. What he is doing is probably illegal. The prices asked by these outside salesmen are, if anything, a little higher than the prices in the commercial shops.

There is always a great crowd in these shops, people who are not there to buy, but to watch others buy. If you look at an article, you are immediately overwhelmed by people who want to see, and want to see whether you will buy. It is a kind of theater to them, we think.

We went back to our green bedroom with its insane mural, and we were conscious of being depressed. We couldn't figure out exactly why, and then it came to us: there is very little laughter in the streets, and rarely any smiles. People walk, or rather scuttle along, with their heads down, and they don't smile. Perhaps it is that they work too hard, that they have to walk too far to get to the work they do. There seems to be a great seriousness in the streets, and perhaps this was always so, we don't know.

We had dinner with Sweet Joe Newman, and with John Walker of *Time*, and we asked them if they had noticed the lack of laughter. And they said they had. And they said that after a while the lack of laughter gets under your skin and you become serious yourself. They showed us a copy of the Soviet humorous magazine, called *Krokodil*, and translated some of the jokes. But they were not laughing jokes, they were sharp jokes, critical jokes. They were not for laughter, there was no gaiety in them. Sweet Joe said he had heard that outside of Moscow it was different, and this we subsequently discovered to be true. There is laughter in the country, in the Ukraine, and on the steppes, and in Georgia, but Moscow is a very serious city.

One of the correspondents was having trouble with his car and his chauffeur. He needed a car, and it is well for a foreigner in Moscow to have a Russian chauffeur. And it did not do him any good to change chauffeurs. His problem was this: his chauffeur drove him very well, but when he was not driving him, he was driving anyone else who was willing to pay a hundred roubles for a short trip. His chauffeur was getting very rich, and the car was taking a beating. There was nothing to do about it, for if he complained his chauffeur was likely to sulk a little bit, and when his chauffeur sulked, something went wrong with his car, and when something went wrong with his car, it was laid up in a garage for two or three weeks. It was better to keep his chauffeur happy if he wanted to be driven in his own car at all. He had tried getting other chauffeurs, but always the same thing happened.

In some cases the chauffeur problem becomes a little ridiculous. Ed Gilmore's chauffeur has a chauffeur of his own who drives him to work.

We wondered if these stories could be entirely true, and we were only finally convinced one day when a man rented us a whole bus. We had to get in from the airport quickly, and we had no choice but a bus. The trip cost us four hundred roubles. It was rather grand riding in from the airport, the two of us, in a bus made to seat thirty people.

It is possible that the chauffeurs of Moscow are very rich and happy people, but they are necessary, since it is difficult for a foreigner to get a driver's license. One correspondent took his examination for a license, but he failed on the question, "What does not belong on an automobile?" He could think of many things that did not belong on an automobile and finally picked one, but he was wrong. The proper answer was "mud."

That evening we saw the American picture *Rhapsody in Blue* at the Embassy. We had seen it before, but this version of it was much more amusing, because the reels got mixed up, and the picture opened with everybody dead; gradually they came to life, until at the end of the picture George Gershwin was a little boy. We liked it much better this way.

Capa constantly used the window of our hotel as a place from which to photograph people in the street. And he lurked behind the curtains with a long lens on his camera, taking portraits of people walking through the rain, and of people shopping at the little place across the street. And he and the man in the repair shop across the street continued their duel of snapping at each other with their cameras.

Neither of us had heard from home for a long time. Letters did not come through, and we decided we would try to telephone New York. This was very difficult, and we finally gave it up. One can telephone New York only if money is deposited to the Russian account in New York, in dollars. This would require that we telegraph someone in New York, say exactly the time we wanted to telephone, and exactly how long we wanted to talk. The cost of this would be computed and the dollars deposited in New York, at which time our telephone call could be put in from Moscow. But since this would take about a week or ten days to accomplish, we decided the simplest thing was just to continue to write letters, and to hope eventually to receive some.

When letters finally did begin to arrive, we found that airmail from New York to Moscow takes from ten days to three weeks. We do not know why it takes so long, for New York to Stockholm is two days, and the rest of the time is from Stockholm to Moscow. This delay of delivery adds to the foreigner's sense of being cut off, of being all alone.

We had begun to brood a little bit, for we had been a week in Moscow and our permits to leave the city had not come through. We thought we might spend the summer waiting for them when suddenly they materialized, and our plan was under way.

Sweet Joe Newman gave us a cocktail party that lasted far into the night. Our plan was to leave at dawn for Kiev. The cocktail party picked up our spirits, and the spirits of about fifty other people.

We found that there was one difficulty about traveling in the Soviet
Union. You cannot go from Kiev to Stalingrad, or from Stalingrad to
Stalino. You must come back to Moscow every time and go out again,
for the transportation system operates out of Moscow like the spokes
of a wheel; and the roads are so torn up by the war that to travel
laterally is nearly impossible, besides taking more time than we
thought we had. Another difficulty is that since the planes fly only
in the daytime, and there is no night flying, they leave very early in
the morning. And after Sweet Joe's cocktail party, it seemed very
early to us indeed.

Chapter 4

SWEET LANA could not go to Kiev with us. Instead, Mr. Chmarsky went as interpreter and guide. A nice little man, and a student of American literature. His knowledge of English was highly academic. Capa, as usual, took liberties with his name and played tricks with it.

Chmarsky again and again would correct him, saying, "Mr. Capa, it is Chmarsky, not Chumarsky."

Whereupon Capa would say, "All right, Mr. Chomarsky."

"No, Mr. Capa, Chmarsky, not Chumarsky, not Chomarsky!"

That went on and on, and Capa joyfully found new pronunciations of his name everyday. Chmarsky was always a little worried by our speech, the curious kind of American double talk that we used. For a while he tried to track it down, and eventually just gave up and did not listen. On certain occasions his plans for us did not materialize— cars ordered did not meet us, planes we met did not fly. And we came to call him the Kremlin gremlin.

"What are gremlins?" he asked.

We explained in detail the origin of gremlins, how they started in the R.A.F., and what their habits were. How they stopped engines in mid-air, iced wings, fouled gas lines.

He listened with great intent, and at the end he held up one finger and said, "In the Soviet Union we do not believe in ghosts." Perhaps we played too hard with him. We hope we did not hurt his feelings.

There is one thing that you can never tell, and that is what time a plane is going to fly. It is impossible to know in advance. But one thing you can know is that it will leave some time early in the morning. Another thing you can be sure of is that you must be at the airfield long before it does fly. Any time you are to take a trip, you must arrive at the airfield in the chilly dark before the dawn, and sit and drink tea for several hours before the plane leaves. At three o'clock in the morning the bell in our room rang, and we were not happy about getting up, for we had been to Sweet Joe's cocktail party, and what we needed was about twelve hours' sleep, and we had had about one hour. We piled the equipment into the back of the car and drove through the deserted streets of Moscow into the country.

We now observed something that was to happen again and again. Drivers in the Soviet Union speed their cars, and then take them out of gear and let them coast. They take advantage of all hills to disengage their gears and coast. We were told that this saved gasoline, and that it is a part of the training of every driver. He is assigned gasoline which is computed to cover a certain distance, and he must make it cover that distance. Consequently he uses every possible trick he can to make his gasoline last. It is just another part of the huge bookkeeping system which is the Soviet Union. It compares with the bookkeeping in the restaurants. The wear and tear on clutch and gear is not taken into consideration, and the saving of gasoline must be very small indeed. To us the practice was rather nerve-racking. The car speeds up to about sixty miles an hour, and then suddenly the clutch is disengaged, and it coasts until it is moving at a crawl. Then it jumps up to sixty miles an hour and coasts again.

In the pre-dawn the Moscow airport was crowded with people, for since all planes leave early in the morning, the passengers begin to collect at the airport shortly after midnight. And they are dressed in all kinds of costumes. Some wear the furs which will protect them from the arctic climate of the White Sea or of northern Siberia; others are in the light clothing which is sufficient for the subtropical regions around the Black Sea. Six hours by air from Moscow you can find almost any climate available in the world.

Being the guests of Voks, we walked through the public waiting-room and into a side room where there was a dining table, some couches, and comfortable chairs. And there, under the stern eye of a painted Stalin, we drank strong tea until our plane was called.

In the large oil portrait of Stalin on the wall, he was dressed in military uniform and wearing all his decorations, and they are very many. At his throat the Gold Star, which is the highest decoration of Soviet Socialist Labor. On his left breast, highest up, the most coveted award of all, the Gold Star of a Hero of the Soviet Union, which corresponds to our Congressional Medal of Honor. Below that, a row of campaign medals, which indicate what actions he has been in. And on his right breast, a number of gold and red enamel stars. Instead of theater ribbons such as our troops wear, a medal is issued for each great engagement of the Soviet Army: Stalingrad, Moscow, Rostov, and so forth, and Stalin wears them all. As marshal of the Soviet armies he directed them all.

Here we may as well discuss something which bothers most Americans. Nothing in the Soviet Union goes on outside the vision of the plaster, bronze, painted, or embroidered eye of Stalin. His portrait hangs not only in every museum, but in every room of every museum. His statue marches in front of all public buildings. His bust is in front of all airports, railroad stations, bus stations. His bust is also in all schoolrooms, and his portrait is often directly behind his bust. In parks he sits on a plaster bench, discussing problems with Lenin. His

picture in needlework is undertaken by the students of schools. The stores sell millions and millions of his face, and every house has at least one picture of him. Surely the painting and modeling, the casting, the forging, and the embroidering of Stalin must be one of the great industries of the Soviet Union. He is everywhere, he sees everything.

To Americans, with their fear and hatred of power invested in one man, and of perpetuation of power, this is a frightening thing and a distasteful one. At public celebrations the pictures of Stalin outgrow every bound of reason. They may be eight stories high and fifty feet wide. Every public building carries monster portraits of him.

We spoke of this to a number of Russians and had several answers. One was that the Russian people had been used to pictures of the czar and the czar's family, and when the czar was removed they needed something to substitute for him. Another was that the icon is a Russian habit of mind, and this was a kind of an icon. A third, that the Russians love Stalin so much that they want him ever present. A fourth, that Stalin himself does not like this and has asked that it be discontinued. But it seemed to us that Stalin's dislike for anything else causes its removal, but this is on the increase. Whatever the reason is, one spends no moment except under the smiling, or pensive, or stern eye of Stalin. It is one of those things an American is incapable of understanding emotionally. There are other pictures and other statues too. And one can tell approximately what the succession is by the size of the photographs and portraits of other leaders in relation to Stalin. Thus in 1936, the second largest picture to Stalin's was of Voroshilov, and now the second largest picture is invariably Molotov.

After four glasses of strong tea our plane was called, and we moved our pile of luggage up to it. Again it was an old brown C-47. People moved their bundles into the plane and piled them in the aisles. Everyone had brought food, loaves of black bread, and apples, and sausage and cheese, and smoked bacon. They always carry food, and we discovered that this was a very good idea. With a loaf of black rye bread in your bag you will not be hungry for two days if anything goes wrong. As usual, the air system did not work, and as soon as the doors were closed the plane became stuffy. There was a puzzling yeasty odor in the plane which I could not identify for a long time. But finally I discovered what it was. It is the odor of black rye bread on people's breaths. And after a while, when you eat the bread yourself, you grow used to it, and do not smell it at all.

Capa had provided books for the trip, and at that time I did not know how he got them. But it came out later that Capa is a thief of books. He calls it borrowing. Casually he puts books in his pocket, and if he is caught at it, he says, "I will return it, I am just borrowing it, I just want to read it." The book rarely gets returned.

He reached his high point with Ed Gilmore. Among the Moscow correspondents books are very precious, and the arrival of a shipment of detective stories or modern novels is an occasion for rejoicing and a time of happiness. It happened that Ed Gilmore had just received a new Ellery Queen. He was five chapters into it when we visited him, and naturally he laid his book aside to talk to us. When we had left he looked for his book and it was gone—Capa had borrowed it. If Capa had borrowed or stolen Ed's lovely wife, Tamara, Ed might have been more deeply shocked, but he could not have been angrier. And to this day I do not think he knows how the Ellery Queen came out. For some time Capa, who had heard rumors of the Gilmore wrath, showed a certain reluctance about seeing him again. Among Moscow correspondents, particularly in the winter, a code of honor has grown up, rather like the code which developed in the West concerning horses, and it is nearly a matter for lynching to steal a man's book. But Capa never learned and he never reformed. Right to the end of his Russian stay he stole books. He also steals women and cigarettes, but this can be more easily forgiven.

We tried to read a little on the plane, and promptly went to sleep. And when we were awakened, we were over the flat grainlands of the Ukraine, as flat as our Middle West, and almost as fruitful. The huge bread basket of Europe, the coveted land for centuries, the endless fields lay below us, yellow with wheat and rye, some of it already harvested, and some of it being harvested. There was no hill, no eminence of any kind. The flat stretched away to a round unbroken horizon. And streams and rivers snaked and twisted across the plain.

Near the villages there were the zigzags of trenches, and the scoops of shell holes where the fighting had taken place. There were roofless houses, and the black patches of burned buildings.

We seemed to fly endlessly over this flat plain. But at last we came to the Dnieper, and saw Kiev, on its cliff above the river, the only eminence for many miles around. We flew over the broken city and landed on the outskirts.

Everyone had told us it would be different once we got outside of Moscow, that the sternness and the tenseness would not exist. And this was true. On the airfield we were met by a number of Ukrainians from the local Voks. They were laughing people. They were more gay and more relaxed than the men we had met in Moscow. There was an openness and a heartiness about them. They were big men, nearly all blond, with gray eyes. They had a car ready to drive us into Kiev.

It must at one time have been a beautiful city. It is much older than Moscow. It is the mother of Russian cities. Seated on its hill beside the Dnieper, it spreads down into the plain. Its monasteries and fortresses and churches date from the eleventh century. It was once a favorite resort of the czars, and they had their vacation palaces here. Its public buildings were known all over Russia. It was a center of religion. And now it is a semi-ruin. Here the Germans showed what they could do. Every public building, every library, every theater, even the permanent circus, destroyed, not with gunfire, not through fighting, but with fire and dynamite. Its university is burned and tumbled, its schools in ruins. This was not fighting, this was the crazy destruction of every cultural facility the city had, and nearly every beautiful building that had been put up during a thousand years. Here German culture did its work. And one of the few justices in the world is that German prisoners are helping to clean up the mess they made.

Our Ukrainian guide was Alexis Poltarazki, a large man, who limped a little from a wound received at Stalingrad. He is a Ukrainian writer, with a fine command of English, and a great sense of humor, a man of warmth and friendliness.

On the way to our hotel we noticed, as everyone does, that the Ukrainian girls are very pretty, mostly blond, with fine womanly figures.

They have flair, they walk with a swinging stride, and they smile easily. While they were not better dressed than the women of Moscow, they seemed to carry their clothes better.

Although Kiev is greatly destroyed while Moscow is not, the people in Kiev did not seem to have the dead weariness of the Moscow people. They did not slouch when they walked, their shoulders were back, and they laughed in the streets. Of course this might be local, for the Ukrainians are not like the Russian; they are a separate species of Slav. And while most Ukrainians can speak and read Russian, their own language is a language apart and separate, nearer to the Southern Slavic languages than to Russian. Many Ukrainian words, particularly farm words, are the same as in Hungarian, and many of their words are duplicated in Czech rather than in Russian.

At the Intourist Hotel our Ukrainian hosts gave us a magnificent lunch. There were fresh ripe tomatoes and cucumbers, there were little pickled fishes, there were bowls of caviar, and there was vodka. We had small fried fishes from the Dnieper, and beefsteaks, beautifully cooked with Ukrainian herbs. There was wine from Georgia, and Ukrainian sausages which are delicious.

There was a fine feeling of friendship in these men. During lunch, they told us, with a great deal of amusement, about an American who had been in Kiev with an international committee. This man, they said, went home to America and wrote a series of articles and a book about the Ukraine. But the thing that amused them was that he did not know much about the Ukraine. They told us: he had rarely been out of his hotel room, he hadn't seen anything, he might as well have written his book without having left America. These Ukrainians said that this book was full of inaccuracies, and they had a letter from his chief agreeing that this was so. They were mostly worried that this man, who was known now as an authority on the Ukraine, might be believed in America. And they told with laughter how one night, near the hotel where he was eating, a car backfired in the street and he leaped back, crying, "The Bolsheviks are shooting prisoners!" And, said the Ukrainians, he probably still believes it.

In the afternoon we walked through the beautiful park which edges

the cliff above the Dnieper. There were huge trees here, and already
the music shells burned by the Germans had been replaced and a
new stadium put up. And among the trees were the graves of the defenders of the city, green mounds with red flowers planted on the tops
of them. There were little theaters, and many benches to sit on.

Far below, the river winds beside the cliff, and across the river is a
sandy beach, where people lie in the sun and swim in the river. Far off
there is the flat land with the ruins of the town which was completely
destroyed in the fighting for the city, wreckage and blackness, and bits
of standing wall. Here is the place where the Red Army came back to
the city and relieved it from its German occupation.

There was an orchestra playing in the park, and many children sat on the benches and listened. There were sailboats on the river, and little steamboats, and people were swimming.

We walked over a footbridge that goes over a road, and below there was a bus stop. And in front of a bus was the finest woman fight we have seen in a long time. The Russian rules for queueing are inexorable. Everyone must stand in line to get into a streetcar or a bus. There are exceptions to this rule: pregnant women, women with children, the very old, and the crippled do not have to stand in line. They go in first. But everyone else must queue up. It seems that below us a man had gone ahead in the queue, and an angry woman was tearing at him to get him back where he belonged. With a certain obstinacy he stayed in his place and got into the bus, whereupon she dived in after him, pulled him out, and forced him back to his place in the queue. She was furious, and the other members of the queue cheered her as she pulled the man out and stood him back in his place. It was one of the few examples of violence we saw during our whole trip. Mostly the people have incredible patience with one another.

We were very tired at dinner that night for we had had very little sleep, and our passion for vodka had been waning until it disappeared entirely.

Our hosts had many questions they wanted to ask us. They wanted to know about America, about its size, about its crops, about its politics. And we began to realize that America is a very difficult country to explain. There are many things about it we don't understand ourselves. We explained our theory of government, where every part has another part to check it. We tried to explain our fear of dictatorship, our fear of leaders with too much power, so that our government is designed to keep anyone from getting too much power or, having got it, from keeping it. We agreed that this makes our country function more slowly, but that it certainly makes it function more surely.

They asked about wages, and standards of living, and the kind of life a workingman lives, and did the average man have an automobile, and what kind of house does he live in, and did his children go to school, and what kind of school.

And then they spoke of the atom bomb, and they said they were not afraid of it. Stalin has said that it would never be used in warfare, and they trust that statement implicitly. One man said that even if it were used it could only destroy towns. "Our towns are destroyed already," he said. "What more can it do? And if we were invaded we would defend ourselves, just as we did with the Germans. We will defend ourselves in the snow, and in the forests, and in the fields."

They spoke anxiously about war, they have had so much of it. They asked, "Will the United States attack us? Will we have to defend our country again in one lifetime?"

We said, "No, we do not think the United States will attack. We don't know, no one tells us these things, but we do not think that our people want to attack anyone." And we asked them where they got the idea that we might attack Russia.

· 57 ·

Well, they said, they get it from our newspapers. Certain of our newspapers speak constantly of attacking Russia. And some of them speak of what they call preventive war. And, they said, that as far as they are concerned, preventive war is just like any other war. We told them that we do not believe that those newspapers they mention, and those columnists who speak only of war, are true representatives of the American people. We do not believe the American people want to go to war with anyone.

The old, old thing came up, that always comes up: "Then why does your government not control these newspapers and these men who talk war?" And we had to explain again, as we had many times before, that we do not believe in controlling our press, that we think the truth usually wins, and that control simply drives bad things underground. In our country we prefer that these people talk themselves to death in public, and write themselves to death, rather than bottle them up to slip their poison secretly through the dark.

They have a great deal of misinformation about America, for they have their yellow journalists too. They have their correspondents who write with little knowledge, and they have their fiery typewriter soldiers.

Our eyes were heavy and we were dying on the vine, and at last we had to excuse ourselves and go to bed. I had been walking a great deal, and my recently broken knee was giving me hell. The muscles at the back were as tight as ropes. I could barely stand on it. As much as I hated to, I had to lie down for a while.

We talked for a while before we went to sleep. If a war should break out between Russia and the United States, these people would believe that we are the villains. Whether it is through propaganda, or fear, or for whatever reason, they would blame us if there is a war. They speak only in terms of invasion of their country, and they are afraid of it, because they have had it. Again and again they ask, "Will the United States invade us? Will you send your bombers to destroy us more?" And never do they say, "We will send our bombers," or "We will invade."

I awakened early and got up to complete my notes. My leg was so stiff that I could barely walk on it at all. I sat down at our desk, which

overlooked the street, and watched the people going by. And there was a girl policeman directing traffic in the street, and she wore boots, and a blue skirt and a white tunic with a military belt, and a cocky little beret on her head. Her nightstick was painted black and white, and she directed traffic with a military snap. She was very pretty.

I watched the women walking in the street, and they moved like dancers. They are light on their feet and they have a beautiful carriage. And many of them are very handsome. Much of the destruction that has been brought on this people is because their land is rich and productive and many conquerors have coveted it. If the United States were completely destroyed from New York to Kansas, we would have about the area of destruction the Ukraine has. If six million people were killed, not counting soldiers, fifteen per cent of the population, you would have an idea of the casualties of the Ukraine. Counting soldiers, there would be many more, but six million out of forty-five million civilians have been killed. There are mines which will never be opened because the Germans threw thousands of bodies down into the shafts. Every piece of machinery in the Ukraine has been destroyed or removed, so that now, until more can be made, everything must be done by hand. Every stone and brick of the ruined city must be lifted and

carried with the hands, for there are no bulldozers. And while they are rebuilding, the Ukrainians must produce food, for theirs is the great granary of the nation.

They say that in harvest time there are no holidays, and now it is harvest time. On the farms there are no Sundays, there are no days off.

The work ahead of them is overwhelming. The buildings to be replaced must be torn down first. An amount of labor that the bulldozer could do in a few days takes weeks by hand, but they have no bulldozers yet. Everything must be replaced. And it must be done quickly.

We went through the blasted and destroyed center of the city, past the corner where the German sadists were hanged after the war. At the museum were the plans of the new city. More and more we were realizing how much the Russian people live on hope, hope that tomorrow will be better than today. Here in white plaster was a model of the new city. A grandiose, a fabulous city to be built of white marble, the

lines classical, the buildings huge, columns, and domes, and arches, and giant memorials, all in white marble. The plaster model of the city-to-be covered a large section of one room. And the director of the museum pointed out the various buildings. This was to be the Palace of the Soviets, this the museum—always the museum.

Capa says that the museum is the church of the Russians. They seem to want great buildings and ornate structures. They like lavishness. In Moscow, where there is no reason for skyscrapers because the space is almost unlimited and the land level, they are nevertheless planning skyscrapers, almost in the New York manner, without the New York need. With a slow, antlike energy, they will build these cities. But now the people come through the wreckage, through the destroyed and tumbled buildings, people, men, women, and even children, they come to the museum to look at the plaster cities of the future. In Russia it is always the future that is thought of. It is the crops next year, it is the comfort that will come in ten years, it is the clothes that will be made very soon. If ever a people took its energy from hope, it is the Russian people.

We went from this little plaster city, so new that it has not even been built yet, to the ancient monastery on the cliff. Once it had been the center of the Russian Church, and one of the oldest religious structures in Russia. It had been magnificent, its buildings and its paintings dating from the twelfth century. But then the Germans came, and this monastery had been the repository of many of the treasures of the world. And when the Germans had stolen most of the treasures, they destroyed the buildings with shell fire to conceal their theft when they left the city. And now it is a great pile of fallen stones and tumbled domes, with little bits of wall paintings showing through. And it will not be rebuilt, it couldn't be. It took centuries to build, and now it is gone. The weeds that follow destruction have sprung up in the courtyards. In a half-ruined chapel, in front of the destroyed altar, we saw a ragged figure of a woman lying prostrate on the ground. And through an open gate, where once only the czar or his family could pass, a wild-eyed, half-crazed woman walked, crossing herself monotonously and mumbling.

One part of the monastery still stands, a chapel where for centuries only the czar and the nobles were permitted to worship. It is heavily painted, a dark and gloomy place. And each worshiper had his little carven stall, for this was the place of a very select religion, and it was easy to see in one's mind the old nobility, sitting in gloomy concentration on a noble future and on a noble heaven, a heaven which was probably as gloomy as this church, with its incense-blackened ceiling and its glimmering gold leaf. And Capa said, "All good churches are gloomy. That's what makes them good."

There is an older church in Kiev, one of the oldest in the world, that was built by Jaroslav the Wise in 1034, and it is still standing, probably because there was nothing of value to steal in it, and so the Germans let it alone. But it, again, is a high, gloomy place.

In a little side chapel, in a small houselike sarcophagus of marble, is the body of Jaroslav the Wise. It is the tradition that Jaroslav had an accident in battle and broke his leg. And his body lay for over a thousand years in the little houselike sarcophagus, and recently the casket was opened, and it was found that the skeleton in the casket had indeed had a broken leg, and everyone was happy, for this was really Jaroslav the Wise. The gloom of the churches threw a gloom upon us.

At luncheon Mr. Poltarazki spoke of the acts of the Germans in the war, of the thousands of people killed. War is no new thing to Kiev. Starting with the raids of the savages from Tartary, it has been a place of war for thousands of years. But no savage tribe, no invader, ever was responsible for the stupid, calculated cruelties of the Germans. They raged through the country like frantic, cruel children. And now the lines of prisoners in their German army uniforms march through the streets, to work at cleaning up the destruction they caused. And the Ukrainian people do not look at them. They turn away when the columns march through the streets. They look through these prisoners and over them and do not see them. And perhaps this is the worst punishment that could possibly be inflicted on them.

In the evening we went to the theater to see the play *Storm*, a nineteenth-century drama enacted in the nineteenth-century manner. The scenery was quaint and old-fashioned, and the acting was old-fashioned too. It is odd that it should be played, but it is a Ukrainian play, and they love their own. The leading lady was very beautiful. She looked a little like Katharine Cornell, and she had great authority on the stage. The story was of a young wife, under the thumb of a powerful Russian mother-in-law, who fell in love with a poet. She went into the garden to meet him while she was still married to another man. All we could see that she did in the garden was to talk a great deal, and once to let the poet kiss the tips of her fingers, but it was crime enough, so that finally she confessed her sin in a church and threw herself into the Volga and was drowned. It seemed to us almost too much punishment for having the tips of her fingers kissed. The play had its secondary plot too. The chambermaid comically paralleled her mistress's tragedy. Her lover, instead of being a poet, was a country bumpkin. It was a traditional play all right, and the audience loved it. It took half an hour to change the sets, so that it was well after midnight when the leading lady finally dropped herself into the river. It seemed odd to us that the people in the audience, who had known real tragedy, tragedy of invasion, and death, and desolation, could be so moved over the fate of the lady who got her fingers kissed in the garden.

The next morning it rained, and Capa feels that rain is a persecution of himself by the sky, for when it rains he cannot take pictures. He denounced the weather in dialect and in four or five languages. Capa is a worrier about films. There is not enough light, or there is too much light. The developing is wrong, the printing is wrong, the cameras are broken. He worries all the time. But when it rains, that is a personal insult addressed to him by the deity. He paced the room until I wanted to kill him, and finally went to have his hair cut, a real Ukrainian pot haircut.

That evening we went to the circus. Every Russian town of any size has its permanent circus in a permanent building. But, of course, the Germans had burned the Kiev circus, so that so far it is under canvas, but still it is one of the most popular places in the city. We had good seats, and Capa had permission to photograph, so he was comparatively happy. It was not unlike our circuses, a single ring and tiers of seats.

It started with acrobats. We noticed that when the acrobats worked on high trapezes there was a hook and line in their belts, so that if they fell they would not be killed or injured, for, as our Russian host said, it would be ridiculous to hurt a man just to give the audience a thrill.

The pretty ladies and the gallant men did their spins and turns on the high wires and on the trapezes. Then there were dog acts and tumblers, and trained tigers, panthers, and leopards performed in a steel cage that was let down over the ring. The audience loved it, and all the while a circus band played away at the universal circus music which does not change.

Best of all were the clowns. When they first came in, we noticed that the audience was looking at us, and we soon found out why. Their clowns are invariably Americans now. One is a rich Chicago woman,

and the Russian idea of what a rich Chicago woman looks like is wonderful. The audience was waiting to see whether we would be annoyed at this satire, but it was really very funny. And just as some of our clowns wear long black beards, and carry bombs, and are labeled Russians, so the Russian clowns labeled themselves Americans. The audience laughed with delight. The rich woman from Chicago wore red silk stockings and high-heeled shoes covered with rhinestones, a ridiculous turban-like hat, and an evening dress covered with bangles, which looked like a long, misshapen nightgown, and she teetered across the ring, her artificial stomach wobbling, while her husband postured and danced about, for he was a rich Chicago millionaire. The jokes must have been very funny, although we couldn't understand them, for the audience howled with laughter. And they seemed to be greatly relieved that we did not resent the clowns. The clowns finished off rich Chicago

Americans and then went into a violent and very funny version of the death of Desdemona, where Desdemona was not strangled, but was almost beaten to death with a rubber knife.

It was a good circus. The children, sitting in the front seats, were lost in circus dreams the way children are. The company is permanent, it does not move about, and the circus goes on all year long, with the exception of a little while in the summer.

The rain had stopped, so after the circus we went to a Kiev night club, called the Riviera. It is on the cliff above the river, with an open-air dance floor surrounded by tables, and the whole overlooking the river, which flows away across the plain. The food was excellent. Good shashlik, and the inevitable caviar, and wines from Georgia. And to our great relief the orchestra played Russian, and Ukrainian, and Georgian music rather than bad American jazz. And they played very well.

At our table we were joined by Alexander Korneichuk, the ranking Ukrainian playwright, a man of great charm and humor. He and Poltarazki began to tell old Ukrainian sayings, and the Ukrainians are famous for them. Almost our favorite is "The best bird is the sausage." And then Korneichuk told a saying which I had always believed was native to California. It is the description by a heavy eater concerning the nature of the turkey, in which he says, "The turkey is a very unsatisfactory bird, it is a little too much for one, and not quite enough for two." Apparently the Ukrainians have been saying it for hundreds of years, and I thought it was invented in my home town.

They taught us a toast in Ukrainian which we like: "Let us drink to make people at home happy." And they toasted again to peace, always to peace. Both of these men had been soldiers, and both of them had been wounded, and they drank to peace.

Then Korneichuk, who had been to America once, said rather sadly that he had been to Hyde Park, and there he had seen pictures of Roosevelt and Churchill, of Roosevelt and De Gaulle, but there he had seen no picture of Roosevelt and Stalin. And he said they had been together, and they had worked together, and why in Hyde Park had they removed the photographs of them?

The music grew faster and faster, and more and more people came to dance, and colored lights were thrown on the floor, and far below the river reflected the lights of the city.

Two Russian soldiers danced a wild dance together, a dance of stamping boots and swinging hands, a dance of the war fronts. Their heads were shaven, and their boots were highly polished. They danced madly, and red and green and blue lights flashed over the dance floor.

The orchestra played a wild Georgian melody, and from one of the tables a girl got up and danced all by herself. And she danced beautifully, and no one else was on the floor while she was dancing. Gradually a few people began clapping in rhythm to the music, and then more, until there was a soft beat of clapping hands to her dancing. And when the music stopped she went back to her table, and there was no applause. There had been no exhibitionism in it, she had simply wanted to dance.

With the soft music, the lights, and the peaceful river below, our friends again began to speak of the war, as though it were a haunting thing they could never get very far from. They spoke of the dreadful cold, before Stalingrad, where they had lain in the snow and had not known how it would come out. They spoke of horrible things they could not forget. Of how a man had warmed his hands in the blood of a newly dead friend, so that he could pull the trigger of his gun.

A poet came to our table, and he said, "I have a mother-in-law, and when the war came to Rostov she would not leave because she had an oriental rug that she treasured." And he said, "We retreated, and we fought the whole war, and we came back to Rostov. I went to her place, and she was still there, and so was the oriental rug."

"You know," he said, "when an army moves into a city there are many accidents, and many people are killed by mistake. And when I went to my mother-in-law's, and she came to the door, the thought flashed through my mind, why shouldn't she have an accident now? Why shouldn't my gun go off by mistake?" And he finished, "It didn't happen. And I have wondered why ever since."

Capa had set up his cameras on the roof of the little pavilion; he was photographing the dancers and he was happy. The orchestra played a sad song from one of Korneichuk's plays. It is the song of the sailors of the Baltic. When they had to retreat, they sank their ships, and this is a song of sadness and a requiem to their sunken ships.

Chapter 5

IN THE morning we looked up the date, and it was August 9. We had been just nine days in the Soviet Union. But so many had been our impressions and sights that it seemed like much more to us.

Capa awakens in the morning slowly and delicately, as a butterfly comes out of its chrysalis. For an hour after he awakens, he sits in stunned and experimental silence, neither awake nor asleep. My problem was to keep him from taking a book or a newspaper into the bathroom, for then he would be there for at least an hour. I began to prepare three intellectual questions for him every morning, questions in sociology, in history, in philosophy, in biology, questions designed to shock his mind into awareness that the day was come.

On the first day of my experiment I asked him the following questions: What Greek tragedian took part in the battle of Salamis? How many legs has an insect? And, finally, what was the name of the pope who sponsored and collected the Gregorian chants? Capa sprang from his bed with a look of pain on his face, sat staring at the window for a moment, and then rushed to the bathroom with a copy of a Russian newspaper which he could not read. And he was gone for an hour and a half.

Every morning, for two or three weeks, I prepared the questions for him, and he never answered one of them, but he got to muttering to himself most of the day, and he complained bitterly that he could not sleep in anticipation of the questions in the morning. However, there was no evidence, except his word, that he could not sleep. He claimed that the horror created in his mind by my questions had set him back intellectually forty years, or, roughly, to minus ten years.

Capa had stolen books in Moscow to bring along, three detective stories, the *Notebooks of Maxim Gorki, Vanity Fair,* and a report of the United States Department of Agriculture for 1927. All these books were returned to someone before we left Russia, but I am quite sure they were not returned to their owners.

On this day, August 9, we went to the farm village called Shevchenko. We called it in the future Shevchenko I, since another farm village we subsequently visited was also called Shevchenko, named after a much beloved Ukrainian national poet.

For a few miles our road was paved, and then we turned to the right and went along a dirt road, cut and torn to pieces. We went through pine forests and over a plain where vicious fighting had taken place. Everywhere there was evidence of it. The pine trees were ripped and ragged from machine-gun fire. There were trenches and machine-gun placements, and even the roads were cut and jagged by the tracks of tanks and pitted by shell fire. Here and there lay rusting bits of military equipment, burned-out tanks, and wrecked trucks. This country had been defended and lost, and the counterattack had fought slowly over every inch of territory.

Shevchenko I has never been one of the best farms because its land is not of the first quality, but before the war it was a fairly prosperous village, a village of three hundred and sixty-two houses, in other words, of three hundred and sixty-two families. It was a going concern.

After the Germans passed over it, there were eight houses left, and even those had the roofs burned off them. The people were scattered and many of them killed, and the men were in the forest, fighting as partisans, and God knows how the children took care of themselves.

But after the war the people came back to their village. New houses were springing up, and since it was harvest time, the houses were built before and after work, and even at night, by the light of lanterns. Men and women worked together to build their little houses. The method was invariable: they built one room and they lived in it until they could build another room. Since it is very cold in the Ukraine in the winter, the houses are built like this: The walls are of squared logs, mortised at the corners. To these logs heavy laths are nailed, and then a thick plaster is applied inside and out to turn the cold away.

There is a hall, which is a combination storeroom and entrance. From there one goes into the kitchen, a white plaster room, with a brick oven and hearth for the cooking. That fireplace and oven is raised about four feet above the floor, and in this the bread is baked, the flat brown cakes of Ukrainian bread, which are very good.

Next to this is the communal room, with its dining table and its decorations on the wall. This is the parlor, and it has the paper flowers, the holy pictures, and the photographs of the dead. And on the walls are the decorations of the soldiers who have come from this family. The walls are white, and there are shutters on the windows to be closed against the winter cold.

Opening off this room are one or two bedrooms, depending on the size of the family. And since these people lost everything, the bedding is whatever they can get now. Pieces of rug, and sheepskin, anything to keep them warm. The Ukrainians are a clean people, and their houses are immaculate.

Part of our misinformation had been that on the collective farms the people lived in barracks. This was not true. Each family had its house and a garden and an orchard where there were flowers, and where there were large vegetable patches and beehives. And most of these gardens were about an acre in extent. Since the Germans had destroyed all the fruit trees, new trees were being planted, apple, and pear, and cherry.

We went first to the new town council house, where we were greeted by the manager, who had lost an arm in the fighting, and his book-keeper, who had just been demobilized from the Army and was still in his uniform, and three elderly men of the farm council. We told them that we knew how busy they were during the harvest, but that we wanted to see part of the harvest ourselves.

They told us how it had been before, and how it was now. When the Germans came, this farm had had seven hundred horned cattle, and now there were only two hundred animals of all kinds. They had had

two large gasoline engines, two trucks, three tractors, and two thresh-ing machines. And now they had one small gasoline engine and one small threshing machine. They had no local tractor. In the plowing they drew one from the tractor station near by. They had had forty horses, and now they had four.

The town had lost fifty men of fighting age and fifty others, of all ages, and there were great numbers of crippled and maimed. Some of the children were legless and some had lost eyes. But the town, which needed labor so dreadfully, tried to give every man work to do that he could do. All the cripples who could work at all were put to work, and it gave them a sense of importance and a place in the life of the farm, so that there were few neurotics among the hurt people.

They were not sad people. They were full of laughter, and jokes, and songs.

The farm raised some wheat, and some millet, and some corn. But it was a light, sandy land, and its main crops were cucumbers and potatoes, tomatoes and honey and sunflowers. A great deal of sun-flower-seed oil is used.

We went first to the fields where the women and the children were harvesting cucumbers. They were divided into battalions and were in competition with one another, each group trying to pick the most cucumbers. The lines of women were stretched across the field, laugh-ing and singing and shouting at one another. They were dressed in long skirts and blouses and headcloths, and no one wore shoes, for shoes are still too precious to use in the fields. The children were dressed only in trousers, and their little bodies were turning brown under the summer sun. Along the edges of the field there were piles of picked cucumbers waiting for the trucks.

A little boy named Grischa, who wore an ornamental hat made of marsh grass, ran up to his mother and cried with wonder, "But these Americans are people just like us!"

Capa's cameras caused a sensation. The women shouted at him, and then fixed their kerchiefs, and settled their blouses, the way women do all over the world before they are photographed.

There was one woman, with an engaging face and a great laugh, whom Capa picked out for a portrait. She was the village wit. She said, "I am not only a great worker, I am twice widowed, and many men are afraid of me now." And she shook a cucumber in the lens of Capa's camera.

And Capa said, "Perhaps you'd like to marry me now?"

She rolled back her head and howled with laughter. "Now you, look!" she said. "If God had consulted the cucumber before he made man, there would be less unhappy women in the world." The whole field roared with laughter at Capa.

They were lively, friendly people, and they made us taste the cucumbers and the tomatoes for quality. The cucumber is a very important vegetable. It is salted, and the resulting pickles are used all winter.

And green tomatoes are salted too, and these are the salads for the people when the cold and the snow come. These, together with cabbages and turnips, are the winter vegetables. And although the women laughed and talked, and called to us, they did not stop working, for this is a good harvest, seventy per cent better than last year, the first really good harvest since 1941, and they have great hopes from it.

We moved on to a flowered meadow where there were hundreds of beehives, and a little tent where the beekeeper lived. The air was filled with the soft roar of bees working in the clover of the meadow. And the old bearded beekeeper came walking rapidly toward us, with nets to put over our faces. We put them on and shoved our hands in our pockets. The bees buzzed angrily about us.

The old beekeeper opened his hives and showed us the honey. He had been a beekeeper for thirty years, he said, and he was very proud. For many years he had kept bees without knowing much about bees. But now he was reading and studying. And he had a great treasure, he had six new queens. He said they came from California. And I judged from his description that they were some California variant of the

Italian black. He said he was very happy with his new bees. He said that they would be more frost resistant, and that they would work earlier and later in the season.

Then he took us into his little tent and closed the flaps, and he cut great slices of the good black sour rye bread of the Ukraine, and put honey on it, and gave it to us to eat. The deep hum of the bees came from outside. And later he opened the hives again and brought out handfuls of bees without fear, as most beekeepers do. But he warned us not to uncover ourselves, for the bees do not like strangers.

From there we went to a field where they were threshing wheat. The equipment was pitifully inadequate. There was an old one-cylinder gas engine running an ancient threshing machine, and their blower they turned by hand. And here again we noticed the shortage of men. There were so many more women than men, and of the men who were there so many were crippled. The engineer who operated the gas engine had all the fingers on one hand gone.

Since the land was not very good, the yield in wheat was not high. The grain came pouring out of the threshing machine on to a large canvas. Children were stationed at the edge of the canvas so that any grains which happened to jump off and fall into the dirt could be put back, for every grain was precious. The clouds had been piling up all morning, and now a sprinkle of rain started. The people rushed up with cloths to cover the pile of wheat.

An argument was going on among several of the men, and Poltarazki translated to us softly. It seemed that they were arguing as to who was to invite us to lunch. One man had the larger table, and the wife of another had baked that morning. One man claimed that his house was just finished, and it was new, and he should be the man to be the host. And so they agreed. But this man had very little to eat from. The rest should contribute glasses, and plates, and wooden spoons. And when it was decided that his house would be used, the women of his house hiked up their skirts and trotted for the village.

Since we have come back from Russia, probably the remark we have heard most is "I guess they put on a show for you; I guess they really fixed it up for you. They didn't show you the real thing." The people in this village did put on a show for us. They put on the same kind of show a Kansas farmer would put on for a guest. They did the same thing that our people do, so that Europeans say "The Americans live on chicken."

They really put on a show for us. They came dirty from the fields, and they bathed and put on their best clothes, and the women got out from the trunks headcloths that were clean and fresh. They washed their feet and put on boots, and they put on freshly laundered skirts and blouses. Little girls collected flowers and arranged them in bottles and brought them into the clean parlor. And delegations of children from other houses came in with water glasses, and plates, and spoons. One woman brought a jar of her special pickles, and the vodka bottles from all over the village were contributed. And a man brought a bottle of Georgian champagne, saved for heaven knows what great occasion.

In the kitchen the women put on a show too. The fire roared in the new white oven, and the flat cakes of good rye bread were baking, and

the eggs were frying, and the borscht bubbling. Outside the rain poured down, so we didn't feel bad, for we were not interfering with their work in harvest time, they couldn't have been working with the grain anyway.

In one corner of the parlor, which is the communal room, there was an icon, a Mary and Jesus, framed and gilded, under a canopy of hand-made lace. They must have buried these things when the Germans came, for the icon was old. There was an enlarged tinted photograph of the great-grandparents. This family had lost two sons in the Army, and their pictures were on another wall, in their uniforms, looking very young, and very stern, and very countrified.

A number of men came into the parlor, and they were neatly dressed, and cleaned, and washed, and they had shaved and they had on their boots. In the fields they didn't wear boots.

Little girls came running through the rain, carrying aprons full of small apples and little pears.

The host was about fifty, with high cheekbones, and blond hair, and wide-set blue eyes. His face was weather-beaten. And he wore the tunic and broad leather belt of the partisan fighter. His face was drawn as though somewhere he had received a terrible wound.

At last the meal was ready. Ukrainian borscht, which is a meal in itself, and hard fried eggs with bacon, fresh tomatoes and fresh cucumbers and sliced onions, and the hot flat cakes of sweet rye, and honey, and fruit, and sausages, were all put on the table at once. And then the host filled the glasses with pepper vodka, a vodka in which pepper grains have been soaked so that it has an aromatic taste. And then he called his wife and his two grown daughters-in-law, the widows of his dead sons, to the table. And he handed each of them a glass of vodka.

The mother of the family made the first toast. She said, "May God bring you every good." And we all drank to her. We ate hugely, and it was very good.

Our host proposed a toast that we were beginning to know very well—the toast to peace among the peoples of the world. It is odd that there was rarely a little personal toast. The toasts were usually to larger things than individual futures. We proposed the health of the family and the prosperity of the farm. And a large man at the end of the table stood up and drank to the memory of Franklin D. Roosevelt.

We were beginning to understand the quality of Roosevelt's memory in the world, and the great sense of tragedy at his death. And I remembered a story that I had heard one time. Within a week of the death of Lincoln, the news of his death had penetrated even to the middle of Africa, sometimes on the drums, and sometimes carried by runners. The news traveled that a world tragedy had taken place. And it seems to us that it does not matter what the Roosevelt-haters think or say, it doesn't even matter, actually, what Roosevelt was in the flesh. What does matter is that his name is throughout the world a symbol of wisdom, and kindness, and understanding. In the minds of little people all over the world he has ceased to be a man and has become a principle. And those men who attack him now, and attack his memory, do not hurt his name at all, but simply define themselves as the mean, the greedy, the selfish, and the stupid. Roosevelt's name is far beyond the reach of small minds and dirty hands.

When the meal was over, there came the time we were beginning to expect. The time of questions. But this time it was more interesting to us, because they were the questions of farmers about farmers and about farms. Again it was clear to us that peoples have a curious composite idea of one another. The question "How does a farmer live in America?" is impossible to answer. What kind of farm? And where? And it is difficult for our people to imagine Russia, with every possible climate from arctic to tropic, with many different races and languages.

These farmers did not even speak Russian, they spoke Ukrainian. "How does a farmer live in America?" they asked. And we tried to explain that there are many different kinds of farms in America, as there are in Russia. There are little five-acre farms, with one mule to work them, and there are great co-operative farms that operate like the state farms of Russia, except that the state does not own them. There are farm communities rather like this village, where the social life is somewhat the same, except that the land is not owned communally. One hundred acres of good bottom land in America is worth a thousand acres of poor land. And this they understood very well, because they are farmers themselves. They had just never thought of America that way.

They wanted to hear about American farm machinery, for that is what they need the most. They asked about combines and seed drills, about cotton-pickers and fertilizer spreaders; about the development of new crops, of cold-resistant grains and rust-resistant wheat; about tractors and how much they cost. Could a man running a small farm afford to buy one?

The farmer at the end of the table told us with pride how the Soviet government lends money to farms, and lends money at very low interest to people who want to build houses on their farms. He told how farm information is available under the Soviet government.

We said that the same thing is true in America, and this they had never heard of They had never heard of the farm loans or of the important work that is done by our Department of Agriculture. It was all news to them. As a matter of fact, they seemed to think that they had invented the system themselves.

Across the road a man and woman were working in the rain, raising the timbers for their roof-tree to the top of newly built walls. And on

the road the children were driving the cows in from pasturage to the barns.

The women in their clean headcloths leaned through the kitchen door and listened to the conversation. And the conversation turned to foreign policies. The questions were sharp.

One farmer asked, "What would the American government do if the Soviet government loaned money and military aid to Mexico, with the avowed purpose of preventing the spread of democracy?"

And we thought for a while and we said, "Well, we imagine we would declare war."

And he said, "But you have loaned money to Turkey, which is on our border, with the purpose of preventing the spread of our system. And we have not declared war."

And our host said, "It seems to us that the American people are democratic people. Can you explain to us why the American government has as its friends reactionary governments, the governments of Franco and Trujillo, the military dictatorship of Turkey, and the corrupt monarchy of Greece?"

We could not answer their questions because we didn't know enough, and because we are not in the confidence of our makers of foreign policy. We told them instead what was being asked in America: the questions about the domination of the Balkans by Communist parties; the questions about, and the denunciations of, the use of the veto by the Russians in the United Nations; the questions about the denunciation of America by the Russian press.

These things seemed to balance each other—they knew no more about their foreign policy than we knew about ours. There was no animosity in their questions, only wonder. Finally our host stood up, and he raised his glass, and he said, "Somewhere in all of this there must be an answer, and there must be an answer quickly. Let us drink to the hope that the answer may be found, for the world needs peace, needs peace very badly." And he pointed to the two who were struggling with the heavy beams to build a roof, and he said, "This winter those two will have a house for the first time since 1941. They must have peace, they want their house. They have three small children who have never had a house to live in. There cannot be in the world anyone so wicked as to want to put them back in holes under the ground. But that is where they have been living."

The host opened the champagne and poured a little of the precious fluid into each of our glasses. The table had become very quiet. We raised our glasses, and no one made a toast. We drank the champagne without speaking. After a while we thanked our hosts and drove away through the war-scarred country. And we wondered whether our host was right, whether there really were people in the world who wanted to destroy the new little houses again, and put the children in caves under the ground.

We slept long the next morning, and when we awakened we discussed the day on the farm, and Capa got his exposed films put away. We were invited to lunch at the house of Alexander Korneichuk and his wife, Wanda Wasilewska, a Polish poetess who is known in America. They live in a pleasant house with a large garden behind it. Luncheon was served on the porch, under a great vine that shaded it. Behind the porch was a square of flowers, roses and flowering trees, and behind that a very large vegetable garden.

Wanda Wasilewska had prepared the luncheon. It was delicious, and there was a great deal of it. There was a vegetable caviar made of eggplant, a fish from the Dnieper cooked in a tomato sauce, strange-tasting stuffed eggs, and with this an aged vodka, yellow and very fine. Then came strong, clear chicken soup, and little fried chickens, rather like our Southern-fried chicken, except that they were dipped in bread crumbs first. Then there was cake, and coffee, and liqueur, and last Korneichuk brought out Upmann cigars in aluminum cases.

It was a beautiful lunch. The sun was warm, and the garden was lovely. And as we sat with the cigars and liqueur, the talk turned to relations with the United States. Korneichuk had been part of a cultural delegation to the United States. On their arrival in New York he and his delegation had been fingerprinted and made to register as agents of a foreign power. The fingerprinting had outraged them, and so they had returned home without carrying out the visit. For, as Korneichuk said, "With us, fingerprinting is only for criminals. We did not fingerprint you. You have not been photographed or forced to register."

We tried to explain then that according to our rule the people of a communist or a socialist state are all employees of the government, and that all employees of foreign governments are required to register.

And he answered, "England has a socialist government, and you don't make every Englishman register, nor do you fingerprint them."

Since both Korneichuk and Poltarazki had been soldiers, we asked them about the fighting which had gone on in the area. And Poltarazki told a story which is very hard to forget. He told of being with a Russian patrol which was sent to attack a German outpost. And he said that they had been so long getting there, and the snow had been so deep, and the cold so severe, that when they finally made their attack, their hands and their arms and their legs were stiff.

"We had nothing to fight with, except one thing," he said. "That was our teeth. I dreamed about that afterward. It was so horrible."

After luncheon we went to the river, and hired a little motorboat, and cruised about under the cliff of Kiev and across to the flat sandy beach where hundreds of people were bathing and lying in the sun. Whole families in colored bathing suits were turning brown on the white sand. And there were many little sailboats on the river, tacking back and forth. There were excursion boats too, loaded with people.

We took off our clothes, and jumped over the side of the boat, and swam around in our shorts. The water was warm and pleasant. It was Sunday and very gay. In the gardens on the cliffs, and in the town, people swarmed. Music was playing in the orchestra shells on top of the cliff. And many young couples walked arm in arm along the river.

In the evening we went back to the Riviera, the dancing place on the cliff, and we watched the night come down over the huge level Ukraine with the silver river twisting away.

There were many more dancers this evening because it was Sunday. And some of them danced almost professionally well. The orchestra played its usual gypsy, and Georgian, and Russian, and Jewish, and

Ukrainian songs. In our honor they did a version of "In the Mood," which was a shattering affair. It was two-thirds over before we recognized it at all. But it was played with great vigor.

The open-air dancing platform was surrounded by a rich hedge of some flowering plant. And in a little cave in this hedge a small boy hid —a little beggar. He would creep out of his cave of flowers and come to the table and beg a little money to go to the movies.

The manager came over and said, "He is our steadiest customer, and he is very rich."

He drove the little boy away gently, but the moment the manager had moved away, he came back and got his money for the movies.

More and more people came to the club, and it was quite crowded. At about ten o'clock a fight started, a rushing, striking, running fight, among a number of young men. But it was not about a girl. It was about soccer, which is a very serious business for the Ukrainians. The men of Kiev feel as strongly about their soccer team as do the Brooklynites about their baseball. The fight raged over the platform for a moment, and then it settled down, and everyone went to a table and had a drink and settled the problem.

We walked back through the parkway. Hundreds of people were still sitting and listening to the music of the orchestras. Capa begged me not to ask him any questions in the morning.

There is an institution here which would be good for us. In the hotels and restaurants, well displayed, there is a complaint book with a pencil on it, and you can write any complaint that you want against the service, or the management, or the arrangements, and you needn't sign it. At intervals an inspector comes around to look over the restaurants, and all public services, and if there are enough complaints against any one man, or against the manager, or against the service, there is a reorganization. One complaint is not taken very seriously, but if the same complaint is repeated a number of times, it is.

And there is another book in the Soviet Union, which we were coming to view with a certain amount of terror. It is the impression book. Whether you have visited a factory, a museum, an art gallery, a bakery, or even a building project, there is invariably an impressions book in which you must set down what you think about what you have seen. And usually, by the time you come to the book, you don't know what you have seen. It is a book obviously intended for compliments. The shock would be great if the remarks and the impressions were not complimentary. Impressions, with me at least, require a little time to cook up. They are not full grown immediately.

We had asked to go to another farm, one on richer land than the one we had seen, and one that had not been as badly destroyed by the Germans. And the next morning we started for it, in another direction from Kiev than the first farm we had visited. Our car was a pre-war Ziss. And as we had driven in it, it had grown progressively more decrepit. Its springs no longer sprang very much, its gears groaned and clattered, its rear end howled like a dying wolf.

We had become interested in the drivers we got. Being a chauffeur is not a servant's job in the Soviet Union at all, but a well-paid and dignified position. The men are mechanics, and nearly all of them have been soldiers—either tank-drivers or pilots. Our driver in Kiev was a serious man who was nursing his dying automobile like a child. None of the new cars had come in from Moscow yet, and no one knew when they would arrive. Every piece of rolling stock had to be kept going long after it should have been sent to the junk heap.

As a car, our vehicle in Kiev didn't amount to much, but as a water heater it was magnificent. We stopped every three miles and filled the radiator from ditches, from little streams, from water holes, and the car promptly turned it into steam. Our driver finally left his water bucket on the front bumper, ready for use.

We went about twenty kilometers on a mildly paved road, and then turned left into gently rolling country. The road was no road at all, but a series of wheel tracks, and since it had rained, the trick was to find the wheel tracks least recently used. In the depressions between the rolls of land there were small ponds, with white herons and storks strolling around their edges. We nursed our boiling car between the ponds, and at each one stopped and let it steam a while, and filled it with fresh water.

Our driver said he had been a pilot during the war as well as a tank-driver. He had one very great gift, he could sleep at any time, and for any length of time. If we stopped the car for five minutes, he went to sleep, and immediately awakened when he was called, wide awake and ready to go. He could sleep for twelve hours and awaken the same way. I remembered the gunners in our bombers who had developed the same gift by sleeping on the way to their targets and on their way home.

We arrived at the farm and village about noon. And this farm was also named Shevchenko. We had to call it Shevchenko II. It was very different from the first farm we had seen, for the land was rich and versatile, and the town had not been destroyed. The Germans had been surrounded here. They had killed all the animals, but had not had time to destroy the village. This farm had raised a great many horses, and when the Germans were finally captured, all the horses and cows, chicken and geese and ducks, were dead. It is hard to imagine these Germans. Hard to imagine what went on in their heads, what their thinking process was, these sad, destructive, horrible children.

The manager of Shevchenko II had been a partisan fighter of note, and he still wore his brown tunic and belt. He was blue-eyed and had iron lines along his jaws.

This was a farm of over twelve hundred people, and a great many of its men were killed. The manager told us, "We can rebuild what houses we lost, and we can raise more animals, but we cannot get our men back, and we cannot give new arms and new legs to our maimed people."

We saw very few artificial limbs in the Soviet Union where so many are needed. Perhaps this industry has not been developed as yet, but it is surely one of the most necessary ones, for many thousands of people have lost arms and legs.

Shevchenko II is a thriving farm. The land is rich and rolling. The crops are wheat and rye and corn. There was a late freeze last spring, and part of the winter wheat was frozen. The people rushed to the earth and prepared it for corn, so that the land would not be lost for the year. And it is good corn land. The stalks stand eight or nine feet high, and the ears are big and full-bodied.

We went out to a threshing machine in the fields where the battalions of people were working with wheat. It was a very large farm, and all over in the distance we could see the people working with scythes, for there were only one small reaper and one small tractor on this farm. Most of the grain was being cut by hand and bound by hand. The people were working furiously. They laughed and talked, but they never paused in their work. And not only were they in competition, but this has been their biggest year for a long time, and they wanted to get the grain in, for their prosperity depends entirely on this.

We went to see the granary where the produce is stored, the bins of sesame for oil, the rye and the wheat. The grain was being distributed: so much for the state, so much put aside for the new planting, and the rest distributed to the people of the community.

The village itself is laid out around the village pond, where people swim, wash their clothes, and water the horses. Little naked boys were riding horses into the pond and swimming them about to get them cleaned. The public buildings are grouped around the pond: the club, which has a small stage and a dancing space and seats; the mill where the local grain is ground; and the office where accounts are kept and letters received. In this office there is a radio-receiver, with a loud-speaker on the roof. The loud-speakers in all the houses in the village are wired to this master set. This is an electrified village, it has lights and it has motors.

The houses of the people with their gardens and orchards climbed up over the small round hills. It was a very pretty little village. The houses were white with new plaster, and the gardens were green and rich, the tomatoes red on the vines, and the corn very high around the houses.

The house where we were to be guests was on the top of the rise, so that we could overlook the rolling country, the fields, and the orchards. It was a house like all the rest, like most of the Ukrainian farmhouses--an entranceway, a kitchen, two bedrooms, and a parlor. It was newly plastered. Even the floors were clean new plastered. The house had a sweet smell of new clay.

Our host was a strong, smiling man of about fifty-five or sixty. His wife, Mamuchka, was just what her name implied. She was the hardest-working woman I have ever seen.

They welcomed us to the house and gave us the parlor for our own. The walls were plastered in pale blue, and on the table there were bottles covered with pink·paper, in which were paper flowers of all colors.

There was obviously more prosperity in this village than in Shevchenko I. The icon was larger and it was covered with lace of pale blue to match the walls. This had not been a large family. There had been only one son, and his picture was very large on the parlor wall, a tinted photograph, and they only mentioned him once.

The mother said, "Graduated in bio-chemistry in 1940, mobilized in 1941, killed in 1941."

Mamuchka's face was very bleak when she said it, and it was the only time she mentioned him, and he was her only son.

Near one wall was an old Singer sewing-machine, covered with a piece of cheesecloth, and against another wall, a narrow bed with a rug for blanket. In the center of the room stood a long table, with benches on either side. It was very hot in the house. The windows would not open. We decided that if we could, without seeming to be discourteous, we would sleep in the barn. For the nights were cool and delightful outside; inside the house we would smother.

We went into the yard and washed ourselves, and then dinner was ready.

Mamuchka is a very famous cook in the village, and a very good one. Her meals were unbelievable. Supper that night began with water glasses of vodka, with pickles and home-baked black bread, and

· 97 ·

Ukrainian shashlik which Mamuchka made very well. There was a great bowl of tomatoes, and onions and cucumbers; there were little fried cakes, full of sour cherries, on which honey was poured, a national dish and delicious. There was fresh milk, and tea, and then more vodka. We ate far too much. We ate the little cherry cakes and honey until our eyes popped.

It was beginning to get dark, and we thought this was the last meal of the day.

In the evening we walked down through the village to the club house. As we passed the pond a boat came across it, and there was music in the boat, a curious music. The instruments were a balalaika, a little drum with a small cymbal, and a concertina, and this was the dance music of the village. The players moved across the little lake in the boat and landed in front of the club house.

It was quite a large building, the club. It had a small stage, and in front of the stage were tables with chess boards and checker boards, and then a dancing space, and then rows and rows of benches for spectators.

There were very few people in the club when we went in, only a few chess players. We learned that the young people come back from the fields, and have their supper, and then rest for an hour, even sleep for an hour, before they come to the club.

The stage was set up for a little play that night. There were big pots of flowers on a table, and two chairs, and, upstage, a large portrait of the President of the Ukrainian Republic. The little three-piece orchestra came in, and set up its instruments, and began to play. The young people drifted in, strong girls, their faces washed and shiny. Only a few young men came.

The girls danced together. They wore bright print dresses, and head-cloths of colored silk and wool, and their feet were almost invariably bare. And they danced with fury. The music had a rapid beat, accentuated by drum and cymbal. The bare feet beat the floor. The boys stood around and watched.

We asked a girl why she did not dance with the boys. She said, "They are good for marrying, but there are so few of them since the war that

a girl only gets into trouble if she dances with them. Besides, they are very bashful." And then she laughed and went back to her dancing.

There were so few of them, young men of marriageable age. There were very young boys, but the men who should have been there dancing with the girls were dead.

The energy of these girls was unbelievable. All day they had been working in the fields, since daylight in fact, and yet after one hour of sleep they were prepared to dance all night. The men at the chess tables played on, unmoved and unbothered by the noise that went on around them.

Meanwhile the company which was to play was preparing the stage, and Capa was setting up his lights to photograph the play. It seemed to us that the girls were a little impatient when the music stopped. They did not want to stop dancing for the play.

It was a little propaganda play, and it was naïve and charming. The story was as follows: There is a girl on a farm, but she is a lazy girl, and she does not want to work. She wants to go to a town, and paint her nails, and use lipstick, and be decadent and degraded. As the play opens, she is engaged in an argument with a good girl, a girl who is a brigade-leader, a girl who is honored for her great work in the fields. The girl who wants to paint her nails slouches around the stage and is obviously no good, whereas the other, the brigade-leader, stands very straight, with her hands at her sides, and declaims her lines. The third member of the cast is a heroic tractor-driver, and the interesting thing is that he really is a tractor-driver, and the play had been held up an hour and a half while he fixed the tractor he had been working with all day. The heroic tractor-driver had one dramatic trick, and only one —he delivered his lines pacing back and forth across the stage, smoking cigarettes.

Now the tractor-driver is in love with the girl who wants to paint her nails. He is really in love with her, and he is in grave danger of losing his soul to her. In fact, as the play progresses, it is obvious that he is almost ready to throw up his job driving a tractor and helping the economy of the people, to move into a city and get an apartment and live softly with the nail-painting girl. But the brigade-leader, standing very straight, delivers a lecture to him.

It does no good. He is obviously distraught, and he is very much in love with the slovenly, no-good girl. He does not know what to do. Shall he give up the girl he loves, or shall he follow her to town and become a bum?

Now the decadent girl goes off stage, leaving the brigade-leader with the tractor-driver. And the brigade-leader, with feminine wile, tells the tractor-driver that this girl does not really love him. She only wants to marry him because he is such an eminent tractor-driver, and she would soon be sick of him. The tractor-driver does not believe this, and

so the brigade-leader says with a flash of inspiration, "I have it. You pretend to make love to me, and when she sees us you will find how much she loves you."

This new idea is accepted. The nail-painter makes an entrance to find the tractor-driver holding the brigade-leader in his arms, and, lo and behold, not what you would expect happens, for the slovenly girl decides that she will become a worker in socialist economy. She will stay on the farm. She turns her fury on the brigade-leader. She says, "I will form my own brigade, not only you can be so eminent and decorated. I myself will become a brigade-leader and wear decorations."

This solves the tractor-driver's problems both amorous and economic, and the play closes with everybody feeling pretty good about the whole thing.

This is the story of the play, but this is not how it really came off. The tractor-driver had only made four or five paces across the stage, and the story had only opened, when Capa discharged his flash bulbs to take his first picture. This broke the play wide open. The nail-painting girl retired behind a bunch of ferns and didn't come out for the rest of the scene. The tractor-driver forgot his lines. The brigade-leader stumbled and tried to pick up the play, and failed. The rest of the play was done like an echo. The actors repeated the lines given by the prompter, so that one had a double version. Every time they nearly got their lines again, Capa set off new flash bulbs and threw them.

The audience was delighted. It applauded wildly every time the flash bulbs went off.

The decadent girl's light nature was indicated both with red nail polish and with strings of glass beads and shiny jewelry. The flash bulbs made her so nervous that she broke her beads and spilled them all over the stage. The play fell apart completely.

We wouldn't have known what it was about, except that the prompter, who was also a teacher, explained it to us later. And the curtain was finally drawn with tumultuous applause. We had the feeling that the audience preferred this version to any they had seen of this play. When it was over, they sang two Ukrainian songs.

The girls wanted to dance. They were restless, and soon the orchestra took up its position again and the whirling dances went on. They were only persuaded by the manager that they should go to bed. It was already a quarter of two, and they had to get up at five-thirty in the morning to work in the fields. But they were reluctant to leave, and they would have danced all night if they had been permitted to.

By the time we had climbed the hill it was two-thirty, and we were ready to go to bed. But this was not Mamuchka's plan. She must have started cooking the moment we left, after having finished what we thought was supper. The long table was laid, and the food was piled upon it. And at two-thirty in the morning we had the following meal: glasses of vodka, and pickles and cucumbers again, and fried fish which had been caught in the village pond, and little fried cakes and honey again, and a beautiful potato soup.

We were dying of overeating and lack of sleep. The house was very hot, and the room uncomfortable. Also we had found out that the narrow bed Capa and I were supposed to occupy was Mamuchka's bed, so we asked permission to sleep in the barn.

They spread new hay for us and put a rug over it, and we lay down to sleep. We left the door open, and it was silently closed. Apparently the fear of night air is here, as it is in most of Europe. We waited a while before we got up and opened the door, but again it was closed very softly. They were not going to let us hurt ourselves by exposure to night air.

The hay in the little barn was sweet. Rabbits in a cage against the wall rustled and nibbled in the dark. On the other side of the mud wall a few pigs grunted comfortably, and Lubka, the cow, stirred in her sleep.

Lubka is the new cow, and not as well liked by Mamuchka as the old cow was. She says she doesn't know why she sold her old cow. That was Katushka, an affectionate form of Katharina. She loved Katushka very much, and she does not know why she sold her. Lubka is a nice cow, but she hasn't the personality, nor does she give quite as much milk as Katushka did. Every morning the village children come by to take the cows to pasture for the day, and Lubka goes out to join the herd, and there is Katushka in the herd. And every evening, when the cows come back, each one turning of its own accord into its own yard, Katushka tries to come into this yard, she still wants to come to her old home, and Mamuchka speaks to her for a little while, then drives her out of the yard.

And she says, "I must have been crazy to sell Katushka. Of course, Lubka is a younger cow, and she will probably live longer, but she is not as nice a cow, she is not as generous a cow as Katharina was."

The night was so short as to be practically nonexistent. We closed

our eyes, turned once, and it was gone. And there were people walking about in the yard beside the barn, the cows were being led out, the pigs were squealing and grumbling in anticipation of breakfast. I don't know when Mamuchka slept. She could hardly have slept at all, for she had been up for hours cooking breakfast.

Capa gave trouble about getting up. He didn't want to do it. But he was finally lifted out of the hay. He sat on a log and stared into space for a long time.

The breakfast must be set down in detail because there has never been anything like it in the world. First came a water glass of vodka, then, for each person, four fried eggs, two huge fried fish, and three glasses of milk; then a dish of pickles, and a glass of homemade cherry wine, and black bread and butter; and then a full cup of honey, and two more glasses of milk, and we finished with another glass of vodka. It sounds incredible that we ate all that for breakfast, but we did, and it was all good, but we felt heavy and a little sick afterward.

We thought we were up early, but the village had been in the fields since the first dawn. We went to the fields where they were reaping the rye. The men with long scythes walking in a line, cutting a great swath. Behind them came the women who bound the grain into bundles with ropes of twisted straw, and after them the children who gleaned the grain, who picked up every straw and every head, so that none was wasted. They worked doggedly, for this is their busiest time. Capa moved about taking pictures, and they looked up and smiled and went back to work. There was no pause. This people worked this way for thousands of years, and then for a little while they were mechanized, and now they have had to go back to hand labor until they can build new machinery.

We visited the mill where they grind the grain for their bread, and went to the office where the records of the farm are kept.

On the edge of the village they were building a brickworks, for it is their idea to have every house of brick, and every roof of tile, for the fire hazard of the thatch has impressed them very deeply. They are glad that they have peat and clay to make the bricks on the grounds. And when their village is rebuilt, they said, they would sell bricks to the neighboring farms. The brickworks will be done before the winter, and when they cannot work on the land they will make bricks. Piles of peat are under roof now for burning.

At noon we stopped in to see a family at lunch: mother, and father, and two children. They had a great bowl of vegetable and meat soup in the middle of the table, and each member of the family had a wooden spoon which he dipped into the central bowl. And they had a large bowl of sliced tomatoes, and a big flat loaf of bread, and a pitcher of milk. These people seemed to be eating very well, and we could tell what the process of good eating was by looking at the leather belts around the tunics of the men, for the lines of other years were on the belts, and now the belts were extended and the old lines were back two, three, and four inches, where the buckle had made its mark in the past.

Mamuchka must have cleared away the breakfast dishes and started immediately to cook again. By four-thirty in the afternoon she had prepared a banquet. This was her little state dinner. She was very proud of her ability, and the village was very proud of her, which is probably one of the reasons she was our hostess. At this dinner the leaders of the village were her guests. There were present at the table the president of the farm, the agricultural expert, called *agronome,* and his wife, a pretty woman, who was the teacher and dramatic coach, the manager of the farm, the male schoolteacher, the father and mother of course, and us. And if we had thought the other meals were huge, this one outdid them all. There was a great carafe of vodka on the table, and we were very tired of vodka, and our stomachs were very weak. We began with black bread, pickles, tomatoes, and vodka, and then there was Ukrainian borscht with sour cream, and a huge stew of meat, cooked in some way so that the spices had gone into the potatoes themselves. And there were little cakes, and honey, and milk. When a plate became only half empty, Mamuchka filled it up again. She nearly fed us to death.

Then the president of the farm made a little speech of welcome, and we made a little speech of thanks. And then they asked if we would mind answering a few questions, because we were the first Americans who had ever come to that farm, and they had a great curiosity about our country. They would like to know some things about it. We told them that America was a huge country, and we knew only a little of it, and possibly many of the questions we wouldn't know the answers to, but we would try. Then the agricultural expert asked us about farming. What crops are grown, and where are they grown? And whether there are experiments with seeds, and do we have stations where experiments are carried on? And are there agricultural schools? He said that every collective farm in the Soviet Union has fields set aside for experiments with soils and seeds, and did we have things like that? And he asked whether the government helped farmers with money and with advice. This question had been asked before, and it was always a little surprising to them when we told of the work our government does with agriculture, not only our federal government, but our state governments. Then the farm manager asked how much land it took to support a family in America, and what its income was in relation to food, and medicine, and clothing; and what equipment there would be likely to be on an American farm, what machinery, and what stock. And he asked what care is being taken of our veterans.

Then the schoolteacher asked us about our government. He wanted to know about the Supreme Court, and how the President is elected, and how the Congress is elected. He asked whether the President has the power to lead the country into war, and what power has the State Department, and how close is the government to the people.

We answered that we did not think the President has very great power, but he may have an oblique power, we didn't know. And they wanted to know what kind of a man Truman is, and we didn't know that. And our host spoke of Roosevelt. He said he was greatly loved by the people of Russia, and trusted, and he said that his death was like the death of a father.

And he asked, "Did you know him? Did you ever meet him?"

And I said, "Yes."

And he said, "Tell about it, how did he speak, and what was his manner? Could you tell some little stories about him that we can understand?"

Then the *agronome* asked about atomic power, not as a bomb, but if anything constructive would be done with nuclear fission in America.

And we said, "We don't know. We think so. We think already many things are being done and many experiments are being made for the use of this power, and also for the use of by-products of fission for medical research. We know that this new thing could change the world if it were properly used, and also it could change the world if it were improperly used."

Then the people around the table spoke of the future of their farm. In a year or two it would be electrified and mechanized. They are very proud of this farm. Soon, they said, the new tractors would begin to come in, and before very long the people of the village would be well fed and well housed, and then the people would not have to work so dreadfully hard. "Come back in a year," they said, "and see how we have progressed. We will be starting to build brick houses, and our club will be of brick, and our roofs will be of tile, and life will not be so hard."

Our driver had been sleeping almost solidly ever since we had arrived. He was a wonderful man with sleep. Now we awakened him, and he got his car running on about four cylinders out of eight.

We said our good-bys. The manager of the farm and the *agronome* rode with us to the crossroads to see us off. The manager asked us to send some of the pictures we had taken of the farm, for they would like to put them up in the club, and this we will do.

On the way in to Kiev we went to sleep in the back of the car, from a combination of weariness and overeating. And we do not know how many times the driver stopped for water, or how many times his car broke down. We rolled out of the car and into bed in Kiev, and slept for about twelve hours.

The next morning we went to the river to see the barges bringing produce from the north and south for the markets at Kiev. There were barges of firewood, and little boats piled high with hay. Great loads of tomatoes, and cucumbers, and cabbages moved on the river and landed at the feet of the city. These were the products of the collective farms, brought in to be sold in the open market. We followed the produce up the cliff to the marketplace, where the sellers sat in long lines with their produce in front of them, old people and children, for the young people were working in the harvest fields.

From the market we went to a gigantic bakery, where the black bread is baked for the whole city. The manager put white coats on us before we could enter. Part of the bakery is in ruins and is being rebuilt and enlarged. The manager told us that while the city was under siege the bakery had continued to work, and even while bombs were falling on the buildings the ovens had turned out bread.

There were mountains of bread. It was a completely mechanized bakery, with mixers, kneaders, baking ovens all automatic. The great chains of black bread come through the oven and drop off and are piled on the carts to go out to the city.

The people were very proud of this bakery, and the manager asked us whether in America we had any such wonderful things. And here we found again something that we had found so often, that Russian people truly believe they invented these things. They love automatic

machinery, and it is their dream to be completely mechanized in practically all their techniques. To them mechanization means ease and comfort, and plenty of food, and a general richness. They love machines as much as Americans do, and a new automobile will draw a crowd to stand around and gaze at it almost with reverence.

In the afternoon I was interviewed for a Ukrainian literary magazine. It was a very long and painful experience. The editor, a sharp-faced alert little man, asked questions that were two paragraphs long. They were translated, and by the time I understood the last part I had forgotten the first part. I answered them as well as I could. This would be translated to the editor, and then the whole thing written down. The questions were highly complicated and highly literary. And when I answered a question, I wasn't at all sure that the translation was getting over. There were two problems. One was my complete difference of background from the interviewer, and the second was my English, probably quite colloquial, which did not register very clearly with the translator who had been trained in academic English. To make sure that I was not misquoted by accident, I asked to have the translation of the Russian back into English. I was right, the answers I was supposed to have given did not very closely approximate what I had said. This was not done on purpose; it was not even the difficulty of trying to communicate from one language to another. It was more than language. It was translation from one kind of thinking to another. They were very pleasant and honest people, but we just could not communicate closely. And this was my last interview; I never tried it again. And when in Moscow I was asked for an interview, I suggested that the questions be given to me in writing, that I be given a chance to think them over, to answer them in English, and to check on the translation. And since this was not done, I was not interviewed again.

Wherever we went, the questions asked us had a certain likeness, and we gradually discovered that the questions all grew from a single source. The intellectuals of the Ukraine based their questions, both political and literary, on articles they had read in *Pravda*. And after a while we began to anticipate the questions before they were asked, for we knew the articles on which they were based almost by heart.

There was one literary question which came up on all occasions. We even knew when to expect it, for our questioner's eyes sharpened, and he leaned forward in his chair and inspected us closely. We knew we were going to be asked how we liked Simonov's play *The Russian Question*.

Simonov is probably the most popular writer in the Soviet Union at the present time. Recently he came to America for a while, and on his return to Russia he wrote this play. It is probably the most performed drama of the time. It opened simultaneously in over three hundred theaters in the Soviet Union. Mr. Simonov's play is about American journalism, and it is necessary to set down a short synopsis of it. It is cast partly in New York, and partly in a place that resembles Long Island. In New York its set is approximately Bleeck's restaurant, near the *Herald Tribune* building. And the play is roughly this:

An American correspondent who, years before, had been to Russia and had written a favorable book about Russia, is employed by a newspaper tycoon, a capitalist, a hard, crude, overpowering, overbearing newspaper baron, a man of no principles and no virtues. The tycoon, for purposes of winning an election, wants to prove through his newspapers that the Russians are going to fight the Americans. He employs the correspondent to go to Russia, and to come back and report that the Russians want to go to war with America. The tycoon offers him an immense amount of money, thirty thousand dollars to be exact, and complete security for the future if the correspondent will do this. Now this newspaperman, who is broke, wants to marry a certain girl and wants to have a little country place in Long Island. He undertakes the job. He goes to Russia, and he finds that the Russians do not want to go to war with the Americans. He comes back and secretly writes his book, and writes it exactly opposite from what the tycoon wants.

Meanwhile, on his advance of money, he has bought the house on Long Island in the country, he has married the girl, and some little security is on the way. When his book is turned in, the tycoon not only kills the book, but makes it impossible for the correspondent to publish it anyplace else. And such is the power of this newspaper baron that the correspondent cannot ever get a job again, and can't have his book or his future writing published. He loses his house in the country; his wife, who has wanted security, leaves him. At this time his best friend, for a reason which is not dramatically exposed, is killed in an altitude flight in a defective airplane. Our correspondent is left broke and unhappy, but with the sense that he has told the truth, and that that is the best thing to do.

This roughly is the play *The Russian Question* about which we were asked so often. And we usually answered in this way: 1) It is not a good play, in any language; 2) The actors do not talk like Americans, and within our knowledge do not act like Americans; 3) While there are some bad publishers in America, they have nowhere near the power that is indicated in this play; 4) No book publisher in America takes orders from anyone, the proof being that Mr. Simonov's own books are printed in America; and last, we wish a good play could be written about American journalism, but this is not it. This play, far from adding to Russian understanding of America and Americans, will probably have an opposite effect.

We were asked about the play so often that after a while we wrote a synopsis of a play which we called "The American Question." We began reading it to our questioners. In our play, Mr. Simonov is commissioned by *Pravda* to come to America and to write a series of articles proving that America is a Western degenerate democracy. Mr. Simonov comes to America, and he finds that America is not only not degenerate, but is not even Western, unless the viewing point is Moscow. Simonov goes back to Russia and secretly writes his conviction that America is not a decadent democracy. He submits his manuscript to *Pravda*. He is promptly removed from the Writers' Union. He loses his country house. His wife, a good Communist girl, deserts him, and he starves to death, just the same as the American must in his play.

At the end of this synopsis, there were usually some chuckles among our questioners. We would say, "If you find this ridiculous, it is no more ridiculous than Mr. Simonov's play *The Russian Question* is about America. Both plays are equally bad, for the same reasons."

While once or twice our synopsis precipitated a violent argument, in most cases it caused only laughter and a change of subject.

In Kiev there is a place called the Cocktail Bar. It is spelled in Russian letters so we couldn't read it, but that is the way it is pronounced, Cocktail Bar. And it is like an American cocktail bar. There is a round bar with stools, and little tables, and some of the young people of Kiev go there in the evening. They have tall drinks which are called cocktails, and they are wonderful drinks. There is the Kiev cocktail, and the Moscow cocktail, and the Tiflis cocktail, and oddly enough they are always pink in color and they always taste strongly of grenadine.

The Russians, when they make cocktails, seem to believe that the more ingredients, the better the cocktail. There was one that we tasted which had twelve different liquors in it. We forgot what it was called. We didn't want to remember. We were a little surprised to find cocktail bars in Russia, since the cocktail is a very decadent drink. And surely the Kiev cocktail and the Moscow cocktail are the most decadent of cocktails that we have ever tasted.

Our time in Kiev was up, and we prepared to fly back to Moscow. The people here had been most hospitable, and most kind and generous, and besides that we had liked them very much. They were intelligent, laughing people, people with a sense of humor, and people with energy. In the ruins of their country they had set out doggedly to build new houses, new factories, new machinery, and a new life. And they said to us again and again, "Come back in a few years and see what we will have accomplished."

Chapter 6

Back in Moscow we indulged a hunger for our own language and our own people, for, kind and generous as the Ukrainians had been to us, we were foreigners. We felt good about talking to people who knew who Superman was, and Louis Armstrong. We went out to Ed Gilmore's pleasant house and listened to his swing records. Pee Wee Russell, the clarinetist, sends them to him. Ed says he does not know how he could spend the winter without Pee Wee's contribution of hot records.

Sweet Joe Newman got some Russian girls, and we went dancing in Moscow night clubs. Sweet Joe is a wonderful dancer, but Capa uses long rabbit leaps, amusing but dangerous.

The Embassy people were very kind to us. General Macon, the Military Attaché, contributed D.D.T. bombs to protect us from the flies when we left Moscow, for in some of the bombed and destroyed areas the flies are troublesome. And in one or two of the places where we had slept, there were other troublesome little visitors. Some of the people in the Embassy had not been home for a long time, and they wanted to know about simple little things like baseball prospects, and how the football season was likely to go, and elections in various parts in the country.

On Sunday we went to the war trophy display, near Gorki Park, along the edge of the river. There were German airplanes of all kinds, German tanks, German artillery, machine guns, weapon-carriers, tank-destroyers, specimens of the German equipment taken by the Soviet Army. And walking among the weapons were soldiers with their children and their wives, explaining these things professionally. The children looked with wonder at the equipment their fathers had helped to capture.

There were boat races on the river, little water-scooters with outboard motors, and we noticed that many of the motors were Evinrudes and various other American makes. The races were among clubs and workers' groups. Some of the boats were raced by girls. We bet on one particularly beautiful blond girl, simply because she was beautiful, but she didn't win. If anything, the girls were tougher and more competitive racers than the men. They took more hazardous turns, and they handled their boats with a fine recklessness. Sweet Lana was with us, and she was dressed in a navy blue suit, and a hat with a little veil, and she wore a silver star in her lapel buttonhole.

Later we went to Red Square, where a queue of people at least a quarter of a mile long stood waiting to go through Lenin's tomb. In front of the door of the tomb two young soldiers stood like wax figures. We could not even see that they blinked their eyes. All afternoon, and nearly every afternoon, a slow thread of people marches through the tomb to look at the dead face of Lenin in his glass casket; thousands of people, and they move past the glass casket and look for a moment on the domed forehead and the sharp nose and the pointed chin of Lenin. It is like a religious thing, although they would not call it religious.

At the other end of Red Square there is a round marble platform, where the czars used to execute people, and now it supports gigantic bouquets of paper flowers and a little colony of red flags.

We had only come in to Moscow for the purpose of getting transportation to Stalingrad. Capa made a contact for developing his films. He would have preferred to bring the films home undeveloped, for facilities and controls in the United States are better. But he had a sixth sense about it, and his hunch turned out to be a very good idea in the end.

As usual we left Moscow not under the best circumstances, for again there had been a late party and we had had very little sleep. Again we sat in the V.I.P. room under the portrait of Stalin, and drank tea for an hour and a half before our plane was ready to leave. And we got the same kind of plane we had had before. The ventilation did not work on this plane either. The baggage was piled about in the aisles, and we took off.

Mr. Chmarsky's gremlin was very active on this trip. Almost everything he laid out or planned did not come off. There was no chapter or committee of Voks in Stalingrad, consequently, when we arrived at the little wind-blown airport building, there was no one there to meet us, and Mr. Chmarsky had to get on the phone to call Stalingrad for a car. Meanwhile we went outside, and we saw a line of women selling watermelons and cantaloupes, and very good ones. We dripped watermelon juice down our shirt fronts for an hour and a half, until a car arrived, and since we used it quite a bit, and it had a certain individuality, we must describe this car. It was not a car but a bus. It was a bus designed to hold about twenty people, and it was a Model A Ford. When the Ford Company abandoned the Model A, the Russian government bought the machinery with which it had been made. Model A Fords were manufactured in the Soviet Union, both for light automobiles and for light trucks and busses, and this was one of them. It had springs, I suppose, but it couldn't have had many or they would have been broken. There was no physical evidence of any springs at all. The driver who was assigned was a fine co-operative man, with an almost holy attitude toward automobiles. Later, when we sat alone with him in the bus, he would simply go over the list of cars that he loved.

"Buick," he would say, "Cadillac, Lincoln, Pontiac, Studebaker," and he would sigh deeply. These were the only English words he knew.

The road to Stalingrad was the roughest area in the whole country. It was miles to the city from the airport, and if we could have gone off the road it would have been comparatively easy and smooth riding. This so-called road was a series of chucks and holes and great deep gushes. It was unpaved, and the recent rains had translated part of the road into ponds. On the open steppe, which stretched away as far as you could see, there were herds of goats and cows grazing. The railroad track paralleled the road, and along the track we saw lines of burned-out gondolas and freight cars which had been fired and destroyed during the war. The whole area for miles, on all sides of Stalingrad, was littered with the debris of war: burned-out tanks, and half-tracks, and troop-carriers, and rusting pieces of broken artillery. The

salvage crews went about the country to draw in this wreckage and cut it up to be used as scrap in the tractor factory at Stalingrad.

We had to hold on with both hands while our bus bumped and leaped over the country. We seemed to go on endlessly across the steppe, until at last, over a little rise, we saw Stalingrad below us and the Volga behind it.

On the edges of the city there were hundreds of new little houses growing up, but once in the city itself there was little except destruction. Stalingrad is a long strip of a city along the bank of the Volga, nearly twenty miles long, and only about two miles wide in its widest part. We had seen ruined cities before, but most of them had been ruined by bombing. This was quite different. In a bombed city a few walls stand upright; this city was destroyed by rocket and by shell fire. It was fought over for months, attacked and retaken, and attacked again, and most of the walls were flattened. What few walls stand up are pitted and rotted with machine-gun fire. We had read, of course, about the incredible defense of Stalingrad, and one thing occurred to us in looking over this broken city, that when a city is attacked and its buildings knocked down, the fallen buildings offer fine shelter to the defending army—shelter, and holes, and nests out of which it is almost impossible to drive a determined force. Here, in this raving ruin, was one of the great turning points of the war. When, after months of siege, of attack and counterattack, the Germans were finally surrounded and captured, even their stupidest military men must have felt somewhere in their souls that the war had been lost.

In the central square were the remains of what had been a large department store, and here the Germans had made their last stand when they were surrounded. This is where Von·Paulus was captured and where the whole siege crumbled.

Across the street was the repaired Intourist Hotel where we were to stay. We were given two large rooms. Our windows looked out on acres of rubble, broken brick and concrete and pulverized plaster, and in the wreckage the strange dark weeds that always seem to grow in destroyed places. During the time we were in Stalingrad we grew more and more fascinated with this expanse of ruin, for it was not deserted. Underneath the rubble were cellars and holes, and in these holes many people lived. Stalingrad was a large city, and it had had apartment houses and many flats, and now has none except the new ones on the outskirts, and its population has to live some place. It lives in the cellars of the buildings where the apartments once were. We would watch out of the windows of our room, and from behind a slightly larger pile of rubble would suddenly appear a girl, going to work in the morning, putting the last little touches to her hair with a comb. She would be dressed neatly, in clean clothes, and she would swing out through the weeds on her way to work. How they could do it we have no idea. How they could live underground and still keep clean, and proud, and

feminine. Housewives came out of other holes and went away to market, their heads covered with white headcloths, and market baskets on their arms. It was a strange and heroic travesty on modern living.

There was one rather terrifying exception. Directly behind the hotel, and in a place overlooked by our windows, there was a little garbage pile, where melon rinds, bones, potato peels, and such things were thrown out. And a few yards farther on, there was a little hummock, like the entrance to a gopher hole. And every morning, early, out of this hole a young girl crawled. She had long legs and bare feet, and her arms were thin and stringy, and her hair was matted and filthy. She was covered with years of dirt, so that she looked very brown. And when she raised her face, it was one of the most beautiful faces we have

ever seen. Her eyes were crafty, like the eyes of a fox, but they were not human. The face was well developed and not moronic. Somewhere in the terror of the fighting in the city, something had snapped, and she had retired to some comfort of forgetfulness. She squatted on her hams and ate watermelon rinds and sucked the bones of other people's soup. She usually stayed there for about two hours before she got her stomach full. And then she went out in the weeds, and lay down, and went to sleep in the sun. Her face was of a chiseled loveliness, and on her long legs she moved with the grace of a wild animal. The other people who lived in the cellars of the lot rarely spoke to her. But one morning I saw a woman come out of another hole and give her half a loaf of bread. And the girl clutched at it almost snarlingly and held it against her chest. She looked like a half-wild dog at the woman who had given her the bread, and watched her suspiciously until she had gone back into her own cellar, and then she turned and buried her face in the slab of black bread, and like an animal she looked over the bread, her eyes twitching back and forth. And as she gnawed at the bread, one side of her ragged filthy shawl slipped away from her dirty young breast, and her hand automatically brought the shawl back and covered her breast, and patted it in place with a heart-breaking feminine gesture.

We wondered how many there might be like this, minds that could not tolerate living in the twentieth century any more, that had retired not to the hills, but into the ancient hills of the human past, into the old wilderness of pleasure, and pain, and self-preservation. It was a face to dream about for a long time.

Late in the afternoon Colonel Denchenko called on us and asked if we would like to see the area of the fighting for Stalingrad. He was a fine-looking man, with a shaved head, a man of about fifty. He wore a white tunic and belt, and his breast was well decorated. He took us around the city and showed us where the Twenty-First Army had held, and where the Sixty-Second Army had supported it. He had brought the battle maps. He took us to the exact place where the Germans were stopped, and beyond which they had been unable to move. And on the edge of this line is Pavlov's house, which is a national shrine and will probably continue to be one.

Pavlov's house was an apartment building, and Pavlov was a sergeant. Pavlov with nine men held the apartment house for fifty-two days against everything the Germans could bring against it. And the Germans never took Pavlov's house, and they never took Pavlov. And this was the farthest point of their conquest.

Colonel Denchenko took us to the edge of the river and showed us where the Russians had stood and could not be dislodged under the steep banks. And all about were the rusting ruins of the weapons the Germans had brought to bear. The colonel was a Kiev man, and he had the light blue eyes of the Ukrainians. He was fifty, and his son had been killed at Leningrad.

He showed us the hill from which the greatest German drive had come, and there was activity on the hill, and tanks were deployed on the side hill. At the bottom were several rows of artillery. A documentary film company from Moscow was making a history of the siege of Stalingrad before the city is rebuilt. And in the river a barge was anchored. The picture company had come down from Moscow on the river, and they lived on the barge.

And now Chmarsky's gremlin got to work again. We said we would like to take photographs of this motion picture while they were making it.

And Chmarsky said, "Very well, tonight I will call them and find out if we can get permission."

So we went back to our hotel, and as soon as we got there we heard the artillery firing. In the morning when he telephoned that phase of the shooting was all over and we had missed it. Day after day we tried to take pictures of this refilming of the siege of Stalingrad, and every day we missed it through one accident or another. Chmarsky's gremlin was working all the time.

In the afternoon we walked across the square to a little park near the river, and there under a large obelisk of stone, was a garden of red flowers, and under the flowers were buried a great number of the defenders of Stalingrad. Few people were in the park, but one woman sat on a bench, and a little boy about five or six stood against the fence, looking in at the flowers. He stood so long that we asked Chmarsky to speak to him.

Chmarsky asked him in Russian, "What are you doing here?"

And the little boy, without sentimentality, in a matter-of-fact voice said, "I am visiting my father. I come to see him every night."

It was not pathos, it was not sentimentality. It was simply a statement of fact, and the woman on the bench looked up, and nodded to us, and smiled. And after a while she and the little boy walked away through the park, back to the ruined city.

In the morning, when breakfast came to our room, we thought some major insanity had taken place. Breakfast consisted of tomato salad, pickles, watermelon, and cream soda. But it was not an insanity, it was just a normal Stalingrad breakfast. We did manage to get the cream soda changed to tea. And after a while we even grew to like tomato salad for breakfast. After all, what is it but solid tomato juice? But we never quite got used to the cream soda.

The square in front of our hotel was very broad, and it was surrounded with wrecked buildings. On one standing wall there was a loud-speaker which played from early in the morning until late at night. It broadcast speeches, and news reports, and there was a great deal of singing. And it played so loudly that we could hear it with the covers over our heads. It played so loudly that it nearly burst its own diaphragm, and often we wished it would.

We wanted to see and photograph the famous Stalingrad tractor factory. For it was in this factory that the men had continued to build tanks when the Germans were firing on them. And when the Germans got too close, they put down their tools, and went out and defended the factory, and then went back and continued working. Mr. Chmarsky, wrestling manfully with his gremlins, said he would try to arrange it for us. And in the morning, sure enough, we were told that we could go to see it.

The factory is on the edge of the town, and we could see its tall smokestacks as we drove out toward it. And the ground around it was torn and shot to pieces, and the tractor factory buildings were half in ruin. We arrived at the gate, and two guards came out, looked at the camera equipment Capa had in our bus, went back, telephoned, and immediately a number of other guards came out. They looked at the

cameras and did more telephoning. The ruling was inflexible. We were not even allowed to take the cameras out of the bus. The factory manager was with us now, and the chief engineer, and half a dozen other officials. And once the ruling was accepted by us they were extremely friendly. We could see everything, but we could not photograph anything. We were very sad about this, because in its way this tractor factory was as positive a thing as the little farms in the Ukraine. Here in the factory, which had been defended by its own workers, and where those same workers were still building tractors, could be found the spirit of the Russian defense. And here, in its highest and most overwhelming aspect, we found the terror of the camera.

Inside the big gates the factory was a remarkable place, for while one group worked on the assembly line, the forges, the stamping machines, another crew was rebuilding the ruins. All buildings had been hit, most of them deroofed, and some of them completely destroyed. And the restoration went on while the tractors came off the line. We saw the furnaces where the metal is poured, and big pieces of German tanks and guns being thrown in for scrap. And we saw the metal come out through the rollers. We saw the molding, and the stamping, and the finishing, and the grinding of parts. And at the end of the line the new tractors, painted and polished, rolled out and stood in a parking lot waiting for the trains to take them out to the fields. And among the half-ruined buildings, the builders, the workers with metal and brick and glass, rebuilt the factory. There had been no time to wait until the factory was ready before starting production again.

We do not understand why we were not permitted to photograph this factory, because as we walked through we found that practically all the machinery was made in America, and we were told that the assembly line and the assembly method had been laid out by American engineers and technicians. And it is reasonable to believe that these technicians knew what they were doing and would remember, so that if there were any malice in America toward this plant in the way of bombing, the information must be available. And yet to photograph the plant was taboo. Actually we did not want photographs of the plant. What we wanted were photographs of the men and the women at work. Much of the work in the Stalingrad tractor factory is done by women. But there was no hole in the taboo. We could not take a picture. The fear of the camera is deep and blind.

Also we could not find out the number of units per day that were turned out, for this would be contrary to the new law, which makes the divulgence of industrial information treason equal to the telling of military information. However, we could find out percentages. We were told that the factory was only two per cent below pre-war production, and if we had wanted to, I suppose, we could have found out what pre-war production was, and thus estimated the number of tractors that were coming off the line. The finished machines are standard, and only one type is made. They are heavy-duty machines, not very large, but capable of doing any ordinary farm work. They are not streamlined or prettified, and there are no extras. We were told that they are very good tractors, but they are not made for looks, for there is no competition. One manufacturer does not compete with another by the use of eye-pleasing forms. And it was in this place that the workers built tanks while the shells tore through the buildings and destroyed the factory bit by bit. There was a kind of terrible allegory in this factory, for here, side by side, were the results of the two great human potentials: production and destruction.

When Capa cannot take pictures he mourns, and here very particularly he mourned, because everywhere his eyes saw contrasts, and angles, and pictures that had meaning beyond their meaning. He said bitterly, "Here, with two pictures, I could have shown more than many thousands of words could say."

Capa was bitter and sad until luncheon, and then felt better. And he felt still better in the afternoon when we took a little riverboat and went for an excursion on the Volga. It is a lovely, wide, placid river at

this time of year, and in this place, and it is the road for much of the transportation of the area. Little tugs, barges loaded with grain and ore, lumber and oil, ferries and excursion boats, cruised about. From the river one could see as a whole the destruction of the city.

On the river there were huge rafts with little towns built on them, sometimes five or six houses, and little corrals with cows, and goats, and chickens. These rafts had come from the far northern tributaries of the Volga, where the logs had been cut, and they moved slowly down the river, stopping at cities and towns that have been destroyed. The local authorities requisition the logs that are needed. In every place where they stopped, the requisitioned logs were cut loose and floated ashore, so that as the rafts moved down the river, they diminished gradually in size. But the process takes so long that the crews who live on the rafts have set up tiny townships on their rafts.

The life on the river was very rich, and it reminded us of Mark Twain's account of the Mississippi of his day. Little side-wheelers rushed up and down the river, and a few heavy, clumsy boats even moved under sail.

We went close to one of the big log rafts, and we saw one woman milking a cow in a little corral, and another hanging out washed clothes behind her house, while the men were cutting loose the logs which would be floated ashore to help in the rebuilding of Stalingrad.

Mr. Chmarsky's gremlin really worked overtime in Stalingrad. First it had been the motion-picture company, and then the factory, and even with the little boat excursion his gremlin was busy. We had wanted a small light boat, in which we could move rapidly up and down, and what we got instead was a large cruiser-like boat of the Russian Navy. And we had it all to ourselves, except for its crew. We had wanted a boat with shallow draught, so that we could move close to the shore, and instead we had a boat which had to stand offshore, because it drew too much water. We had to maneuver among small canoe-like boats, in which whole families brought their produce to the markets of Stalingrad, their tomatoes and their piles of melons, their cucumbers and their inevitable cabbages.

· 130 ·

In one market at Stalingrad there was a photographer with an old bellows camera. He was taking a picture of a stern young army recruit, who sat stiffly on a box. The photographer looked around and saw Capa photographing him and the soldier. He gave Capa a fine professional smile and waved his hat. The young soldier did not move. He gazed fixedly ahead.

We were taken to the office of the architect who was directing the plans for the new city of Stalingrad. The suggestion had been put forward that the city be moved up or down the river, and no attempt be made to rebuild it, because the removal of the debris would be so much work. It would have been cheaper and easier to start fresh. Two arguments had been advanced against this: first, that much of the sewage system and the underground electrical system was probably still intact; and second, there was the dogged determination that the city of Stalingrad should, for sentimental reasons, be restored exactly where it had been. And this was probably the most important reason. The extra work of clearing the debris could not stand up against this feeling.

There were about five architectural plans for restoring the city, and no plaster model had been made yet because none of the plans had been approved. They had two things in common: one was that the whole center of Stalingrad was to be made into public buildings, as grandiose as those projected at Kiev—gigantic monuments and huge marble embankments with steps which would go down to the Volga, parks and colonnades, pyramids and obelisks, and gigantic statues of Stalin and Lenin. These were painted, and in projection, and in blueprints. And it reminded us again that in two things the Americans and Russians are very much alike. Both peoples love machinery, and both peoples love huge structures. Probably the two things that the Russians admire most in America are the Ford plant and the Empire State Building.

While a little army of architects works on the great plans for rebuilding Stalingrad, it also works on little things, on schools and the restoration of villages, and on the design of tiny houses. For the city is being rebuilt on its edges, and thousands of small houses are going up, and many apartment houses are being built on the outskirts of the city. But the center is being left for the time when the plans for the public city can materialize.

We spoke to the chief architect about the people we had seen living underground, and living in bits of ruins, and we asked why they were not on the edge of the city, building houses for themselves.

He smiled very understandingly and he said, "Well, you see these people are in the cellars of the buildings they once lived in, and there are two reasons why they do not want to move, and why they insist that they will not move. One is because they like it there, because they have always lived there, and people hate to move from the things they are used to, even when they are destroyed. And the second reason has to do with transportation. We have not enough busses, we have no streetcars, and if they move they will have to walk a great distance to get to work and to get back, and it seems just too much trouble."

And we asked, "But what are you going to do with them?"

He said, "When we have houses for them to move into, we will have to move them. We hope by that time to have the busses, the streetcars, and the methods to get them to and from their work without a great deal of effort."

While we were in the architect's office an official came in and asked whether we would like to see the gifts to the city of Stalingrad from the people of the rest of the world. And we, although we were museum-happy, thought we had to see them. We went back to our hotel to rest a little, and we had no sooner got there when there was a knock on the door. We opened it, and a line of men came in carrying boxes, and cases, and portfolios, and they laid them down. These were the gifts to the people of Stalingrad. There was a red velvet shield, covered with a lace of gold filigree from the King of Ethiopia. There was a parchment scroll of high-blown words from the United States government, signed by Franklin D. Roosevelt. There was a metal plaque from Charles de Gaulle, and the sword of Stalingrad, sent by the English King to the city of Stalingrad. There was a tablecloth with the embroidered names of fifteen hundred women in a small British town. The men brought the things to our room because there is no museum yet in Stalingrad. We had to look at the giant portfolios, wherein were written in the windiest of language greetings to the citizens of Stalingrad from governments, and prime ministers, and presidents.

A feeling of sadness came over us, for these were the offerings of the heads of governments, a copy of a medieval sword, a copy of an ancient shield, some parchment phrases, and many high-sounding sentiments, and when we were asked to write in the book we hadn't anything to say. The book was full of words like "heroes of the world," "defenders of civilization." The writing and the presents were like the gigantic, muscular, ugly, and stupid statuary that is usually put up to celebrate a very simple thing. All we could think of were the iron faces of the open-hearth men in the tractor works, and the girls who came up from holes under the ground, fixing their hair, and of the little boy who every evening went to visit his father in the common grave. And these were not silly, allegorical figures. They were little

· 134 ·

people who had been attacked and who had defended themselves successfully.

The medieval sword and the golden shield were a little absurd in the poverty of their imagination. The world had pinned a fake medal on Stalingrad when what it needed was half a dozen bulldozers.

We went to visit the apartment houses, both rebuilt and new, for the workers in the factories of Stalingrad. We were interested in wages and rent and food.

The apartments are small and fairly comfortable. There is a kitchen, one or two bedrooms, and a living-room. Black workers, that is unskilled laborers, get five hundred roubles a month now. Semi-skilled

workers one thousand roubles, and skilled workers two thousand
roubles, a month. This does not mean anything except in terms of
food and rent, and rent all over the Soviet Union, when you can get

an apartment at all, is incredibly cheap. Rent in these apartments, with gas, light, and water included, is twenty roubles a month, two per cent of the monthly income of a skilled worker, and four per cent of a semi-skilled worker's pay. Food in the ration shops is very cheap. For the common foods, bread and cabbages, meat and fish, which are the standard worker's food, very little money is necessary. But luxuries, tinned foods, imported foods, are very expensive, and such things as chocolate are almost beyond the reach of anyone. But, again, there is the Russian hope that when there is more food the prices will come down. When there are more luxuries they will become available. For example, the new little Russian car, more or less on the model of the German Volkswagen, when it is in full production and can be distributed, will cost about ten thousand roubles. This price will be fixed, and the cars will be distributed as they are made. When you consider that at the present time a cow costs seven to nine thousand roubles, some idea of the comparable prices can be understood.

There were many German prisoners in Stalingrad, and, as at Kiev, the people did not look at them. They were still in German uniform, rather ragged now. Columns of them trudged through the streets, going to and from their work, usually guarded by one soldier.

We had wanted to go out with the fishermen who catch the big Volga sturgeon from which the caviar comes, but we had no time for that since they fish all night. But we did go to see them bring in the fish in the morning. They were gigantic. There were sturgeon of two varieties, one huge whiskery catfish-looking type, and another with a long shovel nose. There were no real giants that day. The largest one that had been brought in weighed only six hundred pounds. We were told that sometimes they run as high as twelve hundred pounds, and a great mass of caviar comes from them. The caviar is taken out and iced the moment the fish are caught. The fishing is done with very large nets of great strength. The moment the boats touch the shore, the iced caviar is rushed away and distributed by airplane to the large cities of the Soviet Union. Some of the fish are sold locally, but many are smoked and put away, and sold later, and they bring a very high price.

Capa was brooding again; he had wanted to take industrial pictures, and he had not been able to. He felt that not only was this trip a failure, but that everything was a failure, that he was a failure, that I was a failure. He brooded very deeply.

We were growing irritable. Chmarsky's gremlin had been working so much overtime that he was nervous too, and we snapped at him a little, I am afraid. And so he gave us a curious lesson in Marxism, and it ended up in a schoolboy shouting argument. And Capa renamed him Chmarsky the Chmarxist, which did not bring out the best in Chmarsky. It was just that we were irritated at not being able to photograph the tractor factory. If we had been truthful with one another we would have arrived at that conclusion.

And here was the test of the association of Capa and me, for when we got angry we never got angry at each other, we joined forces and got angry at somebody else. During our whole trip we never had a serious argument, and I think this is probably some kind of a record. During our argument Chmarsky said that we were relativists, and we, not much knowing what relativists are, banded together and attacked him from the point of view of relativism fairly successfully. Not that we convinced him, but at least we held our own and were not convinced, and we shouted louder.

We were to leave for Moscow the next day, and Capa did not sleep that night. He brooded and worried about his failure to get the pictures he wanted. And all the good pictures he had got turned sour and foul. Capa was definitely not happy. And since neither of us could sleep very much, we wrote the synopses for two motion pictures.

The next morning we got into our Ford bus and went out to the airport very early. And the gremlin had been at work, for while our plane flew, a mistake had been made, and we had not been booked for it. But there was a later plane from Astrakhan, and we could go on it.

The plane from Astrakhan did not arrive. We drank tea, and ate big biscuits, and were miserable at the hot airport. At three o'clock word came that the plane would not arrive, or, if it did arrive, would not go on to Moscow, since it was too late to get there by daylight. We climbed into our bus to go back to Stalingrad.

We had gone about four miles when an automobile from the airport rushed up on us madly and headed us off. It seemed that the captain of the plane had changed his mind. He would start for Moscow that afternoon. We turned around and went back to the airport, and arrived just in time for a new decision. The captain had decided that the plane would not go. So we put our luggage back in our bus and took the horrible road to Stalingrad again. We were sore in very particular areas from the bouncing on the hard seats of our little bus.

At dinner we were mean to Chmarsky. We blew up, we told him unpleasant things, only part of which were true. We told him he should control his gremlin, that he was being pushed around by his gremlin. We criticized his attitude, and his suits, and his choice of neckties. We were bitterly cruel to him, and it was only because we were feeling miserable from having sat at the hot airport all day.

Mr. Chmarsky was upset. He had done his best, I am sure, but he had no way of defending himself against our raging fury, and also against the two of us, for we fought him as a team, and when one stopped talking, the other took it up. And after he had gone to bed, we felt very sorry about what we had done, because we knew why we had done it. We went to bed with the angelic intention of apologizing in the morning.

In the morning we started very early, for there were some pictures we wanted to take on the outskirts of Stalingrad, pictures of people building their new little houses of boards and plaster, and there were some new schools and kindergartens we wanted to see and photograph. We stopped at a tiny house that a bookkeeper in a factory was building. He was putting up the timbers himself, and he was mixing his own mud for plaster, and his two children played in the garden near him. He was very agreeable. He went on building his house while we photographed him. And then he went and got his scrapbook to show that he had not always been ragged, that he had once had an apartment in Stalingrad. And his scrapbook was like all the scrapbooks in the world. The photographs showed him as a baby, and as a young man, and there were pictures of him in his first uniform when he entered the Army, and pictures of him when he came back from the Army. There

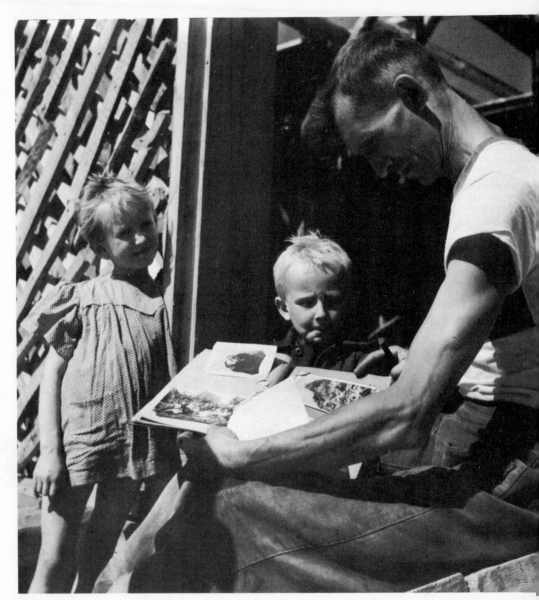

were pictures of his marriage, of his wife in a long white wedding gown. And then there were pictures of his vacations at the Black Sea, of himself and his wife swimming, and of his children as they were growing. And there were picture postcards that had been sent to him. It was the whole history of his life, and all the good things that had happened to him. He had lost everything else in the war.

We asked, "How does it happen that you saved your scrapbook?"

He closed the cover, and his hand caressed this record of his whole life, and he said, "We took very good care of this. This is very precious."

We got back in our bus and again took the road to the Stalingrad airport. We were beginning to know it very well. At the airport the passengers for Moscow had, beside their luggage, string bags in which there were two or three watermelons, for watermelons are hard to come by in Moscow, and there are plenty of very good ones in Stalingrad. We joined them and got a string bag, and each of us bought two watermelons to take with us to the boys at the Metropole Hotel.

The commandant of the airport was extremely apologetic about the mistake of yesterday. He wanted to make us very happy. He saw that we had tea, and he even told a little fib to make us feel happy. He said that we were going on a plane in which there were no other passengers and that it would soon be in from the Black Sea. It developed that when we attacked Chmarsky, Chmarsky had attacked him. Everybody's temper was thin, and the air was full of injustice. But it was hot at the airport, and a hot dry wind laden with particles of dust blew over the steppe. That made people nervous, and so they were mean to each other, and we were just as mean as anyone else.

Our plane finally came in, and it was a bucket-seat plane. And instead of our being the only passengers, it was an overloaded plane. The passengers were mostly Georgians going up to Moscow for the celebration of the eight-hundredth anniversary of the city's founding. They had laid their belongings down the center of the plane, and nearly every seat was taken. They had come prepared in the way of food. They had suitcases full of it.

When we got in, and the doors were shut, the plane became stifling, for, like most bucket-seat airplanes, there was no insulation, and the sun beating on the metal walls heated the inside. The smell was frightful, of people, of tired people. We sat in the metal bucket-seats, which looked like, and were not much more comfortable than cafeteria trays.

At last the plane took off, and as it did, a man sitting next to me opened his suitcase, cut off half a pound of raw bacon which was melting in the heat, and sat chewing it, the grease running down his chin. He was a nice man, with merry eyes, and he offered me a piece, but I didn't feel like it at that moment.

The plane had been hot, but as soon as we made a little altitude the reverse was true. The beads of perspiration on the metal turned to ice and frost. We became freezing cold in the plane. We spent a miserable trip to Moscow, for we had nothing but light clothing, and the poor Georgians in the plane huddled together, for they were from the tropics, and this cold was something they were not used to.

Chmarsky bundled into his corner. We thought he was beginning to hate us, and that he wanted only one thing, to get us into Moscow and to get rid of us. We spent a bad four hours freezing before we landed in Moscow. And Chmarsky's gremlin followed him to the end. The telegrams he had sent for a car to meet us had been misread and there was no car. It would be a matter of two hours' waiting for a car to come for us. But a Greek showed up. In times of stress a Greek always shows up, anywhere in the world. This Greek could make an arrangement for a car, and he did, for a very high price, and we drove in to the Savoy Hotel.

We spoke of how the leaders of a communist or socialist regime must get very tired of the long-living quality of capitalism. Just when you have stamped it out in one place, it comes to life in another. It is like those sandworms which if cut in two go on living, each a separate individual. In Moscow the little clots and colonies of capitalism squirm to life everywhere: the black-market people, the chauffeurs who rent their employers' cars, and the inevitable Greek who shows up with something to rent or sell. Wherever there is a Greek, there is going to be capitalism. Three hundred roubles it cost us to get into Moscow. Our Greek had a fine sense of how much the traffic could stand. I have no doubt that he made a quick estimate of our weariness, our irritation, and our finances, and he set an inexorable price of three hundred roubles, and we paid it.

We had a violent lust for cleanliness, for there had been no bathing in Stalingrad, except with a washcloth, and we yearned for the hot tub, the soak, the shampoo. The statue of Crazy Ella was an old friend to us, and we practically embraced the stuffed bear on the second floor. He didn't look fierce at all to us any more. And our bathtub which rocked on three legs was the most beautiful and luxurious article we had ever seen. In our new-found passion for cleanliness we washed off two or three layers of skin, and Capa shampooed his hair over and over again. He has nice hair, very thick and very black, and because I was still feeling a little mean, when he came out after his third shampoo I remarked that it was rather sad that he was getting a little bald in back. He leaped in the air, and whirled on me, and denied it vehemently. And I took his finger, and placed it down among the hair next to the scalp, and he seemed to feel that there was a bald spot. It was a cruel thing to do, because I had put his finger in a place where he could not possibly see it in the mirror. He went about for a long time secretly feeling the back of his head with his finger. I only did it because I felt mean.

Later Sweet Joe came over and we had a light dinner, and hit the bed, and died. The air of Moscow was strong and cool and made for sleeping, and we didn't get up for many hours.

Mail had come in at last; we had been in Russia only twenty-five days, and it seemed that we had been cut off for years. We read our letters avidly. And although we thought we had been away for so long, people at home who had written didn't think we had been away a long time at all. It was a kind of a shock. We got our equipment together, and our dirty clothes off to be washed, and Capa put his films in order and sent them out to be developed.

He looked at the negatives that had been returned and began to complain bitterly. I might have known it. They were not right. Nothing was right. There was too much grain, this had been left in the developer too long, and this roll had been left in too little. He was furious. And because I had been cruel to him, I tried to reassure him that they were the most wonderful pictures in the world, but he only sneered at me. And because I had been cruel to him, I fixed all of his non-camera equipment: filled his lighter, sharpened his pencils, filled his fountain-pen.

Capa has one curious quality. He will buy a lighter, but as soon as it runs out of fluid he puts it aside and never uses it again. The same is true of fountain-pens. When they run out of ink, he never fills them. A pencil he will use until the point breaks, and then it too is laid aside, and he will buy another pencil, but he will never sharpen a pencil. I flinted and filled his lighters, sharpened all his pencils, filled his pen, and got him generally ready to face the world again.

Before we had gone to Russia, we had not known what kind of equipment would be available, so in France we had bought a wonderful pocketknife, a pocketknife that had a blade to take care of nearly all physical situations in the world, and some spiritual ones. It was equipped with blades that were scissors, with blades that were files,

· 144 ·

awls, saws, can-openers, beer-openers, corkscrews, tools for removing stones from a horse's foot, a blade for eating and a blade for murder, a screw driver and a chisel. You could mend a watch with it, or repair the Panama Canal. It was the most wonderful pocketknife anyone has ever seen, and we had it nearly two months, and the only thing that we ever did with it was to cut sausage. But it must be admitted that the knife cut sausages very well.

We went to the *Herald Tribune* bureau and hungrily read the news reports and the cables for the last two weeks. We read the Embassy hand-outs, and the news reports from the British Information Service. We even read speeches. Capa sniffed through the rooms of the foreign correspondents in the Metropole Hotel and stole books right and left.

We even went to a cocktail party, given by the press division of the British Embassy, and to which an invitation had been only reluctantly issued to us. We conducted ourselves badly. We begged, and borrowed, and whined for cigarettes from everybody we knew, and made outrageous promises about the numbers of cartons we would send once we got home again. Each of us took three baths every day, and we used up all of our soap, and had to beg soap from the other correspondents.

A Legitimate Complaint

BY ROBERT CAPA

I AM NOT happy at all. Ten years ago when I began to make my living by taking pictures of people being bombed by airplanes with little swastikas on them, I saw a few small planes with little red stars shooting down the swastika ones. This was in Madrid during the Civil War, and this made me very happy. I decided then that I wanted to go and see the place where the snub-nose planes and pilots came from. I wanted to visit and take pictures in the Soviet Union. I made my first application then. During these last ten years my Russian friends were often irritating and impossible, but when the shooting became serious they somehow ended up on the side where I was plugging, and I made a great many other applications. The applications were never answered.

Last spring the Russians succeeded in becoming spectacularly unpopular with my side, and considerable plugging was going on to make us shoot this time at each other. Flying saucers and atomic bombs are very unphotogenic, so I decided to make one more application, before it was too late. This time I found a certain support in a man of wide reputation, considerable thirst, and gentle understanding for the gay underdog. His name is John Steinbeck, and his preparations for our trip were very original. First he told the Russians that it was a great mistake to regard him as a pillar of the world proletariat, indeed he could rather be described as a representative of Western decadence, indeed as far west as the lowest dives in California. Also he committed himself to write only the truth, and when he was asked politely what truth was, he answered, "This I do not know." After this promising beginning he jumped out of a window and broke his knee.

That was months ago. Now it is very late at night, and I am sitting in the middle of an extremely gloomy hotel room, surrounded with a hundred and ninety million Russians, four cameras, a few dozen exposed and many more unexposed films, and one sleeping Steinbeck, and I am not happy at all. The hundred and ninety million Russians are against me. They are not holding wild meetings on street corners, do not practice spectacular free love, do not have any kind of new look, they are very righteous, moral, hard-working people, for a photographer as dull as apple pie. Also they seem to like the Russian way of living, and dislike being photographed. My four cameras, used to wars and revolutions, are disgusted, and every time I click them something goes wrong. Also I have three Steinbecks instead of one.

My days are long, and I begin with the morning Steinbeck. When I wake up, I open my eyes carefully, and I see him sitting before the desk. His big notebook is open, and he is imitating work. In reality he is just waiting and watching for my first move. He is terribly hungry. But the morning Steinbeck is a very shy man, absolutely unable to pick up the telephone and make the smallest attempt toward articulate conversation with Russian waitresses. So I give up and get up, pick up the phone, and order breakfast in English, French, and Russian. This revives his spirits and makes him rather cocky. He puts an expression of an overpaid village philosopher on his face and says, "I have a few questions for you this morning." He has obviously spent his three hours of hunger figuring out the damn things, which range from the old Greek table habits to the sex life of the fishes. I behave like a good American, and although I could answer these questions simply and clearly, I stand on my civil rights, refuse to answer, and let the thing go to the Supreme Court. He doesn't give up easily, keeps on bragging about his universal knowledge, tries to provoke me with help and education, and I have to go into exile. I take refuge in the bathroom, which place I simply detest, and I force myself to stay in the sandpaper-lined bathtub filled with cold water till breakfast arrives. This sometimes takes considerable time. After breakfast I get help. Chmarsky arrives. There are no morning and evening phases in Chmarsky's character, he is pretty bad all the time.

· 147 ·

During our day, I have to fight with the hundred and ninety millions who don't want their pictures taken, with Mr. Chmarsky who snobs photography, and with the morning Steinbeck who is so goddam innocent that all questions posed by the curious and hero-worshiping Russian population are answered by a friendly grunt, "This I do not know." After this momentous statement he is exhausted, shuts up like a clam, and big drops of perspiration break out on his fair-sized Cyrano face. Instead of taking pictures, I have to translate Mr. Steinbeck's strange silence into intelligent and evasive sentences, and somehow we finish the day, get rid of Chmarsky, and get home again.

After a short mental strip-tease the evening Steinbeck begins. This new character is perfectly able to pick up the telephone and pronounce words like vodka or beer, understandable to the dumbest waiter. After a certain amount of fluid, he is articulate, fluent, and has many and definite opinions about everything. This goes on till we find a few Americans who have acceptable wives, cigarettes, and native drinks, and still don't refuse to see us. By now he could be described as a rather gay character. If there is any pretty girl in a party, he is definitely ready to protect me and chooses his place right between the girl and me. Around this time he is already able to talk to other people, and if I try to save the innocent girl by inviting her to dance, no broken leg will stop him from cutting in almost immediately.

After midnight his innocence gets coupled with strength. This he demonstrates with one finger. He asks innocent husbands if they know anything about the finger game. The two gentlemen sit down, facing each other across a table, put their elbows firmly on the tablecloth, and clinch their middle fingers. After a certain amount of twisting, Mr. Steinbeck usually gets the husband's fingers down on the tablecloth, and excuses himself volubly. Sometimes, late at night, he tries the game on anybody. Once even on a Russian gent who looked obviously like a general to everybody else but him.

After a certain amount of gentle coaxing, and a long dissertation about dignity, we get home. Now it is past three in the morning. The evening Steinbeck is metamorphosed into his late night version. He is on his bed, holding firmly a thick volume of poetry from two thousand years ago, called *The Knight in the Tiger Skin*. His face is fully relaxed, his mouth is open, and the man with the quiet low voice snores without restraint or inhibitions.

I fortunately borrowed a mystery story from Ed Gilmore, just because I knew that I would be unable to sleep, and would have to read till the morning.

I leave you, gentle American readers, and have to assure your Russian counterparts that everything that Mr. Chmarsky will write about us in *Pravda* is absolutely true.

END OF COMPLAINT

Chapter 7

WHEREVER we had been in Russia, in Moscow, in the Ukraine, in Stalingrad, the magical name of Georgia came up constantly. People who had never been there, and who possibly never could go there, spoke of Georgia with a kind of longing and a great admiration. They spoke of Georgians as supermen, as great drinkers, great dancers, great musicians, great workers and lovers. And they spoke of the country in the Caucasus and around the Black Sea as a kind of second heaven. Indeed, we began to believe that most Russians hope that if they live very good and virtuous lives, they will go not to heaven, but to Georgia, when they die. It is a country favored in climate, very rich in soil, and it has its own little ocean. Great service to the state is rewarded by a trip to Georgia. It is a place of recuperation for people who have been long ill. And even during the war it was a favored place, for the Germans never got there, neither with planes nor with troops. It is one of the places that was not hurt at all.

Inevitably we went in the early morning to the Moscow airport and sat an hour and a half in the V.I.P. room, under the portrait of Stalin, drinking tea. As usual there had been a party the night before, and we had had practically no sleep. We got on our plane and slept until we landed at Rostov. This airfield had been badly broken up, and a great number of prisoners were rebuilding the facilities. In the distance we could see the shattered city which had taken such a pounding during the war.

Then we flew on over the unending plain until at last, in the distance we saw mountains, and it had been very long since we had seen any mountains at all. These were terrific mountains. We picked up altitude and flew very high over the Caucasus. There were high peaks and sharp ridges, and in between there were streams where we could see ancient villages. Some of the peaks were snow-capped even in summer. After so much flat land there was a fine feeling of friendliness about mountains again.

We climbed very high, and in the distance we saw the Black Sea. And our plane came down to it and flew along the edge of the land. It is a beautiful land. The hills come down to the edge of the sea, and on the sides of the slopes there are lovely trees, black cypresses, and a great deal of foliage. And among the hills are villages, and big houses, and hospitals. It might have been the coast of California, except that the Black Sea is not turbulent and violent like the Pacific, and the coast is not rocky. The sea is very blue, and very tranquil, and the beaches are very white.

Our plane flew for a long time along the coast. At last it landed at Sukhum, a strip of level grass along the edge of the sea. The grass was very green, and the airport was lined with eucalyptus trees, the first we saw in Russia. The architecture was oriental, and everywhere were flowers and flowering trees. In front of the little airport was a line of women selling fruits: grapes, and melons, and figs, and fine-colored peaches, and watermelons. We bought some grapes and some peaches and figs. The people on the plane charged at the fruit, for they were people of the north who have never really had enough fruit. They overate, and many of them were bound to be sick later, for their stomachs and their systems were not used to fruit, and an overindulgence can be a rather serious thing, and was.

We were supposed to leave for Tiflis in twenty minutes, but the crew of the plane thought otherwise. They took a car and left to go swimming in the ocean, and they were gone for two hours, while we strolled through the gardens of the airport. We would have liked to go swimming too, but this we could not do, for we did not know that the plane was not going to leave in twenty minutes. The air was warm and moist and salty, and the vegetation was heavy and green and lush. It was really a tropical garden.

These Georgians are different-looking people. They are dark, almost gypsy-looking, with shining teeth, and long well-formed noses, and black curly hair. Nearly all the men wear mustaches, and they are

· 151 ·

handsomer than the women. They are lean and energetic, and their eyes are black and sparkling. We had read and had been told that this is an ancient Semitic people, a people which had come originally from the Euphrates Valley, at a time before Babylon was a city; that they are Sumerians, and that their strain is one of the oldest remaining in the world. They are fiery, proud, fierce, and gay, and the other people of Russia have great admiration for them. They speak always of their strength and vitality, and of their abilities—great cavalry men and good fighters, they say. And the men are triumphant with the women of Russia. They are a people of poetry, of music and dancing, and, according to the tradition, great lovers. And surely they live in a country favored by nature, and just as surely they have had to fight for it for two thousand years.

Just before two o'clock our crew came back, their hair still wet from their swim in the Black Sea. And we wished we had been with them, for we were covered with sweat. It was very hot, and some of our passengers were beginning to feel the effect of an overindulgence in fresh fruit. A few children had been sick already.

We took off again and flew low over the sea, and then began to take on altitude, and climbed very high, and flew over mountains that were gaunt and brown, like the mountains of California. And deep in the creases there were little streams, and we could see the vegetation and the towns along the streams. The mountains were bleak here and forbidding, and they cast the light back blindingly. Then we flew through a pass, the mountaintops level with us, and came over the valley of Tiflis.

It is a huge and dry valley which looks like New Mexico. And when we landed the air was hot and dry, because it is far from the sea, but it was pleasant heat, there was no discomfort in it. And this great level valley, surrounded by the high mountains, seemed almost barren from the air.

We landed at a large airfield. There were many planes—Russian fighter planes. Two of them would take off as two came in, and they buzzed around the field constantly. Perhaps they were patrolling the Turkish border, which is not very far away.

On the high ridge to the west of us there was an ancient fortress, battlemented and huge, and black against the sky.

Mr. Chmarsky was with us again. We had declared a truce: we were nicer to him, and he was nicer to us, than we had been in Stalingrad. He had never been to Georgia either.

We were met by a delegation of the Tiflis section of Voks, and they had a fine big car, and they were nice people. We drove across the flat dry plain to a pass in the mountains. And in the pass lay Tiflis, a beautiful city which has been on the main route of travel from the south to the north for many centuries. The ranges on either side are lined with ancient fortifications, and even the city is dominated by a castle on the ridge. There is a fortress on the other side of the valley too, for through this narrow pass has come every movement and migration of people—Persians, Iranians, Iraqi from the south, and Tartars and other marauders from the north. And in this narrow pass the battles occurred and the fortifications were put up.

Part of the city is very old, and a river runs through the pass, with high cliffs on one side. And on the high cliffs are clustered ancient houses. It is truly an ancient city, for whereas Moscow celebrates this year its eight-hundredth anniversary, Tiflis next year will celebrate its fifteen-hundredth. And this is the new capital, the old capital is thirty kilometers farther along the river.

The streets of Tiflis are wide and tree-shaded, and many of its buildings are modern. The streets climb the hills on either side. And at the very top of the hill, to the west, there is a playground and park, with a funicular railroad that goes straight up the cliff. It is a giant park, with a large restaurant, and it overlooks the valley for many miles. And on the ridge, in the very center of the city, the huge round towers and high battlemented walls of the city fortress stand, ruinous and forbidding.

In the city and on the ridges there are old churches, for Christianity came to the Georgians in the fourth century, and churches which are still in use were built then. It is a city of many ancient stories, and probably many ancient ghosts. There is the story of the Moslem Iranian king who, massing his troops, forced the captive people of Tiflis to the

· 153 ·

bridge over the river, set up a picture of the Virgin, and allowed every one to go free who would spit on the picture. Every one who refused had his head chopped off, and the story is that thousands of heads bumped in the river that day.

The people of Tiflis were better dressed, better looking, and more full of spirit than any we saw in Russia. There was gaiety and color in the streets. The clothing was handsome, and the women wore colored kerchiefs on their heads.

This city is incredibly clean. It is the first clean oriental city I have ever seen. In the river that cuts through the center of the city hundreds of little boys swim. And here there is no destruction, except that which time does to the ancient buildings.

Voks has a very large and efficient organization in Tiflis. For this is a tourist city, and Voks operates not only with foreigners, but with visitors from the other republics of the Soviet Union. They invited us to their building, which is extremely impressive, and even though it was late at night, they served us wonderful cakes and fine Georgian wine, and they wanted to talk and drink with us. But we were awfully tired. We promised that we would talk as much as they wanted later, but we had to go to bed.

During our stay in Georgia Mr. Chmarsky's gremlin hardly operated at all, and that made us feel better toward him, and made him feel better toward us.

We had two large rooms in the Intourist Hotel. They overlooked the street, and there were windows on three sides, so that any moving breeze came through. It was very pleasant. There was only one difficulty: we could not get breakfast. During the whole time we were there we tried to get breakfast early, and we never succeeded. It came when they were ready.

In the morning we got up very early, for the city fascinated us, and we wanted to see a great deal of it. Our driver was, as usual, wonderful, an ex-cavalry man, and he had, of all things, a jeep. The jeep does not bring out the best in anyone, and in a cavalry man it brings out the cowboy. He loved it because it would climb almost straight uphill, because he could whip it around corners, and jump it over culverts. It

· 155 ·

plunged into streams, and splashed water, and came out on the other side. He drove like a mad man, he was afraid of no one. Again and again, in traffic, outraged drivers forced him to the curb, and there would be an exchange of violent Georgian language, and our man would smile and drive off. He won all engagements. We loved him. He was the first man we met in Russia who had the same feeling about policemen that we have. His black curly hair blew wildly about his head when he drove. He never wanted to stop.

He roared the jeep up the hill, into the most ancient part of the city, where the old Georgian wooden houses are preserved. They have a strange architecture, usually two to three stories high, with large open balconies. And the carving and the painting on the walls are exotic.

We climbed the ridge to the old fortification, which has round towers and high thick walls; it might have been impregnable forever if it had not been for artillery, for there was no way to attack it without artillery.

We walked through the tropical garden of the city, beautiful with flowering trees and rare plants, many of which we had never seen before. It was cool there, and a stream flowed beside it.

We did not feel strange in Tiflis, for Tiflis receives many visitors, and it is used to foreigners, and so we did not stand out as much as we had in Kiev, and we felt quite at home.

There are many churches in Tiflis, and it must have been, as it is now, a city of religious toleration, for there are ancient synagogues and Moslem temples, and none of them has ever been destroyed.

High upon the hill, overlooking the city, is David's Church, built, I believe, in the seventh century, simple and beautiful. Our driver rode his jeep as far as he could, and we climbed the rest of the way. And there were many people climbing the twisting trail up to the church, many people going to worship there.

This ancient church is much beloved by the Georgian people, and the graves of the great Georgian writers and composers of music are in the churchyard. Stalin's mother is buried there under a very simple stone. Sitting on the edge of one composer's grave were three elderly women and an old man, and they were singing litanies in an ancient mode, soft weird music.

Inside the old church a service was going on, and there was more singing. The line of people came up, and as they came off the trail and into the churchyard, each one kneeled and kissed a corner of the church.

It was a remote and peaceful place, and the city with its tile roofs was far below. We could see the botanical gardens, which were laid out by Queen Tamara, the fabulous twelfth-century queen, who has left a heroic shadow over the city. Queen Tamara was beautiful, and kind, and fierce. She knew statecraft and building. She built fortresses and encouraged poets and caused musicians to gather together—one of the fairy queens of the world, like Elizabeth, and Catherine of Aragon, and Eleanor of Aquitaine.

· 157 ·

When we came down from David's Church the bells of the cathedral were ringing violently, and we went in. The church was rich and oriental, and its paintings were very black with incense and age. It was crowded with people. The service was being performed by an old man, with white hair and a golden crown, so beautiful that he looked unreal. The old man is called the Catholicus, he is the head of the Church of Georgia, and his robe is of gold thread. There was great majesty in the service, and the music of the large choir was incomparable. Incense rose to the high ceiling of the church, and the sun shone through and lighted it.

Capa took many pictures. It was amazing to see how he could move about silently and photograph without being noticed. And later he went into the choir loft and took more pictures.

By now, in this account, I am beginning to eliminate museums, but we saw them, we saw them every place. As Capa has said, the museum is the church of modern Russia, and to refuse to look at a museum is a little like refusing to visit a church. And they are all more or less alike. There is one section which deals with the past of Russia before the Revolution, from the beginning of history to 1918, and at least half the museum has to do with Russia since the Revolution, with all of the gains made, and the people involved, and the giant pictures of the heroes and of the scenes of the Revolution.

In Tiflis there were two museums. One was the museum of the city, on the ridge over the town, which had very fine miniatures of the ancient houses and plans of the old city. But what was most interesting in this museum was its curator, a man who must have been an actor, for he shouted and postured, he made speeches, he was dramatic, he wept, he laughed loudly. His most successful gesture was a large outward fling of the right hand while he shouted, always in the Georgian language of course, about the glories of the ancient city. He spoke so rapidly that no translation was possible, and it couldn't have been possible anyway, for Mr. Chmarsky did not speak Georgian. We came out of this museum deafened but happy.

On the road along the ridge to this museum is probably the largest and most spectacular picture of Stalin in the Soviet Union. It is a giant thing which seems to be hundreds of feet high, and it is outlined in neon, which, although it is broken now, is said, when working, to be visible for twenty-eight miles.

There were so many things to see, and so little time to see them, that we seemed to rush during the whole visit.

In the afternoon we went to a soccer game between the teams representing Tiflis and Kiev. They played fine, fast, and furious soccer in the great stadium. At least forty thousand people were there, and the crowd was emotional, for these intersectional games are extremely popular. And although the game was rough and fast, and although the competition was very violent, there were practically no flares of temper. Only one little argument happened during the whole afternoon. The score ended two to two, and as the game finished two pigeons were released. In the old days in Georgia, in contests of all kinds, even in fights, a white pigeon was released for victory and a black one for defeat. And these pigeons carried the news to the other cities of the country of Georgia. And this day, since the score was a tie, both black and white were released, and they flew away over the stadium.

Soccer is the most popular sport in the Soviet Union, and the intersectional soccer games carry more excitement and more emotion than any other sports event. The only really heated arguments we heard during our stay in Russia concerned soccer.

We toured the department stores of Tiflis, and they were choked with people. The shelves were fairly well stocked, but prices, particularly of clothing, were very high: cotton shirts, sixty-five roubles; rubber galoshes, three hundred roubles; a portable typewriter, three thousand roubles.

We spent a whole day going about the city to the public swimming pools and to the parks. And in the workers' park we saw a children's train that was charming. It was a real little train, perfect in every detail, and the engineer, the switchman, the station master, the fireman, all were children. They had got their positions in a competition in efficiency, and they ran the train for children or adults. We took a ride on it with a delegation of children from Uzbek, who had come on the invitation of the children of Tiflis, and they were riding the train for the afternoon. The little boy who was engineer was very proud. The station had all the equipment for running a railroad, only on a small scale. And the children were very formal in carrying out their tasks. To be an official on the children's railway is a great honor to a child in Tiflis, and he works hard for the position.

Georgian food is famous all over the Soviet Union, but our hotel had not heard much about it. We were a little tired of its menu, which consisted almost entirely of shashlik and sliced tomatoes. That night Chmarsky and Capa and I decided to experiment with another restaurant. We went to the Tiflis Hotel, where the dining-room is as large as the nave of a cathedral. There were marble columns supporting the roof, there was a very bad loud orchestra, and no food at all. Instead of shashlik we got little bits of fried meat—and sliced tomatoes.

And while we were eating, the waiter came and said, "A lady would like to dance with either one of you gentlemen."

Chmarsky translated for us, and he did not look approvingly at the waiter. He said, "It is undoubtedly a public woman."

And we said, "But what's wrong with a public woman? Is she pretty?"

Chmarsky screwed up his face. He was the only one at the table who could see her. "No," he said, "she is very ugly."

We said, "We think she should be abolished. We think she is a social evil. We think that an ugly public woman is a threat to the whole structure of society, a threat to the home, and security, and mother love, and all things like that."

And Chmarsky nodded his head gloomily and agreed with us. It was practically the first time we had agreed on anything.

And we said, "If, on the other hand, she were pretty, there might be extenuating circumstances. There might be some social injustice involved. If she were pretty, we would advocate investigating her background, to find out what social difficulty has caused her to be a public woman, and to try, perhaps, to induce her to return to private enterprise."

Chmarsky began to regard us with a suspicious, inquisitive eye. He did not trust us very much.

Our backs were to the public woman, but eventually we stole a look, and he was right, she was not pretty, and we don't know whether they abolished her or not.

The summer nights were wonderful in Tiflis; the air soft, and light, and dry. Young men and girls walked aimlessly in the streets, enjoying themselves. And the costumes of the young men were rather nice: tunics, sometimes of heavy white silk, belted at the waist, and long narrow trousers, and soft black boots. They are a very handsome breed, the Georgian men.

From the high balconies of the old houses we could hear in the night soft singing of strange music, accompanied by a picked instrument that sounded like a mandolin, and occasionally a flute played in a dark street.

The people of Georgia seemed to us more relaxed than any we had seen so far, relaxed, and fierce, and full of joy. And perhaps this is why the Russians admire them so. Perhaps this is the way they would like to be.

There was a huge moon over the western mountains, and it made the city seem even more mysterious and old, and the great black castle on the ridge stood out in front of the moon. And if there are ghosts anyplace in the world, they must be here, and if there is a ghost of Queen Tamara, she must have been walking the ridge in the moonlight that night.

Chapter 8

THE Tiflis Writers' Union had asked us to come to a little reception. And it must be admitted that we were frightened, for these meetings have a habit of becoming extremely literary, and we are not very literary people. Besides, we knew by now that the Georgians take their literature very seriously: poetry and music are their great contributions to world culture, and their poetry is very ancient. Their poetry is not read by a few people; it is read by everyone. In their burial places on the hill we had seen that their poets were buried on an equal footing with their kings, and in many cases a poet has been remembered where a king has been forgotten. And one ancient poet, Rust'hveli, who wrote a long epic poem called *The Knight in the Tiger Skin,* is honored almost as a national hero in Georgia, and his verses are read and are memorized even by children, and his picture is everywhere.

We were afraid that the meeting of the writers might be a little rugged for us, but we went. About twenty men and three women received us. And we sat in chairs around a large room and regarded one another. There was a speech of welcome to us, and without transition our welcomer said, "And now Mr. So-and-so will read a short summary of Georgian literature."

A man on my right opened a sheaf of papers, and I could see that it was typewritten and single-spaced. He began to read, and I waited for the translation. A paragraph later I suddenly realized that he was reading in English. I became fascinated, because I could only understand about one word in ten. His pronunciation was so curious that although the words were English all right, they did not sound remotely like English when he said them. And he read twenty typewritten pages.

I got the manuscript later and read it, and it was a concise, compact history of literature in Georgia, from earliest times to the present.

Since most of the people in the room did not speak English at all, they sat and smiled benignly, for to them he was reading in perfect English. When he had finished, the man who had first spoken said, "Have you any questions now?"

And since I had understood very little of what had gone on, I had to admit that I had no questions.

It was quite hot in the room, and both Capa and I had developed a little trouble in the stomach, so that we were not comfortable.

Now a lady stood up, and she too had a sheaf of papers, and she said, "I will now read some translations into English of Georgian poetry."

Her English was good, but because I had a bad cramp in the stomach, I had to protest. I told her, which is true, that I much prefer to read poetry to myself, that I get more out of it that way, and I begged her to let me have the poetry to read when I was alone, so that I could appreciate it more. I think it hurt her feelings, but I hope not. It was true and I was miserable. She was a trifle curt. She said that this was the only copy in existence, that she did not dare let it out of her hands.

Again, as before, there came the questions about American writing. And, as usual, we felt terribly unprepared. If we had known we were going to be asked questions like this before we left America, we might have studied a little bit. We were asked about new writers emerging, and we mumbled a little about John Hersey, and John Horne Burns, who wrote *The Gallery*, and Bill Mauldin, who draws like a novelist. We were dreadfully inadequate at this sort of thing, but the truth of the matter is we had not read very much of modern fiction lately. Then one of the men asked us what Georgians were well known in America. And the only ones we could remember, outside of the choreographer George Balanchine, were the three brothers who collectively had married many million dollars' worth of American women. The name Mdvani did not seem to bring out great enthusiasm among the present-day Georgian writers.

They are very stern and devoted, these Georgian writers, and it is very hard to tell them that although Stalin may say that the writer is the architect of the soul, in America the writer is not considered the architect of anything, and is only barely tolerated at all after he is dead and carefully put away for about twenty-five years.

In nothing is the difference between the Americans and the Soviets so marked as in the attitude, not only toward writers, but of writers toward their system. For in the Soviet Union the writer's job is to encourage, to celebrate, to explain, and in every way to carry forward the Soviet system. Whereas in America, and in England, a good writer is the watch-dog of society. His job is to satirize its silliness, to attack its injustices, to stigmatize its faults. And this is the reason that in America neither society nor government is very fond of writers. The two are completely opposite approaches toward literature. And it must be said that in the time of the great Russian writers, of Tolstoy, of Dostoevski, of Turgenev, of Chekhov, and of the early Gorki, the same was true of the Russians. And only time can tell whether the architect of the soul approach to writing can produce as great a literature as the watch-dog of society approach. So far, it must be admitted, the architect school has not produced a great piece of writing.

The room was very hot by the time our meeting with the writers was over, and we shook hands all around, wiping our palms on our trousers between handshakes, for we were perspiring very freely.

There had been one question they had asked that we wanted to think about further. It had been, "Do Americans like poetry?"

And we had had to reply that the only check we have on the liking or disliking of any form of literature in America is whether the people buy it, and certainly the people do not buy very much poetry. So we had been forced to say that perhaps Americans do not like poetry.

And then they had asked, "Is it that American poets are not very close to the people?"

And this was not true either, because American poets are just as close to the people as American novelists are. Walt Whitman and Carl Sandburg are certainly not very far from the people, but the people just do not read very much poetry. We do not think it makes very much difference whether Americans like poetry or not. But to the

Georgians, whose love for poetry is traditional, the lack of love for poetry is almost a crime.

Old as Tiflis is, it is the new capital. Fifteen hundred years ago the seat of power was about thirty kilometers to the north, and in the afternoon we got in the jeep and our cavalry driver drove us out there. It was a good macadam road, and it was crowded with little wagons pulled by donkeys, and by army trucks, and by soldiers on German motorcycles with side-cars. On the hills on either side were castles and ancient churches, almost inaccessible of approach. And the feeling of ancientness was in these passes which had been guarded against invasions for three thousand years. The road followed the river, and there were two hydroelectric dams, but when Capa wanted to photograph them, the refusal was instant. And just above the dams we came to a bridge that was built by Pompey when the Romans came through this pass, and one of the central supports is still standing in the river.

The name of the ancient capital is Mtskhet, and I cannot pronounce it yet. There is a fifth-century church high up on the peak above the city, half ruinous and very impressive. And to get to it you must climb a goat trail. In the town itself there was a beautiful church, inside high walls. And the walls were castellated and built for defense.

The huge courtyard inside the walls was grass-grown and the walls themselves were stepped, so that in the old days the fighting men could guard the church. The door of the church was of iron, and it was locked with a gigantic padlock. And inside the porch there were many little candles, stuck against the stone of the wall. The method seems to be to light the wrong end of the candle, and when it is burning to press it against the stone so that it sticks, and then to light the other end, so that the burning candle adheres to the stone of the church itself.

A dry hot wind howled through the pass in which the old town stands, and cried against the corners of the church. Off in one corner of the churchyard there was a curious parody. A long, lean, stringy man, dressed in rags, was dancing about. He was of the breed we used to call "touched." In his bony right hand he held a big feather, and with it he gestured while he made a loud speech to three goats who stood watching him and chewing rapidly. He waved his feather, stopped in his speech, and charged at the goats, and they disdainfully stepped aside, like boxers, and then stood and watched again while he spoke to them.

Eventually the caretaker of the church arrived—a dark woman, with a strong aquiline face. She was dressed in a black costume, with a black headcloth that wrapped around her throat, so that only her face showed. Her eyes were dark and brooding. She seemed to be some kind of secular nun. She carried a big key for the padlock. She opened the church, and we went inside the dusky ancient place.

The wall paintings were stiff, and old, and primitive, and their colors were faded. The more recent icons were dark in their gold frames and under their gold filigree. The stern woman began to tell us about the origin of the church.

Now there developed what we were later to call the Tinker to Evers to Chmarsky translation. Chmarsky did not understand the Georgian language. The words had to be spoken to a Georgian, who translated into Russian, and Chmarsky translated the Russian to us. This took a lot longer than normal conversation.

The dark woman told us that this church had been finished in the fifth century, but it had been started long before. And she told us a curious story about its founding, one of the incredible eastern stories one hears so often.

There were two brothers and a sister. And they had heard from the sky, or from the winds, that Jesus Christ had been born and had grown to manhood. There were portents and dreams that told them about him. Finally the two brothers started for Jerusalem, leaving their sister at home in this place. And they arrived on the day of the crucifixion, so they only saw him dead. And these two brothers from this pass in the Georgian mountains were heartbroken, and they begged a piece of the body-cloth of Jesus, and they brought it home to their sister. She was grief-stricken by the crucifixion, and she clutched the cloth, and fell sick and died of sorrow, and her dead hand held the cloth against her heart. Then the brothers tried to release the cloth, but her hand held firm and they could not get it away from her. And so she was buried with the cloth still held in her hand. She was buried right in this place where the church now stands. And almost immediately a plant grew out of the grave and became a giant tree. After a number of years it was desired to build a church in this place to commemorate the event. And woodsmen came and tried to cut the tree, but their axes flew to pieces against its trunk. Everyone tried to cut the tree, and they couldn't make a dent in it. Finally two angels came and cut the tree, and the church was built over the spot. The dark woman pointed to a curious tent-like structure of clay inside the church, and this is where the grave was, she said, and this is where the tree stood.

· 167 ·

And under the clay tent undoubtedly was the body of the holy woman, still clutching the piece of the cloth that had been worn by Jesus.

She told other stories in her austere dry voice, but this was the best story, this was the origin of the church.

The wind whined in through the creaking iron door while she talked. And she said that although the place was deserted now, at various times of the year many thousands of people gather at this church and the courtyard is so crowded that one cannot even sit down or move about. There are people who even climb up on the walls. And during these feasts the service is celebrated in the ancient church. And people come from many, many miles on pilgrimages for these ceremonies, and the church is surrounded by little candles stuck against the walls and burning in the night.

We left the church and saw the iron door locked, and in the corner of the courtyard the "touched" man still waved his feather and addressed his hoarse speeches to the goats.

We went to a monastery on the edge of the town where a colony of monks still live. They have their own chapels and their own communal houses.

These were Christian places when France, and Germany, and England were still pagan. And the Christian stories told here have an Eastern flavor.

This long pass north of Tiflis is an archeologist's heaven, for there are remnants of civilizations for thousands of years. High on the cliffs are the square holes of burial places of remote antiquity. The Soviet government's diggers work all the time at their excavations. Only recently they found a gigantic oil jar filled with golden money—the army pay of an ancient king who had been attacked and had buried his treasure in this place. And everyday the diggers find artifacts that carry the history of Georgia back and back to unsuspected civilizations. In the light of this age, a pier of Pompey's bridge is a comparatively new structure, and the hydroelectric dam is a real newcomer against this background of antiquity.

Capa lined up four objects that he wanted to get on one camera plate: the hydroelectric dam, a statue of Lenin, a fifth-century church, and the square hole of a Sumerian grave. But they wouldn't let him photograph it, because most important of all was the hydroelectric dam, and a photograph of it was considered out of bounds.

We were wind-burned and weary in the evening, and the stomachs of Capa, and Chmarsky, and me were badly upset. We had been drinking a mineral water called Borjoom, which had a pleasant alkaline taste, and we only discovered after it had done its work that it was a mild purgative, and in the quantities we were drinking it, it was much more than a mild purgative. We were quite weak before we found out the cause of our difficulty.

In America there are many hundreds of houses where George Washington slept, and in Russia there are many places where Joseph Stalin worked. The railroad shops in Tiflis have against their outer wall a bank of flowers and a giant plaque proclaiming that in this shop Joseph Stalin once had a job. Stalin is a Georgian by birth, and his birthplace, Gori, about seventy kilometers from Tiflis, has already become a national shrine. We were going to visit it.

It seemed a long way in the jeep, for a jeep seems to go faster than it does. We went again through the windy pass, and out into farther valleys, and through other passes, until at last we came to the town of Gori. It is a town set among the mountains. It is dominated by what we would call a mesa, a tall lone, round mountain, in the middle of the town, and topped by a great castle, which once defended the town and was its place of refuge. The castle is now in ruins. This is the town where Stalin was born, and where he spent his early youth.

The birthplace of Stalin has been left as it was, and the whole thing covered by an enormous canopy to protect it from the weather. The top of the canopy is of stained glass. The birthplace is a tiny one-story house, built of plaster and rubble, a house of two rooms with a little porch that runs along the front. And even so, the family of Stalin were so poor that they only lived in half of the house, in one room. There is a rope across the door, but one can look inside at the bed, the shallow clothes closet, a little table, a samovar, and a crooked lamp. And in this room the family lived, and cooked, and slept. Square golden marble columns support the canopy of stained glass. And this structure is set in a large rose garden. On the edge of the rose garden there is the museum of Stalin, in which is preserved every article that could be gathered that is associated with his childhood and early manhood— early photographs and paintings of everything that he did, and his police photograph when he was arrested. He was a very handsome young man at that time, with fierce wild eyes. On the wall there is a big map of his travels, and the prisons where he was incarcerated, and the towns in Siberia where he was held. His books and papers are here, and the editorials he wrote for small papers. His life has been consistent, and from the very beginning he started the line that has continued to the present day.

In all history we could not think of anyone so honored in his lifetime. We can only think of Augustus Caesar in this respect, and we doubt whether even Augustus Caesar had during his lifetime the prestige, the veneration, and the god-like hold on his people that Stalin has. What Stalin says is true to them, even if it seems to be contrary to natural law. His birthplace has already become a place of pilgrimage. People visiting it while we were there spoke in whispers and tiptoed about. A very pretty young girl was in charge of the museum on the day we visited this place, and after her lecture to the group of us, she went into the garden and cut roses and gave everyone a blossom. And the roses were carefully put away to be saved and treasured as a remembrance of a kind of holy place. No, in all history we do not know anything quite comparable to this.

If Stalin can have this amount of power during his lifetime, what will he become when he is dead? In many speeches in Russia we have heard the speaker suddenly quote a line from a speech of Stalin's that has the stopping quality of the *ipse dixit* of the medieval scholar who put his argument in the lap of Aristotle. In Russia there is no appeal from the word of Stalin, and there is no argument against anything he says. And however this has been accomplished, by propaganda, by training, by constant reference, by the iconography which is ever present, it is nevertheless true. And you can only get the sense of this force when you hear, as we did many times, the remark, "Stalin has never been wrong. In his whole life he has not been wrong once." And the

· 170 ·

man who says it does not offer it as an argument, it is not refutable, he says it as a matter completely true and beyond argument.

We got into the jeep again, and our cavalry man drove us into one of the side valleys, for we wanted to see the vineyards where the Georgian wine comes from. We went into a narrow valley, and again on all the slopes were fortifications. And there were little farms in the valley and on the mountains on both sides. The vineyards climbed up the mountains. The grapes were just coming to ripeness. And there were orchards too, orchards in which there were orange trees, and apples, and plums, and cherries. The road was narrow and rough, and in places streams cut across it. Our driver whooped with joy, for this he loved. He drove at breakneck speed over the narrow roads, and he watched us narrowly to see if we were frightened—and we were. We had to hold on with both hands to keep from being flung out of the jeep. He struck the streams so hard that water cascaded over the whole of the car and drenched us. We went up through a series of little farming valleys with mountain passes between. On every pass there was a fortification where in old times the people of the farms went for protection when an invasion came through.

We stopped at last at a collection of houses in a mountain vineyard, where we had planned to have lunch. About a hundred people were collected, dressed in their best clothes, standing quietly about. And pretty soon four men went into one of the houses, and they emerged carrying a casket. The whole group started up the mountain, weaving back and forth, carrying the dead to be buried high up on the slope. We could see them for a long time, getting smaller and smaller as they zigzagged up the mountain trail to the high cemetery.

We went out into the vineyard and ate a monster lunch which we had brought with us—caviar and sausage, roast saddle of lamb, fresh tomatoes, wine, and black bread. We picked the grapes that were just ready to eat and stuffed ourselves with them. And all of this, incidentally, did not do our weakened stomachs any good. The little valley was green and lush and the air was delightfully warm. There was a good smell of green things all over. And after a while we got back in the jeep and went kayoodling down the road again to Gori.

A visitor to a town in America is taken to see the Chamber of Commerce, the airfield, the new courthouse, the swimming pool, and the armory. And a visitor in Russia is taken to see the museum and the park of culture and rest. In every town there is a park of culture and rest, and we were becoming used to them—the benches, the long plots of flowers, the statues of Stalin and of Lenin, the commemorations in stone of the fighting that was done in this town at the time of the Revolution. To refuse to see the local park of culture and rest would be as bad manners as to refuse to go to see a new real estate development in an American town. Tired as we were from being shaken to death in the jeep, sunburned as we were, for we had no hats, we had to go to the park of culture and rest in Gori.

We walked along the gravel paths and looked at the flowers, and suddenly we became aware of a curious music that was being played at the back of the park. It was almost like bagpipe music, with a background of drums. We walked toward the sound, and saw three men, two playing flutes and one playing a little drum. We soon saw why the music sounded like that of bagpipes, for the flute players puffed their cheeks, and when they drew breath, their filled cheeks kept the music going, so that there was no interval. The music was savage and wild. The two flutists and the drummer stood at the entrance of a high board fence, and the trees around the fence were clustered with children who were looking into the enclosure.

We were glad we had come to the park, for this was the national competition of Georgian wrestling, and it was the day of the finals. For three days the competition had gone on, and today the champions of the republic would be chosen.

Inside the circular board fence was an arena-like place with seats on all sides. The wrestling circle itself was about thirty-five feet in diameter, and the surface was of deep sawdust. At one side was the table of judges, and behind them a little lean-to where the contestants took off their clothes.

The people were very hospitable to us; they made a place for us on a bench, and they cleared the pathway so that Capa could take photographs of the competition.

The two flute players and the drummer sat down in the front row, and the contestants were called. They were dressed in an odd costume—short canvas jackets without sleeves, and canvas belts, and short trunks. They were barefooted.

Each pair of contestants came to the judges' table and was formally recognized. Then they took their places, one on either side of the circle. And at that moment the music started playing its savage melody, with the heavy drumbeat underneath it. The contestants approached each other and joined battle.

It is curious wrestling. Its nearest relative is, I suppose, jujitsu. The contestants are not permitted to grasp any part of the body. The only holds permitted are on the jackets and on the belts. Once the holds are established, it is a matter of tripping, of throwing of weight, of forcing your opponent off balance, until you have thrown him to the ground and pinned him down. During the whole attack and defense, the

savage music plays, and only when one fighter has lost does the music stop.

The contests were not long, usually one minute was enough for one or the other of the fighters to be thrown. And in the instant that one contest was over, another pair approached the judges' table and was recognized. It is a sport which requires incredible speed, and strength, and technique. Indeed, some of the throws were so violent and fast that a man would go sailing through the air at the end of the attack and land on his back.

The audience grew more and more excited as the competition continued and more and more contestants were eliminated. But we had to go. We were to take an evening train for the Black Sea, and before that we had been invited to the opening of the Tiflis Opera. Furthermore, our jeep had developed saddle sores and was giving trouble, and we had seventy kilometers to go before we could even attempt to go to the opera. It was gasoline-line trouble, and we limped back, stopping every little while to blow out the gasoline line.

We were very tired when we got back to Tiflis, so tired that we refused to go to the opening of the opera. My broken knee had taken a dreadful beating in the mad jeep. I was barely able to walk at all. I wanted an hour in boiling hot water to loosen up the painful kneecap.

The station, when we finally got to it, was hot and crowded. We walked along a very crowded train and came at last to our carriage, a 1912 first-class *wagon-lit* of happy memory. Its green velvet was as green as we had remembered. Its dark wood polished and oiled, shining metal and musty smell we well remembered. We wondered where it could have been all these years. The Belgians who built these carriages so many years ago built them for the ages. It was the finest railroad carriage in the world forty years ago, and it is still comfortable, and it is still in good shape. The dark wood grows darker year by year, and the green velvet grows greener. It is a hangover from days of grandeur and royalty.

It was very hot in the train, and we opened the window in our compartment. Immediately a guard came and closed it, scowling at us. As soon as he was gone, we opened the window again, but he seemed to sense that we would rebel. He was back instantly, closing the window and lecturing us in Russian, and shaking his finger in our faces. He was so fierce about this window that we did not dare open it again, although we were smothering in the hot train. His message translated was that on the trip that night we would be going through many tunnels. If the window were open the smoke of the engine would come into the car and get the green upholstery dirty. We begged him to let us open the window, saying we would even help to clean the upholstery, but he only shook his finger more sternly at us and lectured us again. When a Russian rule is established, there are no deviations.

That reminded us of a story that was told us by an American military man in Moscow. He said that during the war when the American plane on which he was traveling landed at Moscow, a sentry was sent with orders to let no one on the plane. And when the time came for the party to board the plane, the sentry let no one on. Our man said that he was nearly shot for trying to, in spite of his orders, and his passes, and his identifications. Finally the sentry was changed, not the orders. The commanding officer explained that orders were fixed and that it was much easier to change sentries than to change orders. Sentry number two had orders "Let people on the plane," while sentry number one had orders "Do not let anyone on the plane." Two sets of orders, or changed orders, might confuse a man. It was much simpler to change sentries. And also it was probably much better for discipline. The man who enforces one order can do it much more faithfully than one who has to make a decision between two.

There was not any doubt about it, the guard on our train did not intend to let us get the window open. We could have smothered, and it wouldn't have made any difference at all. We did not know what the penalty would be for traveling with an open window in our car, but we judged by the seriousness of the guard's attitude that it must be about ten years' imprisonment.

Our train started at last, and we settled in our little sweat box for the night. But the train had no sooner started than it stopped. And all night it stopped about every two miles. We finally fell into a sweaty sleep and dreamed of being caught in a coal mine.

We awakened very early in the morning to find ourselves in a new kind of country, a completely changed country. We had come into a tropical area where the forests stretched down to the tracks, and where we could see bananas growing, and where the air was moist. The land around Tiflis, and the air, had been dry.

The little houses beside the track were swaddled in flowers, and the foliage was dense. Hibiscus in bloom climbed up the hills, and there were orange trees everywhere. It was a most rich and beautiful country. In little patches along the track the corn stood as high as it does in Kansas, twice the height of a man in some places, and there were fields of melons. In the early morning the people came to the entrances of their open and airy houses and watched the train go by. And the women were dressed in brilliant clothing, as tropical people always are. Their head-cloths were red and blue and yellow, and their skirts were bright, figured cloth. We went through forests of bamboo and giant ferns, and through fields of tall tobacco. And now the houses were on stilts, with high ladders to get to the first floor. And under the houses children and dogs played in the early morning light.

The hills were densely wooded with great trees, and every visible thing was covered with lush growth.

And then we came to the area of the tea gardens, probably the most beautiful crop in the world. Low hedges of tea spread away for miles and climbed up over the brows of the hills. Even in the early morning lines of women were picking the new leaves from the tops of the tea plants, their fingers fluttering among the bushes like little birds.

We had awakened very hungry, but it didn't do us any good. There was nothing to eat on the train. In fact, in all the time we were in Russia we did not find anything to eat on any conveyance. You either take your lunch or you go hungry. This accounts for the bundles the travelers take with them: one-tenth clothing and baggage, and nine-tenths food. We tried again to get a window open, but there were tunnels ahead, and we were forbidden again to open them. In the distance, and far below us, we could see the blue of the sea.

Our train came down to the shore of the Black Sea and paralleled it. The whole of this coast is one gigantic summer resort. Every little distance is a great sanatorium or a hotel, and the beaches even in the morning are thronged with bathers, for this is the rest place and this is the vacation place of nearly all of the Soviet Union.

Now our train seemed to stop every few feet. And at every stop groups of people got off, groups who were assigned to one rest house or another. This is the vacation that nearly all Russian workers look forward to. It is the reward for long hard work, and it is the recuperation place for the wounded and the sick. Seeing this country, with its calm sea and its warm air, we realized why people all over Russia said to us again and again, "Just wait until you see Georgia!"

Batum is a very pleasant little tropical city, a city of beaches and hotels, and an important shipping point on the Black Sea. It is a city of parks and tree-shaded streets, and the breeze from the sea keeps it from being too hot.

The Intourist Hotel here was the finest and most luxurious in the Soviet Union. The rooms were pleasant and newly decorated, and each one had a balcony with chairs. The full-length windows made it possible to open whole rooms to the outside. After the night in an old

· 177 ·

museum-piece of a coach, we looked longingly at the beds, but they were not for us. We barely got away with a bath. Our time was running short, and we had to see a great deal in a very short time.

In the afternoon we visited several of the rest houses. They are large palaces set in magnificent gardens, and nearly all·of them look out to the sea. It would be dangerous to be experts in these things. Nearly everyone who has ever traveled in Russia has become an expert, and nearly every expert cancels out every other expert. We must be very careful in what we say about these rest houses. We must repeat only what we were told in the ones we saw, and even then we'll bet we get an argument from somebody.

The first one we visited looked like a very luxurious hotel. It was at the head of a long set of steps that led up from the beach, and it was surrounded by great trees, and in front of it was an enormous porch overlooking the water. This one was owned by a Moscow branch of the electricians' union, and the people who stayed in it were electricians. We asked how they got to come, and we were told that in every factory, in every workshop, there is a committee which includes not only representatives of the factory workers, but a company doctor. A number of factors are taken into consideration by the committee which designates the people who are to come on vacation. There is length of service, there is physical condition, there is quality of tiredness, and there is reward for service beyond that which is required. And if a worker has been sick and needs a long rest, the medical section of his factory committee designates him for a trip to a rest house.

One part of this rest house was set aside for single men, another for single women, and a third part for whole families, who had apartments for their vacations. There was a restaurant where everyone ate, and there were game rooms, and reading-rooms, and music rooms. In one game room people were playing chess and checkers; in another a fast ping-pong game was going on. The tennis courts were crowded with players and spectators, and the stairs were lined with people climbing up from the beach or going down to swim. The hotel had its own boats and fishing equipment. Many of the people simply sat in chairs and looked off toward the sea. There were recuperating illnesses here, and there were the results of industrial accidents, sent down to get well in the warm air of the Black Sea. The average vacation was twenty-eight days, but in cases of illness the stay might be protracted for as long as the factory committee wished.

We were told that very many of the unions maintain rest houses on the sea for their members. This rest house could take about three hundred people at a time.

We drove a few miles down the coast to a sanatorium, a place that again looked like a giant hotel. And this was a state sanatorium for tuberculars and people troubled with other pulmonary difficulties. It was part hospital and part rest house. It was a very pleasant sunny place. The bed-ridden patients had their beds pulled out on balconies overlooking the gardens and the sea, and the ambulatory cases wandered about, listening to music and playing the inevitable chess, which is a game second only to soccer in importance.

The patients in this house were designated by the medical boards of their districts. This was a place of rest. When we came to it it seemed to be almost deserted, for all of the patients were in their beds. But while we were there a bell rang, and gradually they emerged to stroll about.

We were told that there were many hundreds of such sanatoriums on the edges of the sea, and driving along the coast road we could see a great many of them among the trees on the hillside slopes.

While we were driving, a heavy tropical rain began, and we went back to our hotel and finally got a couple of hours sleep. We were awakened by an unusual kind of music. There would be a passage of clarinet marmalade, played in unmistakable Benny Goodman style. Then the passage would stop, and a second clarinet would take up the same passage, but not in unmistakable Benny Goodman style. In a half doze it took us some time to realize what was happening in one of the rooms near us. Someone was listening to a passage of a Benny Goodman record, and then trying to imitate it, with only a modest amount of success. It went on and on, one passage repeated again and again and again. It is only when one sees the mess that is made of American swing music by most Europeans that one is able to realize how definite, how expert, and how unique American music is. Perhaps our musicians would have the same difficulty with the intricate rhythms and melodies of Georgian music. Certainly the Russians have plenty of trouble with ours, but they bring great enthusiasm to bear. We had not heard much American swing music in Tiflis, but in Batum there was a good deal. The hotels were filled with it, for many of the visitors had come down from Moscow where it is played more often.

In the evening we were invited to a concert on the seashore by what was called the Tiflis jazz orchestra. In a little band shell beside the beach, the orchestra took its place, and it played its version of American jazz—"Shine," and "China Boy," and "In the Mood"—always "In the Mood." When Capa and I came in to the concert, we were given huge bunches of flowers to hold, and we felt a little silly. Neither of us is quite the type to listen to a concert peering over the edge of fifteen pounds of gladioli. They were big bouquets, and there was nothing we could do with them. We couldn't put them down, we had to peer through the spikes of flowers at the orchestra on the platform.

We realized why they could not play American music well. Our swing music is invented and improvised. The musician puts himself and his imagination into his playing, whereas this Russian orchestra slavishly imitated records that it heard, and such records are not imitatable. If they wanted to play swing music, they should have taken perhaps the theme of "Dinah" and improvised on it, in which case they would have had music. It wouldn't have been American swing music, but it might have been Georgian swing music.

It was with relief that the orchestra turned to its own music and played the wild dances of the Georgian hills. And we were relieved too, because they were at home, and it was music. And after it was over, the leader and several of the players came back to the hotel with us to have dinner. The leader was a wiry, enthusiastic man, and with our Tinker to Evers to Chmarsky translation we tried to tell him about the background of American swing, how it had developed and what it was. He was fascinated with its theory, and he and his players would break into explosive explanations in Georgian. The idea that around a simple melody the musicians became creators of music, not to be written down, not to be preserved, but simply to be played, was new to him. And as he and his players listened, they grew more and more excited about the idea. We told them there was no reason why an American theme should be used. A Georgian theme with the same improvisation would be just as good, and probably an idea that they could better carry out. After a while they jumped up, and said good-by, and left us. And we imagine that somewhere in the night, on the shore of the Black Sea, there was some wild experimenting with improvisation in the American manner.

We never seemed to get enough sleep, but it was not entirely that which wearied us. We were on the go all the time, we were never able to settle back and think about things. Capa's cameras had been snapping like firecrackers, and he was getting a lot of exposed film. Maybe it was something like this. We were seeing things all the time, we were having to see things all the time. For us, in a normal inefficient kind of an existence, we'd only see things a little part of the time, and the rest of the time we would just relax and not look at anything. But with our limited time on this trip, we had to see something every minute, and we were getting extremely tired. And there was one other thing too. We were living a life which for virtue has only been equaled once or twice in the history of the world. Part of this was intentional because we had too much to do, and part of it was because vice wasn't very available. And we are fairly normal specimens. We love a well-turned ankle, or even a few inches above the ankle, clad, if possible, in a well-fitting nylon stocking. We are fond of all the tricks, and lies, and falsities that women use to fool and snare innocent and stupid men. We like these things very much—nice hair-dos, and perfume, and beautiful clothes, and nail polish, and lipstick, and eye-shadow, and false eyelashes. We had a definite hunger to be tricked and fooled. We like intricate French sauces, and vintage wines, and Perrier-Jouet champagne, approximately 1934. We like sweet-smelling bath soap, and soft white shirts. We like gypsy music played by a whole bloody battalion of violins. We like the crazy skirl of Louis Armstrong's trumpet, and the hysterical laughter of Pee Wee Russell's clarinet. And we were leading a life of limpid virtue. We were consciously circumspect. The most common attacks on foreigners in the Soviet press are on the basis of drunkenness and lechery. And while we are only reasonably alcoholic, and no more lecherous than most people, although this is a variable thing, we were determined to live the lives of saints. And this we succeeded in doing, not entirely to our satisfaction.

There might have been one other thing that made us tired, and that was our conversation, which had been consistently kept on a high intellectual level. We do not mean to state categorically that Russians are stuffy, non-alcoholic, non-lecherous people. In their more private moments we don't know if they are or not, but it is just possible that we were all showing off for each other a little bit, like housewives putting on a puff at a party. At any rate, at this time we were not only extremely tired, but we felt the squirm of decadence working under our skins.

In the morning it was raining very hard, a warm soft rain. We turned over and went back to sleep. At about ten o'clock the sun broke through, and our committee came to take us to a state tea farm.

We drove along the seashore, and then up through a cleft in the green mountains into a back valley, where the lines of dark green tea bushes stretched for miles, and here and there were groves of orange trees. It was a lovely piece of country, and it was the first state farm we had visited.

Here again we cannot make generalities, we can only tell what we saw and what we were told. The state farm was run like an American corporation. It had its manager, and its board of directors, and its employees. The farm workers lived in apartment houses, new, and clean, and pleasant. Each family had its own apartment, and if the women worked in the fields, there were crèches for their children to stay in. And they had the same status as people who worked in factories.

It was a very large farm, with its own schools and its own orchestras. The manager was a businesslike man, who might easily have been a manager of a branch factory of an American company. It was very different from the collective farms, for in the latter each farmer has a share in the profits of the collective. This was simply a factory for growing tea.

The men worked with the conditioning of the land. Tea-picking
was done mostly by the women, for their fingers were clever. The
women moved across the field in long lines, and they sang and talked
as they worked, and they were very pictorial. Capa took a great many
pictures of them. And here, as everywhere, there were decorations for
proficiency. There was one girl who had won a medal for her speed
in picking tea, and her hands worked like lightning over the tea bushes,
picking the fresh light green leaves and putting them in the basket she
carried. The dark green of the tea bushes and the color of the women's
clothes made a very pretty scene on the hillside. At the bottom of the
hill there was a truck to receive the fresh picked tea and take it to the
processing plant.

· 183 ·

We followed the truck to the tea factory, which is worked entirely by automatic machinery. Macerators bruise the tea and let it oxidize, and endless belts go through the drying ovens. The factory is operated almost entirely by women. The director is a woman, and the tasters. Women work the machines where the tea is macerated and oxidized, and women tend the big ovens where the tea is dried. Women grade and pack it. The only men are those who move the crates of packaged tea.

The director of the plant, a handsome woman of about forty-five, is a graduate of an agricultural school in her specialty. And her factory puts out many grades of tea, from the finest small top leaves to the bricks of tea which are sent out to Siberia. And since tea is the most important beverage of the Russian people, the tea gardens and the tea factories are considered one of the most important industries of the region.

When we left, the director gave each of us a large package of the finest product of the region, and it was excellent tea. We had long since given up coffee, because what coffee there was, was not good. We had taken to drinking tea, and from now on we made our own tea for breakfast, and ours was much better than any we could have bought.

We stopped at a little crèche where fifty or sixty tiny children were dancing on the green grass—the children of the women who were working in the tea fields. And Capa found a beautiful little girl, with long curls and huge eyes, and he wanted to photograph her, but she became embarrassed, and cried, and would not be comforted. He photographed a little boy, who cried too. Capa is the children's friend. The teacher said that the girl was hard to comfort because she was not a Georgian child, she was a Ukrainian orphan who had been adopted by a Georgian family, and she felt strange because she could not speak the language yet. And many of the Georgian families have adopted children from the destroyed areas, for this rich country was not touched, and the people feel a responsibility toward the rest of the nation. Here and there we stopped at little houses to visit. And they had their gardens and their orchards around them. And in every place we ate a handful of hazelnuts or some country cheese and fresh black bread;

a pear just picked from the tree over the house, or a bunch of grapes. We seemed to be eating constantly, and we could not refuse. And we tasted Georgian vodka, which we do not recommend to anyone, for it has a fuse in its tail. It is a veritable rocket of a drink, and our stomachs just couldn't take it. Actually it is not vodka at all, but what we used to call *grappa,* that is distilled wine. It was much too violent for us.

When our stomachs were beginning to bulge with food, the manager of the farm caught up with us. He was a tall, straight, spare man, in a partisan uniform and a stiff cap. He asked us to stop by at his house for a bite to eat, God help us! We explained, through Chmarsky and another interpreter, that about one more bite to eat and we would explode. It was returned to us that it was only a token bite, and that he would take it as a great courtesy if we would visit his house and have a glass of wine with him.

We had just about begun to believe that Russia's secret weapon, toward guests at least, is food. But we surely could not refuse to have a bite to eat and a glass of wine. And so we went with him to his house, a neat little house on a hill.

And we should have known. There were more people standing about on the neat clipped grass of his yard than were justified by a simple bite to eat and a glass of wine. Two handsome girls came out of the house with jugs of water. They poured it over our hands, we washed our faces and hands. The girls held out white towels embroidered in red for us to dry ourselves.

And then we were invited to step into the house. Through a hallway we went, and into a large room. The room was hung with woven materials in brilliant colors; some of the designs reminded us of Indian blanketry. The floor was covered with a kind of matting, rather like Mexican *petate.* It was the vision of the table that nearly killed us. It was about fourteen feet long, and it was loaded with food, and there were about twenty guests. I think it is the only meal or dinner we ever attended where fried chicken was an hors d'oeuvre, and where each hors d'oeuvre was half a chicken. It went from there to a cold boiled chicken over which was poured a cold green sauce, delicious with spices and sour cream. And then there were cheese sticks and tomato

· 185 ·

salads and Georgian pickles. And then there was a savory stew of lamb, with a thick sauce. And then there was a kind of fried country cheese. There were loaves of flat Georgian rye bread piled up like poker chips, and the center of the table was loaded with fruit, with grapes, and pears, and apples. And the frightful thing about it was that everything was delicious. The flavors were all new, and we wanted to taste all of them. And we were nearly dying of overeating. Capa, who prides himself on a thirty-two-inch waist, and who will not let out his belt, no matter what happens, was getting a puffed look under the chin, and his eyes were slightly popped and bloodshot. And I felt that if I could just go two or three days without eating anything, I might return to normal.

I remembered and finally understood a story that had been told me by an Englishman. He was sent to America during the war on some kind of purchasing job, and he had headed toward the Middle West. And every place he went he was stuffed. He ate three and four dinners a day. His luncheons sank him, and between meals people slipped things into his mouth. They were sorry for him because there was so little food in England. They wanted to feed him up so that he could last a while just on his accumulated fat. At the end of three days he was ill, but he had to keep going. At the end of a week he was in desperate condition. His stomach, which was used to the austere food of England, was in complete revolt, and as he got sick the people got sorrier and sorrier for his hunger, and fed him more and more. At first, being an honest man, he tried to explain that so much food was killing him, but that was just disbelieved. And then he lied a little bit, and said he didn't feel right about eating so much food when his people at home did not have such good things. And they laughed at him for that, and he had to go on eating. He said that at his approach to a farm the massacre of chickens was pitiful, and that he himself had found feathers on his razor when he shaved in the morning. At the end of a two weeks' visit, he collapsed and was taken to a hospital where they pumped him out. And the doctor warned him that in his condition, even though he felt terribly hungry, he shouldn't eat too much. And he laughed crazily, and turned over, and buried his head in the pillow. At the time I had thought this story was an overstatement, but more and more I was beginning to believe that it was an exact story.

We were introduced to the twenty guests, and we sat down. And here our problem began. If we did not eat, we were urged to eat, and if we did eat, our plates were replenished instantly. And meanwhile the decanters of local wine were passed, and it was a delicious wine, light and full of flavor, and it probably saved our lives. After a few glasses of wine our host stood up, and his wife came from the kitchen and stood beside him, a handsome black-eyed woman with a strong face. The manager drank our health, and drank the health of the United States. And then he appointed his best friend table-master, and this, we were told, is an old Georgian country custom, that the host appoints his friend the master of speeches. And from then on no toast may be made by anyone at the table. If someone wishes to propose a

toast, he must pass the word to the table-master, who is usually chosen because of his ability to make speeches. Then the toast is made by the table-master. This saves the guests a great deal of speaking.

The new table-master made quite a long speech. And it must be remembered that even a short speech was long the way it had to be here, for every sentence had to be translated from Georgian to Russian, and from Russian to English. And God knows what ideas were lost or confused on the way, particularly as this dinner progressed. The table-master was a local farm economist, and after the usual courteous remarks in his first speech he got into his own hobby. He deplored the accidents and the misunderstandings that were forcing the Americans and the Russians apart, and he had, he said, an answer to this, and his answer was trade. He said that a trade treaty should be established between Russia and America, for Russia needed desperately the things that America could manufacture—the farm machinery, the tractors, the trucks, the locomotives. And he suggested that the United States might need some of the things that Russia produced, and he mentioned precious stones, and gold, and wood pulp, and chrome, and tungsten. He had apparently been thinking and brooding on this problem for a long time. It is very probable that he did not know many of the difficulties which stood in the way of such an understanding, and we must admit that we did not know them either.

Since we were foreigners and could not pass a written note to the table-master, we were permitted to answer his toast. And we proposed a toast to the abolishment of curtains of all kinds—of iron curtains, and nylon curtains, and political curtains, and curtains of falsehood, and curtains of superstition. We suggested that curtains were a prelude to war, and that if war should come it could be for only one of two reasons —either through stupidity, or through intent, and if it was through intent on the part of any leaders, then those leaders should be removed, and if it was through stupidity, then the causes should be more closely inspected. And we proposed that since no one, not even the most stupid and belligerent of men, could imagine that a modern war could be won by anyone, then any leader on any side who seriously proposed war should be hunted down as an insane criminal and taken out of circulation. Capa has seen a great deal of war, and I have seen a little, and both of us feel very strongly on the subject.

At the end of our toast the wine fairly leaped from the decanters, and everyone at the table stood up, and everyone insisted on touching his glass to the glass of everyone else at the table. And there was the intimate Georgian toast. Each man holding a glass links his arm with his neighbor's arm and drinks from his own glass. The women leaned in from the kitchen, and around the entranceway the neighbors had gathered, and the wine decanters were passed out to them.

The Georgians we met are like the Welsh. In any group of, say, ten men, there would be at least seven fine voices. And at this table now the singing broke out, magnificent choral singing. They sang the songs of the Georgian shepherds of the mountains, and the old fighting songs. And the voices were so good, and the chorus was so good, that they seemed to be almost a professional group, and they were not. And then the tempo quickened, and two men took chairs, and turned them over their knees, and used them for drums, and the dancing started. The women came out of the kitchen and danced, and the men leaped up from the table and danced. And the music was the chorus of male voices, and the patted chair bottoms, and the clapping of hands.

It was magnificent dance music. Sometimes a man would dance alone, and sometimes a woman alone, and sometimes they danced together, in formal quick steps, traditional dances of Georgia. And this is how it was when we stopped for just a bite to eat and a glass of wine in a Georgian farmhouse. We had to tear ourselves away.

As our car dashed down the hills back to Batum, it began to rain again.

We were taking the train to Tiflis that night, and we were supposed to go to the theater before train time. And so heavy were we with fatigue, and food, and wine, and impressions, that the theater left not very much mark on us. It was *Oedipus Rex* played in Georgian, and our eyes were barely open enough to see that Oedipus was a handsome man with a flashing gold tooth, and that his red wig was magnificently red. He played on a staircase, up and down and up and down. He declaimed his lines with force and beauty. And when Oedipus beat his own eyes out, and tore his bloody shirt, our eyes were almost closed, and we propped them open. The audience spent half its time turning and looking at us, the visiting Americans. We were only a little less rare than visiting Martians here, and we couldn't have appeared to advantage, for we were half asleep. Our host led us out of the theater, and pushed us into a car, and got us up the stairs of the train, and we were like sleepwalkers. We didn't have any quarrel with the guard that night about open windows. We fell into our berths and went to sleep almost immediately.

In these terrific Georgians we had met more than our match. They could out-eat us, out-drink us, out-dance us, out-sing us. They had the fierce gaiety of the Italians, and the physical energy of the Burgundians. Everything they did was done with flair. They were quite different from the Russians we had met, and it is easy to see why they are so admired by the citizens of the other Soviet republics. Their energy not only survives but fattens on a tropical climate. And nothing can break their individuality or their spirit. That has been tried for many centuries by invaders, by czarist armies, by despots, by the little local nobility. Everything has struck at their spirit and nothing has succeeded in making a dent in it.

Our train got into Tiflis about eleven o'clock, and we slept until just a little before that time, and struggled into our clothes, and went to our hotel, and slept some more. And we did not eat, not even a cup of tea did we have, for there was one more thing we had to do before we flew back to Moscow the next morning. That night we were to be given a party by the intellectuals and the artists of Tiflis. And if this seems to be turning into a record of eating, that is accurate. It was not that we seemed to be eating practically all of the time—we were.

Just as the body can become flooded, and inattentive to rich food and wines, so that the perception of spices and vintages disappears, so can a mind become drowned with impressions, overwhelmed with scenes, imperceptive of colors and movements. And we were suffering both from overeating, overdrinking, and overseeing. It is said that in a foreign country impressions are sharp and accurate for a month, and then they become blurred, and the reactions are not accurate again for five years, so that one should stay either one month or five years in a country.

We had the feeling that we were not seeing things sharply any more. And we had a certain terror of the dinner of the intellectuals of Georgia that night. We were so tired, and we did not want to hear speeches, particularly intellectual speeches. We did not want to think about art, or politics, or economics, or international relations, and particularly we did not want to eat or drink. We wanted mainly just to go to bed and sleep until plane time. But the Georgians had been so kind to us, and so pleasant, that we knew that we had to go to this dinner. It was the one formal thing they had asked us to do. And we should have trusted the Georgians and their national genius more, because the dinner did not turn out at all like what we had suspected it might.

Our clothes were in outrageous condition. We hadn't brought very many, you can't when you fly, and our trousers hadn't been pressed since we had entered the Soviet Union. And little accidents of food were upon our coats. Our shirts were clean but badly ironed. We were far from beautiful examples of overdressed America. But Capa washed his hair, and that had to do for both of us. We sponged the more removable spots from our clothes, and put on clean shirts, and we were ready.

They took us in the funicular railway straight up the cliff to the great restaurant at the top which overlooks the whole of the valley. It was evening when we went up, and the city was lighted below us. And the evening sky was golden behind the black Caucasus peaks.

It was a big party. The table seemed about a mile long. It was set for about eighty people, for the dancers of Georgia were there, and the singers, and the composers, and the makers of motion pictures, and the poets and novelists. The table was covered with flowers and beautifully decorated and set, and the city was like strings of diamonds below the cliff. There were many handsome women singers and dancers.

The dinner started, as all such dinners do, with a few stuffy speeches, but the Georgian nature, and the Georgian genius, couldn't tolerate it, and it went to pieces almost immediately. They just are not stuffy people, and they could not contrive to be for very long. Singing broke

· 191 ·

out, individual singing and group singing. And dancing broke out. And the wine passed. And Capa did his famous *kazatzki*, which is not graceful, but it is remarkable that he can do it at all. Perhaps the sleep we had got gave us new life, and perhaps the wine helped a little, for the party went on very late into the night. I recall a Georgian composer who raised his glass, and laughed, and said, "To hell with politics!" I recall trying to do a Georgian dance with a handsome woman who turned out to be the greatest Georgian dancer in the world. I recall group singing in the street finally, and that the militia came to see what the singing was about, and joined the chorus. Mr. Chmarsky was a little gay. He was as strange to Georgia as we were. Language barriers went down, national boundaries went down, and there was no need of translators any more.

We had a wonderful time, and this dinner which we had looked forward to with horror and reluctance turned out to be a magnificent party.

In the dawn we dragged ourselves back to our hotel. There was no purpose in going to bed, for our plane would leave in a very few hours. We were half dead packing our bags, but some way we got to the airport, we will never know how.

It was the old routine of getting to the airport in the dark before the dawn. And our hosts came down in a big car to take us there. They looked a little green around the gills, and we felt that way. The all-night party had not given us a great deal of energy at the end. We came to the airport with our baggage, and our cameras, and our films, just in the pre-dawn, and as usual went to the restaurant and had tea and big biscuits. On the starting line at the other end of the field the Russian military fighter craft took off in pairs and went out on patrol duty.

Mr. Chmarsky was tired and a little inattentive. On our side of the field a big transport plane, again a C-47, warmed up and people got into it, and we asked if it was our plane, and we were told that it was not. And it took off. In an hour we inquired again about our plane. Now it seemed it was our plane that had taken off. The Kremlin gremlin was at work again. We complained a little bitterly. No one had told us we were to go on that plane. Even Chmarsky became indignant, and he had a long and explosive conversation with the commandant of the airport, a conversation that had a great many hand gestures, and the use of those Russian words that have consonants we cannot pronounce. It sounds like a series of firecrackers. Mr. Chmarsky threatened to report the whole incident to whatever place you report such incidents, and the commandant was sad. And then his face lighted up and he said, "You will go in a special plane. It is being readied now."

And we were properly impressed and very happy about it, because we'd never gone anyplace in a special plane in our lives, and we rather imagined we could stretch out on the floor and go to sleep. The plane was to leave in one hour. It would take that long to be made ready. Back to the restaurant we went, and had more tea, and more big biscuits.

At the end of an hour we made another inquiry. And it seemed that an engine needed a little work, and it might just possibly be thirty-five minutes more before we took off in our "special plane."

Our hosts meanwhile were wilting and dying on the vine. We tried to get them to go back to Tiflis and go to bed, but they were very courteous and they would not. They would see us off to Moscow. Two more glasses of tea, and forty-five minutes, and we inquired again. It seemed, said the commandant, that a delegation of Turks, representing the Turkish government, were on their way to Moscow to take part in the celebration of the eight-hundredth anniversary of that city. And they were going to go on the plane with us, if we did not mind; they were to share our special plane, if we would permit it. Now we have no great liking for the Turkish government, but when it was put to us that way, we couldn't refuse a whole sovereign nation's representatives the right to go on our little special plane to Moscow. We were very big about it, we granted the permission.

"Let them board the plane, and they can go with us," we said.

There was just one bit of trouble, they were not here yet. They were still in Tiflis, they would be out in half an hour.

Back to the restaurant we went, and had two more glasses of tea, and more big biscuits. The sun rose, and the air became hot, and the Russian patrol craft took off and came in. We had that sandy feeling under the eyes that comes from complete and overwhelming fatigue. And at the end of an hour we went back to the commandant, and even Mr. Chmarsky was getting quite excited by now. Where were the Turks?

Well, it seemed that their train had not reached Tiflis yet. It had been delayed somewhere along the line, and since they had been promised permission to go on our plane, the commandant did not think that he could very well leave the Turkish delegation stranded here, and would we mind waiting perhaps another half hour.

The level of the tea in our bodies had reached the thorax. And we went back to the restaurant, and drank another glass, and it bubbled out of our mouths. Chmarsky put his head down in his hands, and I reminded him of our definition of gremlins, and of his answer that in the Soviet Union they do not believe in ghosts.

I said, "Mr. Chmarsky, do you believe in ghosts now?"

And he raised weary eyes, and then banged his fists on the table, and ran out to the commandant, shouting.

Our hosts from Tiflis were now squatting on the ground under a tree in the garden of the airport, sound asleep. But we couldn't go to sleep, because our plane was to leave in thirty-five minutes.

Two and a half hours later the Turks' baggage arrived—twenty fat suitcases in a truck—but no Turks. And it developed that after an all-night trip on the train the Turks had felt a little sandy, a little grainy, and they had gone to a hotel to take a bath, and have some breakfast, and rest up a little bit. The commandant was very sorry, it was an international matter, and if we wouldn't mind letting the Turks on our plane, we would make him the happiest man in the world, and incidentally probably save his job and his reputation.

Again we were magnanimous. And we had discovered one scientific truth: we knew exactly how much the human system can hold, and we had reached that point.

At twelve-thirty the Turks arrived. They were fat Turks—four men and two women. We didn't know what they were going to do with twenty great suitcases for a stay of at the most two weeks. We thought perhaps they had brought folding harems with them. They swaggered through the airport, and got in the plane, and the door was about to close when we besieged the plane ourselves. There was a little altercation at the door, but the Turks finally let us in. It turned out that it was not our plane at all, it was the Turks' plane. And we were not letting them ride with us, they were letting us ride with them, and they didn't like it a bit. We didn't want to remind them that we, as American taxpayers, were providing dollars to preserve the democracy of their great state. All we wanted to do was to get on that plane and get the hell out of Tiflis. Mr. Chmarsky was crying a little bit by now, and shaking his fist at everything that moved. He had a plan to write letters to all of the Moscow papers concerning the incident.

We finally were permitted in the plane, and the Turks—they were well-rounded, well-upholstered Turks—settled in their seats with grunts of distaste at our presence. They glanced suspiciously at our luggage. We must say that they were the nicest-smelling Turks we have ever encountered. Everyone of them smelled like a two-dollar haircut. And I have a feeling that while we waited at the hot airport they had been bathing in attar of roses.

We waved heavily to our hosts of Tiflis. They had been very kind and hospitable to us, and we had been of considerable nuisance to them. And our friend the cavalryman-driver waved violently. Nothing tired him out.

It was close in the plane, for the air-conditioning system, as usual, was out of order, and the smell of attar of roses was overwhelming. Our plane lumbered into the air and began to climb rapidly to get through the Caucasus. On the ridges we could see the castles and fortifications of antiquity.

It is a magical place, Georgia, and it becomes dream-like the moment you have left it. And the people are magic people. It is true that they have one of the richest and most beautiful countries in the world, and they live up to it. And we understood thoroughly now why Russians had always said to us, "Until you have seen Georgia, you have seen nothing."

We flew over the Black Sea, and stopped again at Sukhum, and this time our crew did not go swimming. The line of women was still there selling fruit, and we bought a great box of peaches to take to the correspondents in Moscow. We purposely got them firm, so that they would not all ripen at once. The sad thing was that they did not ripen at all. They simply rotted in the condition in which we got them.

We flew over the secondary range of the Caucasus and came down into the interminable flat lands. We did not land at Rostov, but flew directly on to Moscow. And it was cold in Moscow, for the winter was approaching very fast.

Mr. Chmarsky was a very nervous man. This time we had nearly finished him off. And even Chmarsky's gremlin was tired. There were no difficulties at the airport. We were met. The car was waiting, and we got into Moscow without any difficulty at all. We were very happy to see our room in the Savoy, with the crazy monkey, the insane goats, and the impaled fish. The bust of Crazy Ella winked and nodded to us as we walked up the stairs to our room, and the stuffed bear on the second floor drew himself up and saluted us.

Capa got into the bathtub with an old British financial report, and I went to sleep while he was still there. For all I know he spent the night in the tub.

Chapter 9

MOSCOW was in a state of feverish activity. Great gangs of men were covering the buildings with gigantic posters and portraits of the national heroes, acres in extent. The bridges were strung with electric light globes. The walls of the Kremlin and its towers, and even its battlements, were outlined in electric lights. Every public building was floodlighted. In every public square dance stands had been put up, and in some of the squares little booths, made to look like Russian fairy-tale houses, had been erected for the sale of sweets, and ice-cream, and souvenirs. A special little dangling metal buttonhole ornament was official, and everyone wore one of them.

Delegations from many countries were arriving almost hourly. The busses and trains were loaded. The roads were full of people coming into the city, carrying not only their clothes, but food for several days. They have been hungry so often that they take no chances when they move, and everyone carries a few loaves of bread. Bunting and flags and paper flowers were on every building. The individual commissariats had their signs on the buildings housing their offices. The subway trust put up a huge map of the subways of Moscow, and at the bottom a little subway train that ran back and forth. This attracted crowds, who stared at it all day and late into the night. Wagons and trucks loaded with foodstuffs, with cabbages, with melons, with tomatoes, with cucumbers, rolled into the city—the gifts of the collective farms to the city on its eight-hundredth anniversary.

Everyone in the street wore some medal, or ribbon, or decoration reminiscent of the war. The city boiled with activity.

I went over to the *Herald Tribune* office and found a note from Sweet Joe Newman. He was held up in Stockholm, and he asked me to cover the party for the *Herald Tribune,* since he couldn't get back to do it.

Capa was working feverishly over his films, criticizing his work himself, the quality of the developing, everything. He had an enormous number of negatives by now, and he spent hours in front of the window, looking through the negatives, and bitching badly. Nothing was correct, nothing was right.

We called Mr. Karaganov at the Voks office and asked him to find out exactly what we had to do to get the films out of Russia. We thought there might be some censorship, and we wanted to know what it was enough in advance so that we could make preparations for it. He assured us that he would go to work on it immediately and would let us know.

On the night before the celebration we were invited to the Bolshoi Theater, but we weren't told what it would be. By some fortunate accident we were unable to go. We heard later that it was six hours of speeches, and no one could leave, for there were members of the government in the government box. It was one of the happiest accidents that ever happened to us.

The restaurants and cabarets were packed with people, and many of them were set aside for the delegates who had come from the other republics of the Soviet Union and from other countries, so that we couldn't get in at all. As a matter of fact it was very difficult to get

dinner that night. The city was simply mobbed with people, and they
walked slowly about the streets, stopping in one square to listen for
a while to the music, and then trudging on to another square. They
looked, and trudged, and looked. The country people were wide-eyed.
Some of them had never seen the city before, and no one had ever seen
the city so lighted up. There was some dancing in the squares, but
not a great deal. Mostly the people trudged and stared, and trudged
on and stared at something else. The museums were so packed that you
couldn't get in at all. The theaters were mobbed. There was no building on which there was not at least one huge picture of Stalin, and the
picture second in size was that of Molotov. Then there were huge
portraits of the presidents of the different republics, and of the other
heroes of the Soviet Union, their size graduated down.

Late in the evening we went to a little party at the house of an American Moscow correspondent who has been in Russia for many years.

He speaks and reads Russian easily, and he told us a great many stories about some of the difficulties of running a house in present-day Russia. And just as with hotel serving, most of the difficulties came from the inefficiency of a bureaucratic system—so many records and so much bookkeeping made it almost impossible to get any repairs done.

After dinner he took a book from his shelves. "I want you to listen to this," he said, and began reading slowly, translating from Russian. And he read something like this—this is not an exact transcription, but it is close enough.

"The Russians of Moscow are highly suspicious of foreigners, who are watched constantly by the secret police. Every move is noticed and sent into central headquarters. A guard is placed on all foreigners. Furthermore, Russians do not receive foreigners in their houses, and they seem to be afraid even to talk to them very much. A message sent to a member of the government usually remains unanswered, and a further message is also unanswered. If one is importunate, one is told that this official has left the city or is sick. Foreigners are permitted to travel in Russia only after great difficulty, and during their travels they are very closely watched. Because of this general coldness and suspicion, foreigners visiting in Moscow are forced to associate with each other exclusively."

There was a good deal more in this vein, and at the end our friend looked up and said, "What do you think of it?"

And we said, "We don't think you can get it past the censor."

He laughed. "But this was written in 1634. It is from a book called *Voyages in Muscovy, Tartary and Persia,* by a man named Adam Olearius." And he said, "Would you like to hear an account of the Moscow conference?"

And he read from another book something like this: "Diplomatically the Russians are very difficult to get along with. If one submits a plan, they counter it with another plan. Their diplomats are not trained in the large world, but are mostly people who have never left Russia. Indeed, a Russian who has lived in France is considered a Frenchman; one who has lived in Germany is considered a German, and these are not trusted at home.

"The Russians cannot go diplomatically in a straight line. They never get to the point, they argue in circles. Words are picked up, and bandied, and tossed, until in the end a general confusion is the result of any conference."

After a pause he said, "And that was written in 1661 by a French diplomat, Augustin, Baron de Mayerburg. These things make one much less restless under the present setup. I don't think Russia has changed very much in some respects. Ambassadors and diplomats from foreign countries have been going crazy here for six hundred years."

Quite late in the night our host tried to drive us home, but halfway there his car ran out of gasoline. He got out and stopped the first motorist who came by. There was a quick exchange of Russian. He gave the man a hundred roubles, and we got in and were driven home by this stranger. And we found that this can nearly always be done. Almost any car becomes a taxi late at night, for a very high price. This is very fortunate, for there are practically no regular taxis on run. The taxis usually cover a route and take the car full. You must say where you are going, and the taxi driver will tell you whether he is going in that direction. They operate a little like streetcars.

In addition to all the decoration a great deal of new equipment was coming out in celebration of the anniversary. Big new electric street-cars, trackless streetcars, were put on the streets for this celebration. The Ziss automobile plant released many beautiful new cars, which were almost exclusively put to the use of the big delegations from foreign countries.

Although it was only September 6, it was becoming very cold in Moscow. Our room was freezing, and the heat would not be turned on for a month. We wore our overcoats when we were not in bed. The other correspondents in the Metropole Hotel were unpacking their electric heaters which had been put away for the summer.

Almost at dawn on the day of the celebration Capa was out raging through the streets with his cameras. He had a Russian cameraman with him now to facilitate his movements about the city and to explain to policemen that he was all right. And in Red Square he had a militia man assigned to him to make things easy and to stop any unpleasantness. He photographed buildings, and displays, and crowds, and faces, and groups of trudging people, and he was as happy as it is possible for him to be when he is working.

In many streets little sidewalk restaurants were set up—one directly across from our hotel—two little tables, with white cloths on them, and vases of flowers, and a big samovar, and a glassed-in display counter for little sandwiches (open-face sandwiches with sausage and cheese), jars of pickles, and small pears and apples, all for sale.

It was a brilliant cold day. The elephants from the circus paraded through the streets, preceded by clowns. There was not to be any military parade on this day, but there was a big show scheduled for the stadium, and to that we went in the afternoon.

It was a show of mass formations of factory workers in brilliant costumes. They did group calisthenics and marches. They made figures on the field. There were races, some for women and some for men, competitions in shot-putting and in volley ball. There was a showing of dancing horses, beautifully trained horses, which waltzed, and polkaed, and bowed, and pirouetted.

Someone important in the government was there, but we couldn't see him, whoever he was, for the state box was on our side of the stadium. In fact we have almost a record. In the whole time we were in Russia we didn't see one single important person. Stalin had not come up to the celebration from his place on the Black Sea.

The show in the stadium went on all afternoon. There were parades of bicycles, and races of motorcycles, and finally there was a last show that required a great deal of preparation. A line of motorcycles rode around the track. In the seat was the motorcycle driver, and standing on each motorcycle was a girl in tights, and each girl held a great red flag, so that when the motorcycles went at full speed, the huge flag flapped behind. This parade circled the track twice, and that was the end of the show.

We started back from the Dynamo Stadium because I had to do my *Tribune* piece for Joe Newman, and Capa had to get back into the crowds to keep his camera clicking. And halfway back we blew a tire,

and we had to walk the rest of the way. Capa got caught in the crowd, and I didn't see him until much later. I finally made it to the *Tribune* office, did my piece, and sent it over to the censor.

We had dinner that night with Mr. and Mrs. Louis Aragon, who were at the National Hotel. They had a room with a balcony that overlooked the huge square in back of the Kremlin. From there we could see the fireworks which went off almost constantly, and we could hear the salutes of artillery that continued at intervals all evening. The square in front of us was one packed mass of people. There must have been millions of them, milling slowly and eddying back and forth across the square. In the middle of the square there was a bandstand where speeches were made, and music played, and there were singers and dancers. The only place we have ever seen people so closely packed together is in Times Square on New Year's Eve.

It was very late at night before we could even force our way through the people back to our hotel. And many hundreds of thousands of

peoples still trudged through the streets, back and forth, looking at
the lights and watching the electrical displays.

I went to bed, but Capa put his hundreds of rolls of film away, and
got out his negatives, and when I went to sleep he was still staring at
the light through his negatives, complaining bitterly that nothing had
gone well. He had discovered that one of the cameras he had been
using all day had developed a light leak, and he thought that all of his

films were probably ruined. This did not make him a very happy man, and I was so sorry for him that I determined not to ask him a single intellectual question the next morning.

Our time was getting very short, and we still had many things that we wanted to do. We wanted to see the Russian writers who when we had first arrived had all been out of town, on the Black Sea, or in Leningrad, or in the country. And we wanted to see theater and ballet and ballet schools. Capa had many pick-up shots to make. And every day or two we called Voks and asked whether our pictures had been cleared, because this was becoming a worry to us. We couldn't get any information about what we had to do about the pictures, and we knew that some kind of request was bound to be made. And no information came back, except that they were working on it. Meanwhile the drawers in our room were crowded with rolls and strips of developed film.

The deep fall had arrived, and the winter was fast approaching. In the country around Moscow a blue mist hung close to the fields, and everywhere the people were digging potatoes and storing cabbages.

A kind of coldness was creeping up between Capa and me, for an odor had come into our room, and it seemed to each of us that it was the odor of not quite clean clothing. We thought we were clean, we bathed a great deal, we sent our laundry out regularly, and yet this smell increased. We began looking at each other with narrowed eyes, and making slightly disparaging remarks about each other. The smell got worse and worse. We had to keep a window open. It was only after the third day that we discovered what it was. General Macon had given us some D.D.T. bombs, and one of these bombs had not been quite tightly screwed down, so that a tiny vapor of it was impregnating the room with its odor. And because we did not expect an odor, each of us thought it was the other. The smell of Aerosol, if you know what it is, is a rather pleasant clean smell, but if you don't know what it is, it is rather disgusting. We were very glad when we discovered the source of the evil and closed it off, and the room soon regained its beauty.

On the night after the celebration Ed Gilmore, who with time had forgiven Capa for stealing his Ellery Queen, invited us to dinner. And his wife is not only beautiful, she is also a beautiful cook. We spent an evening of happy, well-fed, mildly alcoholic decadence, for Ed Gilmore had a number of newly arrived swing records from America. We drank Martinis and ate crisp little *piroschki*, and late in the night we danced a little. It was a good evening, and we honor Ed Gilmore for his ability to forgive Capa's crime against him. The next day Sweet Joe Newman got back from Stockholm with very delicate gifts. He brought a fountain-pen, and some cigarette lighters, and cigarettes, and canned delicacies, and a few bottles of Scotch whisky, and a suitcase full of toilet paper. It was very good to have him back.

Moscow was settling into its winter stride. The theaters were opening, the ballet would begin, the shops were beginning to sell the thick cotton quilted clothing and the felt boots that people wear in winter. Children appeared in the streets in caps with earflaps, and with fur-lined collars on their thick coats. At the American Embassy technical sergeants who were experts in electricity were busily rewiring the whole building. Last winter the wiring burned out, and without the electric heaters they were used to, the Embassy staff had to work in overcoats.

We went to dinner at a house where five young American officers of the Military Attaché's staff lived. It was a very good dinner, but they do not live very happy lives, for they even more than the others are restricted in their movements, and they must live the most circumspect of lives. I presume that the Russian Military Attaché in America is rather carefully watched too. In front of their house stands a permanent militia man in uniform, and every time they leave their house they are accompanied by invisible followers.

Inside the pleasant house we sat at dinner with the American officers, and we had American food—a leg of lamb, and green peas, and a good soup, and salad, and little cookies, and black coffee. And we thought how four hundred years ago, perhaps in a house like this, British and French officers, young men in gold and red uniforms, had sat over their port, while outside in front of the gate the Russian guard in a helmet carried a pike and watched over them. These things do not seem to have changed very much.

Like all tourists, we made the trip to the little town of Klin, seventy kilometers from Moscow, to visit the home of Tchaikovsky. It is a pretty house, set in a large garden. The lower floors are now used as library, as storehouse for music manuscripts, and as a museum. But the upper floor where the composer lived has been left just as it was. His bedroom is as he left it—a big dressing gown hanging beside the narrow iron cot, a small writing table under a window. The ornate dressing table and mirror with the drape of heavy paisley presented to him by a feminine admirer stands in a corner, with his hair tonic still on it. And his living-room with the grand piano, the only one he ever owned, has not been changed. Even his desk has his little cigars in a bowl, and his pipes, and stubs of pencil. The pictures of his family are on the walls, and out on a little glass porch where he took his tea there is a clean sheet of music manuscript paper. His nephew is the curator—a handsome old man now.

He said, "We want to make Tchaikovsky's house seem as though he has just stepped out for a walk and would soon return."

This old man lives mostly in the past. He spoke of the musical giants as though they were still alive—of Moussorgsky, and Rimski-Korsakov, and Tchaikovsky, and the rest of the great group. And the house was indeed full of the presence of the composer. The piano is tuned and played once a year. It is played by the best pianist available, and the music is recorded. Mr. Tchaikovsky, the nephew, played for us for a while, and the piano was mellow and a little out of tune.

We looked at the manuscripts in the library. The notes are stabbed on the paper, cutting into the staffs with a terrible haste, and whole sections are crossed out. And on some pages only eight bars remain, and the rest are viciously eliminated with a destroying pencil. And then we looked at the manuscripts of other composers, neatly inked, no note crossed out. But Tchaikovsky wrote as though every day might be his last, and every note. He was frantic to get his music down.

The old man sat with us in the garden later, and we spoke of the composers of the present day, and he said a little sadly, "Competent men, yes; good craftsmen, yes; honest and intelligent men, yes; but not geniuses, not geniuses." He looked down the long garden where Tchaikovsky had walked every day, winter or summer, after he had finished his daily work.

The Germans had come to this pleasant house, and they had made a motor pool of it, and tanks were in the garden. But the nephew had moved the precious manuscripts in the library, and the pictures, even the piano, safely away before the Germans came. And now it is all back—a strange, haunted place. From the window of the caretaker's cottage came the notes of someone practicing on a piano, the exercises of a child, hesitant and stumbling, and the strange and passionate loneliness of the frantic little man who lived exclusively for music filled the garden.

Our time was growing very short. Our lives had become jerky. We rushed from one thing to another, trying to see everything in our last few days. We visited the University of Moscow, and the undergraduates did not look unlike ours. They congregated in the halls, and laughed, and rushed from class to class. They paired off, boy and girl, just as ours do. The university was bombed during the war, and the students rebuilt it while the war went on, so that it was never closed.

The ballet had opened, and we went nearly every night—the loveliest ballet we have ever seen. It started at seven-thirty and did not finish until after eleven. The casts were huge. A commercial theater could not support such ballet. Such performance, and training, and sets, and music, must be subsidized or they cannot exist. There is no way to make.the sale of tickets pay for this kind of production.

We also went to the Moscow Art Theater, and saw Simonov's play *The Russian Question*. And perhaps we made a mistake in seeing this play, or perhaps this production was not of the best. We found it, for our taste, overacted, overemphasized, unreal, and stylized—in a word, hammy. The character of the American publisher would have reduced an American audience to helpless laughter, and the Russian idea of American newspapermen was only slightly less fantastic than Ben Hecht's. But this play has been unbelievably successful. And its picture of American journalism is taken as absolute truth by nearly all of its audiences. We wish we could have seen other plays, and other casts, to see whether overemphasis is general, but there was no time. We can only say that by New York standards *The Russian Question* is not good.

Mr. Simonov is without question the most popular writer in the Soviet Union today. His poems are known and recited by the whole population. His war reporting was as generally read as Ernie Pyle's was in America. And he himself is a very charming man. He invited us to his country house. It is a simple, comfortable little house, set in a large garden. There he and his wife live quietly. His house is not luxurious, it is very easy. We had an excellent lunch. He loves fine cars, and he has a Cadillac and a jeep. His vegetable garden, orchard, and poultry-yard furnish his table. He seems to live a good, simple, comfortable life. He has his enemies of course, of the kind drawn against him by his popularity. He is the darling of the government, and has been decorated many times, and he is generally beloved by the Russian people.

He and his wife were charming and kind. We liked them very much. And as with all professionals, our criticism of his play had no personal emphasis. We played darts later on, and danced, and sang. And we went back to Moscow very late at night.

Moscow was still in a flurry of activity, for all of the great portraits, and the flags, and the buntings had to come down quickly, before rain should set in, or the color would run. They had to be used again for the celebration of the thirtieth anniversary of the November Revolution. This is a big year for celebration in Moscow. The lights on the buildings, and on the Kremlin, and on the bridges were left up, because the rain could not hurt them, and they too would be needed again on the seventh of November.

We had wanted to see the inside of the Kremlin, everyone does, and we had even wanted to photograph it, and finally our permission came through, but the permission to photograph could not be arranged. No pictures could be taken, no cameras could be carried inside. We did not get the special tour, but only the usual tourists' route. However, that was what we wanted. Mr. Chmarsky was our guide again, and oddly enough Mr. Chmarsky had never been inside the Kremlin either. It is not a permission readily granted.

We approached the long, heavily guarded causeway. There were soldiers at the entrance. Our names were taken, and our permissions scrutinized, and then a bell rang and a military escort went with us through the gate. We didn't go to the side where the government offices are. We walked inside the huge place, past the old cathedrals which have been there for so long, and we went through the museums in the giant palace which was used by so many czars, from Ivan the Terrible on. We went into the tiny bedroom that Ivan used, and into the little withdrawing rooms, and the private chapels. And they are very beautiful, and strange, and ancient, and they are kept just as they were. And we saw the museum where the armor, the plate, the weapons, the china services, the costumes, and the royal gifts for five hundred years are stored. There were huge crowns covered with diamonds and emeralds, there was the big sledge of Catherine the Great. We saw the fur garments and the fantastic armor of the old boyars. There were

· 212 ·

the gifts sent by other royal houses to the czars—a great silver dog sent by Queen Elizabeth, presents of German silver and china from Frederick the Great to Catherine, the swords of honor, the incredible claptrap of monarchy.

It became apparent, after looking at a royal museum, that bad taste, far from being undesirable in royalty, is an absolute necessity.

We saw the painted hall of the warriors of Ivan where no woman was permitted to enter. We climbed miles of royal staircases, and looked into the great halls of mirrors. And we saw the suite where the last czar and his family had lived, uncomfortably amidst too much furniture, too much decoration, and too much dark polished wood. For a child to have to grow up and live with all of this monstrous collection of nonsense must have made a certain kind of adult out of him, and one can understand more readily the character of princes after seeing the kind of life they must have lived in the midst of all this mess. When the little czarevitch wanted a gun, could he have a twenty-two rifle? No, he had a little blunderbuss handmade of silver, with pieces of ivory driven into it, with jewels for sights—an anachronism in the twentieth century. And he couldn't go out and hunt rabbits, he sat on the lawn and swans were driven by for him to shoot at.

Just two hours in this royal place so depressed us that we couldn't shake it all day. What must a lifetime in it have done! Anyway, we saw it, and I suppose we are glad, but horses couldn't drag either of us back. It is the most gloomy place in the world. And it was easy to imagine while walking through these halls and these staircases how murder could rise so easily, how father could kill son and son father, and how any real external life could become so remote as to be non-existent. From the windows of the palace we could look over the walls of the Kremlin, out to the city, and we could imagine how these imprisoned monarchs must have felt toward the city. Directly below us in Red Square was the great marble stand where they used to cut off the heads of their subjects, probably out of their own terror. We walked down a long ramp and out of the heavily guarded gate with a sense of relief.

We ran away from that place and back to the Metropole Hotel, to the

Herald Tribune offices, and we grabbed Sweet Joe Newman, and went down to the cabaret, and ordered four hundred grams of vodka and a huge lunch. But it took a long time to get over the feeling the Kremlin had put upon us.

We never did see the government offices which are on the other side. That is a place where tourists are never taken, and we don't even know what it looked like, except for the tops of the buildings which could be seen over the wall. But we were told that a whole community lives in there. Some of the high government officials have apartments there, and their servants; and the caretakers, the maintenance crews, and the guards, all live inside the walls. Stalin, however, we were told, does not live in the Kremlin, but has an apartment somewhere, and no one seems to know where it is, and no one seems to pay much attention to where it is. Mostly now though, it is said, he lives on the Black Sea, in a climate of perpetual summer.

One of the American correspondents told us that he had seen Stalin driven through the street one day, and he said he was sitting in the jump seat, and he was leaning back at a curious angle, and he looked very stiff. "I wondered at the time," he said, "whether it was Stalin or whether it was a figure. He did not look natural."

Capa brooded over his films every morning, and nearly every day we called Voks and asked what the procedure was going to be to get our films out, and every day we were told that they were working on it and we were not to worry. But we did worry, for we had heard all of the stories of how films are confiscated, and how none is ever allowed out. We had heard them, and I suppose unconsciously we believed them. On the other hand, Mr. Karaganov of Voks had not let us down once, and had not told us an untruth once. And so we depended upon him.

And now the Moscow Writers' Union asked us to a dinner, and this worried us, for here would be all the intellectuals, all the writers whom Stalin has called "the architects of the Russian soul." It was a terrifying prospect.

Our trip was almost done now, and we were a little frantic. We didn't know whether we had got all the things we came for. There is only so much that one can do and see. Language difficulties were maddening. We had made contacts with many Russian people, but were the questions we had wanted answered actually answered? I had made notes of conversations, and of details, even of weather reports, for later sorting out. But we were too close to it. We didn't know what we had. We knew nothing about the things American papers were howling about— Russian military preparations, atomic research, slave labor, the political skulduggery of the Kremlin—we had no information about these things. True, we had seen a great many German prisoners at work, cleaning up the wreckage their Army had created, and this did not seem too unjust to us. And the prisoners did not seem to us either overworked or underfed. But we have no data, of course. If there were large military preparations, we didn't see them. There certainly were lots of soldiers. On the other hand, we had not come as spies.

At the last we tried to see everything in Moscow. We ran to schools,

we spoke to businesswomen, actresses, students. We went to stores where the queues formed to buy everything. An issue of phonograph records would be announced and a line would form, and in a few hours the records would be sold out. The same thing happened when a new book went on sale. It seemed to us that clothing improved even in the two months we had been there, and at the same time the Moscow papers announced the lowering of prices on bread, vegetables, potatoes, and some textiles. There was always a rush on the stores, to buy almost anything that was offered. The Russian economy which had been turned almost exclusively to war production was slowly clanking into peacetime production, and a people which had been deprived of consumer goods, both needed and luxurious, crowded the stores to buy. When ice-cream got to a store, a line formed many blocks long. A man with a box of ice-cream would be rushed, and his goods sold so quickly that he could hardly take the money fast enough. The Russians love ice-cream, and there never was enough of it to go around.

Every day Capa inquired about his pictures. He had nearly four thousand negatives by now, and he was worrying himself sick. And every day we were told that it would be all right, that the rule was in process of being arrived at.

The dinner given us by the Moscow writers was held at a Georgian restaurant. There were about thirty writers and officials of the Union there, among them Simonov and Ilya Ehrenburg. By this time I had reached a point where I could not drink vodka at all. My system revolted against it. But the dry Georgian wines were delicious. The kinds of wines had numbers. Thus one got to know that number sixty would be a heavy red wine, number thirty a thin white wine. These numbers are not correct, but we found that number forty-five, a dry, light, fine-tasting red wine was good for us, and we always ordered it. There was a comparatively dry champagne that was good too. The restaurant had a Georgian orchestra and some dancers, and the food was the same as in Georgia—for our taste, the best in Russia.

We were all dressed up in our best clothes, and ours were pretty beat up and sloppy. In fact we were a disgrace, and Sweet Lana was getting to be a little ashamed of us. There were no dinner clothes. In fact, in

· 216 ·

the circles we traveled in we never saw dinner clothes. Perhaps the diplomats have them, we don't know.

The speeches at this dinner were long and complicated. Most of the people at the table had some language beside Russian, either English, or French, or German. They hoped we had enjoyed our stay in their country. They hoped we had got the information we came to get. They drank our health again and again. We answered that we had not come to inspect the political system, but to see ordinary Russian people; that we had seen many of them, and we hoped we could tell the objective truth about what we had seen. Ehrenburg got up and said that if we could do that they would be more than happy. A man at the end of the table then got up and said that there were several kinds of truth, and that we must tell a truth which would further good relations between the Russian and the American people.

And that started the fight. Ehrenburg leaped up and made a savage speech. He said that to tell a writer what to write was an insult. He said that if a writer had a reputation for being truthful, then no suggestion should be offered. He shook his finger in his colleague's face and told him in effect that his manners were bad. Simonov instantly backed Ehrenburg, and denounced the first speaker, who defended himself feebly. Mr. Chmarsky tried to make a speech, but the argument went on and drowned him out. We had always heard that the party line was so strict among writers that no argument was permitted. The spirit at this dinner did not make this seem at all true. Mr. Karaganov made a conciliatory speech, and the dinner settled down.

My abandoning of vodka in the toasts and the substitution of wine made me much happier in the stomach, although I probably was regarded as a weakling, but I was a healthier weakling. Vodka just didn't agree with me. The dinner concluded about eleven o'clock in good feeling. No one else ventured to tell us what to write.

Our passage was booked now. We were to leave in three days, and still there was no clearance of our pictures. Capa was a brooding mass of unhappiness. The people at the American Embassy and the correspondents had been so kind to us that we felt we ought to give a cocktail party. Poor Stevens of the *Christian Science Monitor* had one of the few houses in Moscow. The rest lived in hotels. So Stevens got chosen to give the party. There was not much he could do about it, even if he had wanted to. We made a guest list and found that at least a hundred people had to be invited, and Stevens's living-room could comfortably hold about twenty. But there was no help for that. We thought perhaps some wouldn't come, but we were wrong. A hundred and fifty came. Parties are very desirable things in Moscow. It was a gay party too, but there wasn't much drinking. The room was so crowded that you could hardly get your arm up to your mouth, and once you did you couldn't get it down again. Stevens never got to see much of his party; quite early he got trapped in a corner, and he never escaped from it.

Our profound thanks are due to the Embassy staff and the correspondents. They gave us every possible help and encouragement. And we think they are doing a very good job under trying and difficult conditions. For one thing, they are not losing their heads as so many people are in the world. It is probably the touchiest political scene in the world today, and far from the most pleasant. Our compliments go to the whole group, from the Ambassador to the T/5 who was rewiring the Embassy.

We were to leave on Sunday morning. On Friday night we went to the ballet at the Bolshoi Theater. When we came out there was a rush telephone call for us. It was Mr. Karaganov of Voks. He had finally got word from the Foreign Office. Our films had to be developed and inspected, every single one of them, before they could leave the country. He would put a crew to work developing the pictures—three thousand pictures. We wondered how it could have been done if we had had to do it at this last moment. They did not know that all the pictures had already been developed. Capa packed up all his negatives, and early in the morning a messenger came for them. He spent a day of agony. He paced about, clucking like a mother hen who has lost her babies. He made plans, he would not leave the country without his films. He would cancel his reservation. He would not agree to have the films sent after him. He grunted and paced the room. He washed his hair two or three times and forgot to take a bath at all. He could have had a baby with half the trouble and pain. My notes were not even requested. It wouldn't have made much difference if they had been, no one could have read them. I have trouble reading them myself.

We spent the day visiting and promising to send various scarce articles to various people. Sweet Joe was a little sad to see us leave, we think. We had robbed him of cigarettes and books, had used his clothes and his soap and his toilet paper, had outraged his slender stock of whisky, had violated his hospitality in every possible way, and still we think he was sorry to see us go.

Half the time Capa plotted counterrevolution if anything happened to his films, and half the time he considered simple suicide. He wondered if he could cut off his own head on the execution block in Red Square. We had a sad little party in the Grand Hotel that night. The music was louder than ever, and the bar girl we had named Miss Sichass (Miss Hurry-up) was slower than ever.

We got up in the dark to go to the airport for the last time. We sat for the last time under the portrait of Stalin, and it seemed to us that he was smiling satirically over his medals. We drank the usual tea, and Capa by now had the jerks. And then a messenger arrived and put a box in his hands. It was a tough cardboard box, and the lid was sewed on with string, and over the knots were little leaden seals. He was not to touch the seals until we had cleared the airfield at Kiev, the last stop before Prague.

Mr. Karaganov, Mr. Chmarsky, Sweet Lana, and Sweet Joe Newman saw us off. Our baggage was much lighter than it had been, for we had given away everything we could spare—suits, and jackets, some cameras, all the extra flash bulbs, and the unexposed film. We climbed into the plane and took our seats. It was four hours to Kiev. Capa held the cardboard box in his hand, and he was not allowed to open it. If the seals were broken it would not pass. He weighed it in his hand. "It is light," he said miserably. "It is only half heavy enough."

I said, "Maybe they put rocks in it, maybe there aren't any films in there at all."

He shook the box. "It sounds like films," he said.

"It could be old newspapers," I said.

"You son-of-a-bitch," he remarked. And he argued with himself.

· 219 ·

"What would they want to take out?" he asked. "It wasn't anything that could hurt."

"Maybe they just don't like Capa pictures," I suggested.

The plane flew over the great flat lands with their forests and fields, and the silver river winding and twisting. It was a beautiful day, and the thin blue mist of autumn hung close to the ground. The hostess took pink soda to the crew, and came back and opened a bottle for herself.

At noon we coasted into the field at Kiev. The customs man gave our baggage a cursory inspection, but the box of film was instantly picked up. They had a message concerning it. An official cut the strings while Capa looked on like a stricken sheep. And then the officials all smiled, and shook hands, and went out, and the door closed, and the engines turned over. Capa's hands shook as he opened his box. The films seemed to be all there. He smiled and put back his head, and he was asleep before the ship could get into the air. Some negatives had been taken, but not many. They had removed films that showed too much topography, and the telephoto picture of the mad girl of Stalingrad was gone, and the pictures which showed prisoners, but nothing that mattered from our point of view was withheld. The farms and the faces, the pictures of the Russian people, were intact, and those were what we had gone for in the first place.

The airplane crossed the border, and early in the afternoon we landed in Prague, and I had to awaken Capa.

Well, there it is. It's about what we went for. We found, as we had suspected, that the Russian people are people, and, as with other people, that they are very nice. The ones we met had a hatred of war, they wanted the same things all people want—good lives, increased comfort, security, and peace.

We know that this journal will not be satisfactory either to the ecclesiastical Left, nor the lumpen Right. The first will say it is anti-Russian, and the second that it is pro-Russian. Surely it is superficial, and how could it be otherwise? We have no conclusions to draw, except that Russian people are like all other people in the world. Some bad ones there are surely, but by far the greater number are very good.